How
Stocks
Work

How
Stocks
Work

David L. Scott

McGraw-Hill

New York   Chicago   San Francisco   Lisbon   London   Madrid
Mexico City   Milan   New Delhi   San Juan   Seoul
Singapore   Sydney   Toronto

ISBN 0-07-136389-0

1. Stocks. 2. Investments. 3. Investment analysis. I. Title.

HG4661 .S347   2001
332.63'22—dc21   2001031701

McGraw-Hill

A Division of The *McGraw·Hill* Companies

1 2 3 4 5 6 7 8 9 0   DOC/DOC   0 9 8 7 6 5 4 3 2 1

ISBN 0-07-136389-0

Printed and bound by R. R. Donnelley & Sons Company..

 This book was printed on recycled, acid-free paper containing a
minimum of 50% recycled, de-inked fiber.

McGraw-Hill books are available at special quantity discounts to use as
premiums and sales promotions, or for use in corporate training programs. For
more information, please write to the Director of Special Sales, McGraw-Hill
Professional's, Two Penn Plaza, New York, NY 10121-2298. Or contact your
local bookstore.

CONTENTS

PREFACE

The foundation for intelligent investing in stocks, or any investment, is a fundamental understanding of the asset; what it represents, how it is bought and sold, why it has value, how it is taxed, and how the risks of ownership can be evaluated. It seems reasonable to assume that anyone would take the time and make the effort to gain knowledge about the basics of stocks before investing their hard-earned money. It would seem reasonable, but it isn't necessarily so.

Over the years, I have talked with many individuals who chose to invest in stocks without fully understanding what they were buying, especially with regard to the potential risks of their investment. Investing with little study was particularly prevalent in the booming 1990s when stock prices appeared to have no upper limit and first-time investors flocked to put their money in equities. The investment truth of the decade was "stocks have historically provided higher returns than other investments, so individuals should concentrate their investments in equities."

Keep in mind that two decades earlier, investment gurus were saying the same thing about real estate. A weak stock market and an economy that had experienced unusually high inflation occasioned this. The same song, but a different verse. The beat goes on. A once-over-lightly approach to investing often produces the desired results so long as the overall market continues moving upward. Buy an overpriced home in the late 1970s, and it didn't really matter because rising real estate prices bailed out most of the buyers. A bull market in stocks, especially the powerful bull market in technology stocks that occurred in the 1990s, overcame foolish and inappropriate investment choices. Only when the bear started rearing its ugly head in March 2000 and the market headed south did the chickens begin coming home to roost. The experience was especially disheartening to individual investors who had loaded up with the technology darlings of Wall Street.

How Stocks Work doesn't tell you how to get rich by investing in stocks. At least, not how to get rich in a few years. I freely admit I am unable to accomplish such a task. You will not find information about how to use someone else's money in order to gain untold personal wealth. In short, this book has no get-rich-quick schemes. Rather, *How Stocks Work* provides basic information about stocks as investment vehicles. The topics are especially valuable for individuals who are relatively new to investing and for investors who have already committed money to stocks without fully understanding what these securities represent. What factors cause stocks to gain or lost market value? What are the risks of investing in shares of stock? How are stocks investments taxed? Why and how do companies issue stock? *How Stocks Work* addresses these and other questions that tend to puzzle many investors.

It is important to keep in mind that stocks should comprise only one segment of your total investment portfolio. It isn't enough to diversity your holding among stocks in different industries or stocks issued by companies that operate in different regions of the world. A portion of your funds should be invested in fixed-income assets such as bonds or certificates of deposit, and a portion in tangible assets such as real estate. Bonds and certificates of deposit are conservative investments that lack excitement and produce relatively low returns, but these assets have a place in every individual's portfolio. Stocks may provide a superior return over long periods of time, but the time period may not coincide with your own investment horizon. Many individuals who were new to investing in early 2000 and chose to devote most of their funds to Internet stocks are unlikely to recover their initial investment, let alone earn a positive return, no matter how long their investment horizon. Diversification among stocks and among investment vehicles makes sense to all but the most daring investors.

Perhaps most important, use caution and common sense when you choose an investment. Common sense and time for reflection will seldom fail you.

David L. Scott
Valdosta, Georgia

1

CHAPTER

WHAT STOCK REPRESENTS

Chapter summary

Why companies issue shares of stock ... Restrictions on corporate stock issues ... The rights of stockholders ...Why corporations sometimes repurchase shares of their own stock ... Types of stock issued by companies ... Comparing preferred and common stock ... Tracking stocks ... The importance of dividends to stockholders ... Stock dividends vs. cash dividends ... The effect of stock splits ...

What does a share of stock represent?

A share of stock represents a single unit of ownership of a particular business. Some businesses issue thousands of shares of stock while other businesses have hundreds of millions or even billions of shares of outstanding stock. Petroleum giant ExxonMobil

Corporation has nearly 3.5 billion outstanding shares of stock that are owned by over a quarter million different shareholders. Some individual investors own 10 or 12 shares while institutional investors such as a mutual fund will often own hundreds of thousands of shares. A shareholder's relative ownership position in a company depends both on the number of shares the stockholder owns and on the total number of shares of the company that are outstanding. One hundred shares of stock represent a significant portion of the ownership of a business with 10,000 shares of ownership, but a much less significant stake in a company with 3.5 billion shares of outstanding stock.

Why do businesses issue shares of stock?

Businesses issue shares of stock, or ownership, in return for contributions of work, ideas, money, or anything else that can improve the economic circumstances of the businesses. The majority of shares are issued in return for money that is used to acquire assets such as equipment, real estate, and items held for resale, and to pay expenses such as wages, utilities, and taxes. Imagine an enterprising person who wants to start a new business. Unless the business is very small or the person starting the business is independently wealthy, the founder will need to recruit outside investors, perhaps including yourself, who are willing to contribute some of the money required to get the business off the ground. You and the other investors are likely to seek an ownership stake in the business in return for providing some or maybe all of the money that is required. Shares of stock issued by the business and held by you and the other investors represent an ownership stake in the business. The founder will almost certainly retain some of the shares, while you and the other investors will own the remainder. Once the company issues shares of ownership to outside investors, the business becomes their company as well as the founder's company. An owner who is able to raise sufficient funds and at the same time retain ownership of over half of the firm's shares of stock will remain in control of the business. Exhibit 1-1 provides information about the number of owners and the number of outstanding shares for selected corporations.

How do I acquire shares of stock?

Most individuals must employ the services of a broker to acquire shares of stock. Brokers, sometimes called *stockbrokers*, might have more formal titles, such as "financial consultants" and "financial executives," depending on the firm where they are employed. Firms that have access to the financial markets where stocks are traded employ brokers to assist customers with their investments, including orders to buy and sell shares of stock. Many individual investors have opened online brokerage accounts that facilitate the buying and selling of stocks without the need to interact with a broker.

EXHIBIT 1-1

Number of Owners and Outstanding Shares of Select Corporations

Company	Number of Shareholders	Shares Outstanding (in Millions)
Boeing Corporation	160,000	888
Broadwing	23,197	216
Cinergy	65,553	159
Coca-Cola	394,603	2,479
ExxonMobil	772,614	3,754
GenCorp	11,900	42
Microsoft	107,824	5,332
Phelps Dodge	27,671	79
Procter & Gamble	291,965	1,304

Is a certificate required to prove I am a shareholder of a company?

Most investors choose to leave certificates for shares of stock they have purchased in the custody of their brokerage firm rather than ask for delivery of the certificates. The brokerage company with which you do business will credit your account for shares of stock you own and send regular reports with a record of assets being held in your account. Some investors prefer to take delivery of stock certificates, but this is a personal choice, not a necessity. In fact, many brokerage firms charge an extra fee to deliver a certificate for shares of stock their customers purchase.

Does the money I pay to purchase shares of stock go directly to the company that issued the shares?

The answer depends on whether the shares you purchase are part of an original issue by a company seeking to raise capital or from another investor like yourself who has decided to sell shares the investor purchased at an earlier date. Your money will go to the company if the shares are part of an original issue. On the other hand, if the shares are not part of a new issue of stock, your money will go to another investor who has decided to sell the shares. In most instances you will be purchasing shares of stock from another investor rather than from the issuing company. Many corporations issued all of their outstanding shares of stock when the companies were initially formed many years ago. Younger companies may have issued shares within the last couple of years. Once a corporation has issued stock, investors can only buy shares directly if the firm decides to later issue additional shares. Otherwise, shares in the firm must be purchased from shareholders who decide to sell shares they purchased at an earlier date.

What about stock trades that are reported in the media?

Stock transactions reported in the newspapers each morning and on various Internet Web sites during the day represent trades between investors, not direct purchases of shares from corporations issuing stock. Investors sometimes buy shares of stock directly from an issuing company, but these purchases are not reported in daily trading statistics. Most likely, the money you invest when purchasing shares of stock will go to another investor, not the company that issued the shares you are buying. Buy 100 shares of Coca-Cola and your money will not go to Coca-Cola but to someone who has decided to sell 100 shares of Coca-Cola stock they already owned. Likewise, money you receive when shares are sold will come from another investor who has purchased the shares of stock you sold. Transactions between investors are reported in the daily trading data reported by the media.

How does a company benefit if its stock can only be purchased from another investor?

Companies would find it difficult or even impossible to issue new shares of ownership if investors were concerned they would be unable to readily resell the stock they purchased. Would you buy shares of AT&T, Wal-Mart, or Microsoft if you were uncertain a buyer could be located when you were ready to sell? The *liquidity*, or ability to dispose of an investment, is a very important consideration for most investors who may later need money for other purposes. Although the company whose shares you purchase is unlikely to receive the money you pay to buy its stock, the firm does benefit from knowledge among investors that its stock enjoys an active secondary market and can be resold by shareholders without great difficulty. Companies often issue stock on more than one occasion, so the market price and liquidity of its outstanding shares is of continuing importance to a firm's directors, who may decide to issue additional shares. In addition, it is likely these directors are also shareholders of the firm.

Is a company limited in the number of shares it may issue?

A company's directors authorize a stated number of shares at the time the firm is organized. For example, a corporate charter may permit the firm to issue up to a maximum of 10 million shares of stock. The directors are not required to issue all the shares that have been authorized, and may choose to hold a portion of the shares in reserve to issue at a later date when additional funds are needed. For example, a corporation may initially issue 5 million shares even though 10 million shares have been authorized. Directors must gain the approval of the firm's stockholders in order to issue additional shares beyond the number authorized in the corporate charter. The requirement for shareholder approval to increase the number of authorized shares protects the shareholders' ownership position from being diluted by additional shares that can result in lower earnings per share and reduced voting power for existing shareholders. Obtaining the approval of shareholders for additional authorized shares is generally not a problem for a company's directors.

Do current shareholders have first right to buy additional shares that are issued?

Some corporate charters specify that existing shareholders be given first right to buy any additional shares that are issued in proportion to shares they already own. For example, a shareholder who owns 5 percent of a company's outstanding stock would be permitted to purchase 5 percent of any new shares. Current shareholders are not required to buy any of the new shares, but they are at least given an opportunity to purchase new shares prior to the stock being offered to outsiders. Being able to buy new shares in proportion to the shares you own allows you to maintain your proportional ownership of the corporation. Shareholders are said to have a *preemptive right* if the company in which they own stock is legally required to offer them first chance to buy shares that are part of a new issue. Not all companies provide their shareholders with the preemptive right. In fact, companies whose owners enjoy a preemptive right sometimes ask their shareholders to give up the right. Companies claim the preemptive right results in a lengthy and expensive process for issuing new shares of stock at the same time that it reduces flexibility in seeking additional financing.

Do any guarantees come with being a stockholder?

The stockholders of a corporation enjoy few guarantees. There is no guarantee that your money will be returned on a specific date, as exists when you invest in a certificate of deposit or a U.S. savings bond. Likewise, stockholders other than those who buy shares of preferred stock (a special type of stock discussed later in this chapter) have no guarantee they will receive any regular income payments, as occurs when money is invested in savings accounts or corporate bonds. In the worst case, there is no guarantee the company that issued the shares of stock you purchased will remain financially viable and remain in business. Even large companies can experience failure and leave their owners holding a worthless certificate. The lack of a guarantee with regard to income and principal is a substantial and important risk for individuals who choose to invest in shares of stock.

What happens to the value of my stock if the issuer goes out of business?

In the event the issuer of your stock goes out of business, you will recover only what remains after everyone else with a financial claim against the company has been paid. Lenders who provided credit must be paid, suppliers must be paid, employees must be paid, the government must be paid, the outside lawyers must be paid, and, finally, you and the remainder of the owners will have a claim to what is left if, in fact, anything remains. Often, companies fail without sufficient financial resources to pay even their debts. When a company goes out of business, stockholders are often left high and dry, especially if the business has been losing money for several years. If nothing remains for the stockholders, your stock is likely to end up worthless and you can frame the certificate as a keepsake or use it as wallpaper. In some corporate failures, shares of stock can be traded for another security of a reorganized company.

Do companies ever repurchase their stock?

Companies sometimes repurchase their own shares of stock, although the repurchases are at the company's option and usually not on a regular basis. Shareholders should not and cannot expect the company that issued their shares to agree to repurchase these shares whenever shareholders desire a return of their funds. Corporations often utilize the proceeds from stock issues to acquire long-term assets, such as equipment and buildings, that they expect to utilize for many years. Managers would be unable to effectively operate their businesses if they were continually worried that a substantial number of stockholders might suddenly demand a return of their money. Companies issue shares of stock in order to raise permanent capital that can be used without concern that unhappy or financially strapped shareholders will require that their shares be redeemed. On the other hand, a company's directors may decide from time to time to use the firm's surplus funds to buy back shares of stock, but the purchases will be at the option of the company, not the stockholders. Don't invest in stock in the belief that you can redeem your shares in the same manner a U.S. savings bond can be submitted for early redemption.

Why do companies repurchase their own shares?

The directors of a company may feel that the market price is too low and investors are undervaluing the firm's stock. Repurchasing stock results in fewer outstanding shares, so the firm's income is spread among fewer units of ownership. In other words, earnings per share are likely to increase as a result of a share repurchase. In addition, fewer shares outstanding will reduce the total amount of dividends the company pays. Keep in mind that a company cannot normally force its stockholders to sell their shares back to the firm. Rather, the firm will hire a company that specializes in major financial transactions to go into the market and gradually buy up shares of stock over a period of time. Alternatively, the directors may choose to have the company go directly to the stockholders and offer a premium price for a specified number of shares. Controversy exists as to whether buying back shares is in the long-run interests of a firm's shareholders.

Do all companies make shares of ownership available for purchase?

Some companies are privately owned, in which case no shares of stock are available for the public to purchase. For many years shares of Coors, the well-known Colorado brewer of beer, were unavailable to individual investors because the founder's family owned all of the firm's stock. Shares become publicly available in the 1970s when the company issued shares of ownership to the general public. Family members and employees currently own all of the stock of Publix, a large Florida-based grocery chain, so that no shares are available for purchase by the investing public. Some companies are wholly owned by another company. For example, Southern Company, a large Atlanta electric utility holding company, owns all the common stock of Alabama Power, Mississippi Power, Georgia Power, and Gulf Power, four large electric utilities in the Southeast. Investors can purchase shares of Southern Company whose stock is traded on the New York Stock Exchange, but investors cannot purchase the stock of those four power companies owned by Southern Company. Mutual companies do not issue shares of ownership that are available for purchase. Rather, their customers own mutual companies such as State Farm, an insurance company that is owned by its policyholders. Mutual companies sometimes decide to convert to stock companies so they can raise capital by selling shares of stock to the public.

How do companies keep track of who owns their shares?

Most large companies require outside assistance to maintain a current list of their shareholders. Firms called *transfer agents* are paid by companies to maintain a current list of their owners and to take care of transferring shares when stock is sold by one investor to another. Keep in mind that a company must know the identities and addresses of its owners in order to send financial reports and dividend payments to the appropriate people. Maintaining an accurate list of shareholders can be a daunting task because the owners of many corporations are continually changing. Consider a company in which millions of shares of stock are traded each day. Some investors buy shares of stock only to shortly sell these same shares to someone else, hopefully at a higher price. Most large companies do not have sufficient staff or the expertise to maintain an ongoing record of shareholders.

What rights do I have as a stockholder?

As a stockholder and part owner of a company, you have a voice in selecting the directors who oversee the business. At least, you probably have a voice in the selection of directors. Most public companies permit their stockholders to vote for the directors who are charged with selecting the managers and providing strategic oversight of the company's operations. The importance of your voice in selecting a firm's directors will depend on the number of shares you hold in relation to the total number of outstanding shares. The greater the proportion of the firm's shares you own, the more sway you will have in selecting the directors and influencing corporate policy. In truth, most individual shareholders have little voice in the management of a large corporation. Owning 300 shares of 300 million outstanding shares gives you little clout in influencing a firm's financial or operating policies. Over half the outstanding shares of many corporations are held by institutional investors such as mutual funds and pension funds. Institutional shareholders tend to vote with a firm's management.

Do I have other rights as a stockholder?

The stockholders of a company have a claim to the firm's income, including income earned during the period the shares are owned, as well as past income that has been retained by the firm for investment in additional assets. A company's board of directors may or may not declare dividends during the time you are a shareholder. If dividends are declared, you will receive a check, the amount of which depends on the size of the dividend the directors have declared and the number of shares you own. Most companies declare and pay dividends four times per year. Profits retained by the firm rather than paid to the owners as dividends can be used to pay debts or acquire additional assets, either of which should increase the value of the company and, hopefully, the market value of the shares you own.

When do I have to buy a company's stock in order to receive a dividend that has been declared?

The day before the *ex-dividend date* is the last day you can purchase shares of stock and receive the dividend that has been declared. Buy shares on the ex-dividend date, and the person who sold you the stock will receive the next dividend payment. The ex-dividend date is two business days prior to the stock-of-record date that will be established by directors when the dividend is declared. Information on the declared dividend and ex-dividend date is available in many financial publications and Web sites. Keep in mind that the stock price is likely to decline on the ex-dividend date because new buyers of the stock will not receive the already declared and upcoming dividend payment. All things equal (as economists like to say), a stock should sell at a higher price when a buyer has the right to the dividend payment. Exhibit 1-2 provides a listing of important dividend dates that are relevant to a company's stockholders. Most stockholders are primarily interested in the date that shares must be purchased in order to receive the dividend (one day prior to the ex-dividend date) and the date the dividend is to be paid (the payment date). A month or more may separate the date a dividend is declared by a company's directors and the date the dividend is actually paid to shareholders

EXHIBIT 1-2

Importatnt Dividend Dates

Declaration date: The date directors publicly announce information about the firm's next dividend. The announcement includes the amount of the dividend, the date the firm will use to determine who is to receive the dividend, and the date the dividend is to be paid.

Ex-dividend date: The first date new buyers of the firm's stock will not receive the dividend that has been declared. Only shares purchased prior to the ex-dividend date have the right to the declared dividend. Newspapers typically place the letter x beside a stock that traded ex-dividend.

Stockholder-of-record date: The date an investor must be listed as a stockholder on the firm's books in order to receive the upcoming dividend. The stockholder-of-record date is two business days after the ex-dividend date.

Payment date: The date the company pays the dividend to stockholders listed on the firm's books as of the stockholder-of-record date. The payment date is likely to follow the declaration date by a month or more.

As a stockholder am I permitted to vote on the firm's dividend?

A firm's directors decide whether a dividend will be paid and, if so, how much and when. Stockholders indirectly influence the dividend decision by electing the directors. Of course, a stockholder can contact the company and convey his or her feeling about the firm's dividend. Dividend decisions by a firm's directors apply to all of the company's stockholders, who are not given an option to turn down a dividend that has been declared. Likewise, each stockholder will receive the same dividend per share no matter how many shares are owned. Companies that have been in business for many years tend to have consistent dividend records that allow investors to have a good idea of future dividends in the near term. Dividends that will be declared several years in the future are more difficult to project. Some companies increase dividends on a regular basis, while other companies pay no dividend and may not plan to pay a dividend in the foreseeable future. If dividends are an important consideration in your investment decision, it is important to research the dividend record of any companies in which you are considering investing.

Can a company's directors reduce dividend payments to the shareholders?

Directors can and do reduce dividend payments. Directors generally don't want to cut dividends because the action is likely to upset stockholders and other investors who were considering purchasing the firm's shares. A reduction in the dividend, especially if it is unexpected, is also likely to result in a decline in the firm's stock price. Valid reasons exist for a firm's directors to reduce or eliminate dividend payments to shareholders. A firm may be experiencing severe financial difficulties that cause the directors to believe the company requires all the available cash to maintain normal operations and pay creditors.

Firms sometimes reinvent themselves and implement new strategic policies regarding growth and reinvestment. For example, telecommunication companies tended to reduce their dividend payouts (dividends as a proportion of earnings) as they moved from being heavily regulated to becoming very competitive. Extra funds were needed for investment in new assets in order to compete in the rapidly changing business environment. Retaining a greater proportion of earnings was considered a good place to generate these funds.

Do companies conduct meetings for their owners?

Companies have an annual meeting for their stockholders. Most stockholders don't have the time or don't want to incur the travel expense to attend an annual meeting. Keep in mind that the company in which you own shares will not pay your expenses to attend the annual meeting, unless, of course, you are a director. As a shareholder you will receive information about the time and place of the meeting, along with an explanation of items that will be presented for shareholder approval. You will also receive the company's annual report, which contains financial and other information about the firm's operations during the past year.

Can I participate in the election of directors if I fail to attend the annual meeting?

Only a small proportion of stockholders of most large companies attend the annual meeting. To accommodate shareholders who are unable or unwilling to attend, companies send a proxy statement and ballot prior to the scheduled date of the meeting. You are expected to read the proxy statement, mark your ballot, and return the ballot in a postage-paid envelope. The proxy statement includes information about the nominees for the directors' positions and the details of any shareholder resolutions or issues that must be approved by owners. The ballot must be returned prior to the annual meeting. The ballot you send will permit someone appointed by the firm to cast your votes as you direct. The company will have a record of the number of shares owned by each shareholder, and your votes will be weighted according to the number of shares you hold.

Does a company issue only one type of stock?

Most companies issue a single type of ownership security, called *common stock*. A company may initially issue millions or tens of millions of shares of common stock and years later, when more funds are required, issue millions of additional shares. Shares of the same class of stock are identical, so that shares issued subsequent to the initial offering cannot be differentiated from the original shares. Some companies issue a second class of common stock with somewhat different privileges compared to the regular common stock. For example, a company may issue a second class of common stock with full rights to dividend payments but without voting rights for directors' positions. Having two classes of common stock outstanding is unusual, but it does occur, often when the company's founding family members or another small group of owners do not wish to share control of the company with other shareholders. In general, however, companies issue only a single class of common stock. All the shares are identical when only a single class of stock has been issued.

Will I be required to submit my certificate when a company in which I own stock changes its name?

Whether you are required to send in your stock certificate in exchange for a new certificate depends on the reason for the name change. You must submit your shares if the company in which you own stock is purchased by another firm. Likewise, you will need to remit your shares in the event the firm in which you own stock merges with another company to form an entirely new corporation. Shareholders of Amoco were required to submit their stock in exchange for new stock when British Petroleum purchased Amoco. On the other hand, shareholders of Standard Oil Company of New Jersey were not required to exchange their stock when the firm changed its name to Exxon (now ExxonMobil). Rather, certificates with the new name gradually replaced old certificates as investors sold shares and the transfer agent issued certificates with the new corporate name to investors who purchased the stock. The firm in which you own stock will inform you if it is necessary for any reason to submit your shares.

Do corporations issue any other type of stock?

Some companies issue a special class of ownership called *preferred stock*, which is very different from common stock and appeals to an entirely different type of investor. Preferred stock nearly always pays a fixed dividend, the amount of which is established at the time the shares are issued. Dividends are paid quarterly for both common stock and preferred stock. Unlike dividends paid on common stock, however, the dividend payment for an issue of preferred stock remains the same quarter after quarter for as long as the stock remains outstanding. For example, a company may issue preferred stock that is entitled to dividends of $6.00 per year, or $1.50 per quarter. Owners of this stock will receive a quarterly dividend of $1.50 per share the first year the stock is issued and a quarterly dividend of $1.50 per share every quarter thereafter regardless of whether the issuer becomes wildly successful and earns huge profits. With respect to the current income an investor receives, preferred stock has more similarity to a bond or certificate of deposit than to common stock that is subject to varying dividend payments. Unlike a bond, however, preferred stock does represent ownership, and the dividends are not a legal liability of the company. In addition, preferred stock has no maturity date on which the issuer is scheduled to repay the principal amount, or face value, to investors. A firm's directors must meet and declare each dividend, even for preferred stock. Companies that encounter serious financial difficulties may reduce or eliminate dividends to their preferred stockholders at the same time the directors make every effort to continue paying interest to the firm's creditors.

In what respect is preferred stock actually preferred to common stock?

Preferred stockholders enjoy a priority to any dividend payments by the company. That is, dividends to preferred stockholders must be paid in full prior to any dividend payments being made to common shareholders. In this respect, preferred stock is indeed preferred because holders of preferred shares must be paid first. In addition, in the event the firm is liquidated, preferred stockholders generally have priority in any financial recovery compared to common stockholders. The claim of preferred stockholders is subordinated to the claims of all of a firm's creditors, but the rights of preferred owners rank ahead of common stockholders. Again, preferred stockholders have a preferred status relative to common stockholders in the event a company is liquidated. Invest in preferred stock, and you are likely to receive more dividend income compared to when you invest in common stock, at least initially, but your possibilities for gains in value are much more limited.

Why does a firm issue preferred stock?

Companies issue preferred stock in order to lock in a financial expense at the same time they gain some flexibility. Preferred stock allows a firm to nail down a fixed dividend expense that, in case of financial difficulty, can be deferred. Directors of a company with preferred stock must vote whether to pay a dividend to investors who own the stock. A vote to pay the dividend is generally automatic. However, the fact that directors are permitted to defer the dividend offers important flexibility if the firm faces severe short-term financial difficulties. Issuing preferred stock in place of additional shares of common stock can also benefit the company's current owners. The fixed dividend to preferred stockholders can work to the advantage of common stockholders, who are not required to split rising profits among a greater number of common shares that would result from a new issue of common stock. In other words, preferred stock provides leverage for common stockholders, who may enjoy a higher return compared to when additional common stock is issued. Although an issue of debt also allows a firm to pin down a fixed expense, creditors have a legal right to be paid, so deferral of interest and scheduled principal payments is generally not an option no matter how bad things become for the company. Conversely, if the economic fortunes of a company go downhill, common stockholders will suffer if preferred stock has been issued because the preferred stockholders will be at the head of the line for dividend payments.

Can preferred stockholders sell their shares back to the company?

Like common stock, preferred stock is considered permanent capital. Companies issue shares of preferred stock in order to raise capital that can be used for acquiring long-term assets and repaying debt. Thus, most companies are in no financial position to redeem shares of preferred stock whenever shareholders decide they want their money back. Preferred stockholders who wish to liquidate their investment must find other investors to purchase their shares. Locating other investors to buy preferred stock is no different from the position of common stockholders who wish to sell their shares.

I recently read about a tracking stock. In what ways does this differ from regular stock?

A *tracking stock* is a special and relatively rare type of owner-ship share that tracks (hence the name) the performance of a company's subsidiary. An investor who purchases a tracking stock takes a financial position in a particular segment of a company, rather than the company as a whole. A firm may issue a tracking stock when the directors believe the investment com-munity is not properly valuing the company's regular stock, especially with regard to a particular segment of the firm. Gen-eral Motors Class H common stock is a tracking stock issued by GM for its Hughes subsidiary, one of the firm's fastest-growing and most promising segments. General Motors allocates a por-tion of Hughes' earnings to the tracking stock in order to deter-mine earnings per share. Although holders of a tracking stock have a financial interest in a particular subsidiary, the sub-sidiary remains under the control of the parent company's directors, who determine the dividends that will be paid to holders of the tracking stock. If tracking stock sounds like "fuzzy" ownership, it is. This special stock generally tracks the economic fortunes of a company segment, although holders of the stock do not have the rights accorded to most common stockholders. Critics of tracking stock claim directors of the issuing company can have a conflict of interest between investors who own the firm's regular shares and investors who hold the firm's tracking stock.

What are penny stocks?

Stocks selling at a very low price are called *penny stocks,* although there is no universally agreed upon price below which a stock must sell in order to qualify as a penny stock. Some individuals consider that only stocks trading for under a dollar a share should qualify as a penny stock. Other investors classify all stocks trading for less than $5 per share as penny stocks.

There is agreement that a stock must sell at a relatively low price to qualify as a penny stock; it's just that no unanimous agreement exists on exactly how low. Penny stocks are generally considered very risky investments, with prices that are sometimes subject to being manipulated both by the dealers who serve as market makers and by individual investors who attempt to profit from price movements. When considering the purchase of low-priced stocks, it is indeed buyer beware.

What is restricted stock?

In the United States, federal regulations require that most stock be registered with the U.S. Securities and Exchange Commission (SEC) before shares can be sold to the general public. Companies will sometimes issue unregistered stock directly to an investor or small group of investors through a private placement rather than offer the stock to the public. Stock issued without registration is called *restricted stock*, or *letter stock*, because the buyer must provide the SEC with a letter stating that the shares will be held for investment and not resold within a specified time. In some instances institutional investors are permitted to trade restricted stock within the defined period. Restricted stock is not traded on the securities exchanges and is of more interest to institutional investors than to individual investors. It is unlikely you will come into contact with restricted stock.

In what respects is stock different from other financial assets?

Stock is the only financial asset that represents ownership of a business. Bonds, another popular financial asset owned by many investors, represent loans to a business or government entity. Purchase a bond, and you have become a creditor who is entitled to periodic interest payments and the return of the principal amount of the loan. All of the payments promised by a bond, both interest and principal, are relatively certain. As a bondholder, you know exactly how much money you will receive and when it will be received. Shares of stock offer no such promises. As a part owner in the business that issued the stock, you will participate in the successes and failures of the business. As a shareholder, it is often difficult to forecast cash distributions and how much you will receive if you decide to sell your shares.

Why should I consider owning shares of stock?

Most individuals invest in stock because they believe the shares will increase in value. Increases in the market price of a stock mean you will be able to sell the shares of stock at a price higher than you paid. Most investors are willing to pay $30 per share for a stock because they believe the stock will increase in price so they can later sell the shares for $35, or $40, or more. Investors who purchase stocks for their potential for gaining value tend to view dividend distributions as an added bonus. Most stocks pay dividends that are relatively meager compared to the stock price, so that only a gain in share value can justify an investment in the stocks. Many companies do not pay any dividends to their stockholders. Exhibit 1-3 provides a comparison of the annual dividend and stock price for the common shares of some better known publicly traded companies. Notice that Dell Computer and Microsoft, companies with prospects for high growth in revenues and income, choose to retain all of their earnings for reinvestment. American Electric Power and Philip Morris, two firms with more limited capital needs, provide their owners with an above-average dividend yield, which is measured by dividing the annual dividend by the stock price. Low dividend yields for shares of General Electric, Pfizer, and Home Depot indicate that investors are expecting gains in market value to supplement the meager return they will earn from dividends.

EXHIBIT 1-3

Market Price, Dividends, and Divident Yield for Select Stocks
(Early 2001)

Stock	Market Price	Dividend	Dividend Yield
American Electric Power	$ 41	$ 2.40	5.85%
Dell Computer	26	0	0
ExxonMobil	79	1.76	2.23
General Electric	47	0.64	1.36
General Motors	56	2.00	3.57
Home Depot	41	0.16	0.39
Microsoft	61	0	0
Pfizer	41	0.44	1.07
Philip Morris	43	2.12	4.93
Wolverine World Wide	15	0.14	0.93

Do some investors buy stocks for dividend income?

Investors interested primarily in current income are likely to attach great importance to a stock's dividend payment. Investors who are retired and live partly off their investment income tend to prefer stocks that pay an attractive dividend relative to the market price of the stock. Income-oriented investors generally view increases in market value as a secondary concern because they rarely plan to sell the stock. A strong and stable dividend with a possibility of periodic increases is their most important concern. Still, income-oriented investors are in the minority, and most individuals search for stocks that offer the promise of an increase in market value. Most stocks with substantial dividend payments have limited prospects for gains in share price.

Do companies pay dividends in anything other than cash?

Companies sometimes choose to pay a stock dividend in place of a cash dividend. A stock dividend is the payment of a dividend in additional shares of stock. For example, suppose a firm in which you own 100 shares of stock declares a 3 percent stock dividend. Three percent of 100 shares is three shares, so you will receive an additional three shares. The certificate will arrive in the mail in the event you hold the certificate for the 100 shares. Otherwise, the additional shares will be credited to the account in which your shares are being held. A stock dividend is generally paid when a company is short of funds or has a need to use all available cash for reinvestment or debt repayment. A company that pays a stock dividend is divided into more ownership units, with a resulting decline in the value of each share of stock.

Can the stockholders of a company expect to receive anything other than dividends? For example, can they obtain discounts on products or services the company sells?

If you are asking whether you can buy stock in St. Louis brewer Anheuser Busch and expect to buy a 12-pack of Budweiser at half price, the answer is no. Likewise, Disney shareholders don't gain admission to Disney World at half price. A relatively small and seemingly decreasing number of companies do provide their shareholders with nominal gifts or discounts on their products or services. For example, shareholders of Union Pacific Corporation receive a colorful train calendar each year in December. Not a big deal, but a nice calendar is better than nothing. And while Anheuser Busch doesn't sell beer to stockholders at a discount, it does provide its shareholders with a 15 percent discount off the admission to the SeaWorld and Busch Gardens amusement parks that it owns. Gifts and discounts to shareholders, if available, are of nominal value and should not

play a part in determining the companies in which you choose
to become a shareholder.

What factors determine the value of a share of common stock?

The value of a single share of common stock depends both on the
overall value of the business and the total number of shares of
stock that are outstanding. Large corporations worth billions
of dollars often have millions or even hundreds of millions of
outstanding shares of stock, so a single share represents a very
small proportion of the overall ownership and total value of the
business. On the other hand, the share value can be relatively
high for a small corporation with few shares of outstanding
stock. Both the overall value and the number of shares of ownership affect the value of each share of a firm's stock. Stock valuation is discussed more completely in Chapter 6.

What happens to my stock if another company acquires the company in which I own shares?

If the directors and your fellow shareholders agree to the acquisition, you will have no choice but to surrender your shares in
return for cash or shares in the acquiring company, depending on
the agreement that has been reached between the directors of the
two firms. The acquiring company will purchase all of the shares
from you and the other owners, and the stock of the acquired firm
will cease trading. In most buyouts, you will receive shares of
stock in the acquiring company in a swap that results in no immediate tax liability on your part. If your shares are purchased for
cash, you will be required to pay a tax on the difference between
the money you receive and your cost basis of the shares that are
sold. In a stock swap, you and the other shareholders of the
acquired company become shareholders in the acquiring company, which will end up after the acquisition with more shares

outstanding. Regardless of how payment is made, shares in the acquired company are no longer available for sale or purchase. Shares of stock in Chrysler Corporation were no longer traded following the merger of the company with Daimler Benz. Likewise, stock in Amoco Corporation disappeared after British Petroleum purchased all of Amoco's shares.

Why do companies sometimes split their shares?

The majority of investors seem to be attracted to stocks that trade within a certain price range. For example, many investors avoid purchasing stocks that trade for over $100 per share, partly because the investors cannot afford to acquire a hundred shares at a time. Likewise, some investors feel that stocks trading below a certain price, say $1 or $2 per share, should be avoided because they must be risky. To attract investors to their stock, companies tend to establish a price range in which their shares will trade. For example, the directors of a company may decide that the firm's stock is most attractive to investors when the stock trades in a $40 to $80 price range. Directors of another company may believe that $10 to $30 per share is the optimal price range for the firm's stock. A company's directors can split the firm's stock and reduce its price without penalizing shareholders by splitting the stock. That is, the company issues additional shares of stock to stockholders in proportion to the shares they already own. Directors of a company may declare a two-for-one split, for instance, meaning the company will issue one additional share for each share currently owned. Own 200 shares, and a two-for-one split means you will receive an additional 200 shares, without being required to provide the company with any additional capital. In other words, the company issues additional shares without a corresponding increase in assets or income. Doubling the number of shares with no corresponding change in assets or earning capability should cause the price of the stock to fall to half the price at which it sold prior to the split. If you owned 200

shares of stock selling at a price of $30 per share before the two-
for-one split, you will own 400 shares of stock selling at a price
of $15 per share following the split. Either way, you have $6000
worth of stock.

Will a stock's dividend remain the same following a split?

A stock split will almost certainly result in a reduction in the
per-share dividend. Consider that, depending on the size of
the split, two or three times as many shares will be outstanding
following a stock split. Companies would never choose to split
their stock if they were expected to maintain the same per-share
dividend. More likely, the dividend will be adjusted downward
in proportion to the split. A two-for-one split can be expected to
result in a per-share dividend that is half the per-share dividend
prior to the split. In some splits, the company will slightly boost
the aggregate dividend. For example, a company that pays
a per-share dividend of 80 cents might pay a dividend of 42
cents per share following a two-for-one split. Your dividend
check will increase, but not by much.

Do companies ever reduce the number of shares?

Companies sometimes reduce the number of shares by purchasing shares of their stock in the market or directly from
shareholders. Repurchase of shares is a fairly common method
for reducing the number of shares in hopes that the stock price
will increase. Less frequently, companies will undertake a
reverse split in which they issue new shares in exchange for
a multiple of their outstanding shares. For example, a one-for-
three reverse split will cause a shareholder will receive one new
share for each three shares that are surrendered. Reverse splits
are designed to prop up a company's stock price and are nearly
always utilized when the stock price has declined to a level the

directors deem unacceptable. Some marketplaces will not list stocks that trade below a specified price. Companies with financial difficulties are most likely to engage in a reverse split to prop up the stock price and thereby make their stock appear less troubled.

Why does a reverse split cause an increase in a stock's price?

A reverse split reduces the number of outstanding shares of ownership without affecting the overall value of the business. A one-for-four reverse split reduces the number of outstanding shares by 75 percent, which should cause each share to sell for four times the price prior to the split. Stockholders are unlikely to gain from this paper shuffling because a reverse split causes each shareholder to own one-fourth as many shares, with each share worth four times the previous price.

What is a spinoff?

Companies sometimes decide to separate, or spin off, a subsidiary whose stock will trade independently of its former parent company. In a spinoff, the parent company sends its shareholders stock of a newly independent company that was formerly a subsidiary. Owners of the former parent company will then hold shares in two smaller companies rather than one large company. Shares of the former parent company will decrease in price following the spinoff because part of the firm (the former subsidiary) has essentially been given away and trades separately from the parent. Directors that decide on a spinoff are generally expecting that the two stocks trading separately will have more value than the parent's stock prior to the separation. Spinoffs generally have no tax consequence for stockholders so long as none of the shares are sold.

2 CHAPTER

FINANCIAL STATEMENTS AND STOCK VALUES

Chapter summary

The income statement, balance sheet, and statement of cash flows are the three major financial statements easily available to investors ... Stockholders are generally most interested in the data contained in a company's income statement ... Companies are permitted some discretion in the methods used to account for assets, liabilities, and income ... Financial analysts tend to consider cash flow to be a more important variable than income ... Financial statements sometimes present an imperfect picture of a firm's financial position and performance

Why are financial statements important?

Financial statements serve as a window through which shareholders, creditors, and other interested parties are able to observe and evaluate a company's operations. Financial statements provide information about the resources available to a company, the financing that has been utilized by the business to pay for these resources, and the success or failure of the firm's managers in earning an adequate return for the owners. The statements can be used to compare a firm's operations to the operations of similar companies, and to determine if operations at a company are improving or deteriorating relative to past periods.

What types of financial statements are available to individual investors?

The three major business financial statements are the balance sheet, the income statement, and the statement of cash flows. These statements are included as part of a company's annual and quarterly reports to shareholders. The financial information provided in the statements must also be filed by the company with the Securities and Exchange Commission, the federal agency with primary responsibility for regulation of the securities markets. A variety of other financial statements are available, but the balance sheet, income statement, and statement of cash flows are likely to provide most of the financial information in which you have an interest.

How do I locate the financial statements of a particular company?

Companies routinely send financial reports to their shareholders. Your brokerage firm should forward the reports if your shares are being held in "street name" in your account. In addition, many firms, hoping to attract new owners, will honor the requests of individuals who ask for annual or quarterly reports. Most companies with publicly traded stock include the most recent financial statements on their corporate Web sites. Look for a link to shareholder information or financial data on a company's main Web page. Several comprehensive brokerage firm Web sites and finance-related Web sites publish financial information for most large publicly held firms. Public libraries often subscribe to publications such as the *Value Line Investment Survey*, Moody's *Handbook of Common Stocks*, and Standard & Poor's *Stock Reports*, which contain substantial amounts of corporate financial information. Locating financial information is less of a problem than interpreting the financial data that is available. Chapter 12 is devoted to a more comprehensive discussion of financial information.

What information is most important to shareholders?

As owners, shareholders are particularly interested in the earnings—also called *income, or profit*—reported by a company. Many individual and professional investors evaluate a stock mostly on the basis of earnings the company is *expected* to report. Earnings forecasts are, at least in part, based on earnings that have been reported in the past. Investors are pleasantly surprised when a company reports higher-than-expected earnings, and the same investors tend to be disappointed when a company reports lower-than-expected earnings. The income a company reports can have a major impact on the firm's stock price because so many investors utilize current and past events in order to project the future. Thus, the report of higher- or lower-than-expected earnings is likely to cause an increase or a decrease, respectively, in the price of a company's stock. The relationship between earnings and stock values is discussed in Chapter 6.

Do companies report a single measure of earnings?

Companies report several levels of earnings. *Gross profit*, the largest amount of earnings reported by a firm each period, is the dollar amount of revenues less the cost of producing these revenues. Gross profit does not take into account many cash and noncash expenses such as depreciation, selling expenses, administrative expenses, or financing costs. This measure of profit is used to evaluate a company's pricing and efficiency. The next level of earnings is *operating income,* which is calculated after deducting depreciation and operating expenses such as selling and administrative expenses from gross profit. Operating income represents earnings before deducting interest expense on debt and income tax obligations. Financial analysts often utilize operating income to evaluate a firm's economic health. Operating income represents the income a firm has earned regardless of how its assets are financed. The third level of earnings, *pretax income*, is calculated by deducting interest expense from operating income. Pretax income is the amount of income available to the firm's shareholders before deducting income taxes. The bottom line for shareholders is *net income after taxes* (also called *net profit*), which represents the amount a firm earns after all expenses, interest, and taxes have been deducted. Net profit is available for the firm's managers to reinvest or distribute to owners. All four measures of earnings are reported in the financial press, and financial analysts use each earnings figure in evaluating different aspects of a company's financial performance.

Is any other information particularly important?

Members of the financial community are always interested in the amount of sales or revenue a company reports. In fact, revenue is the main measure used for measuring the economic health of many newly formed companies that have not yet become profitable. Increasing revenues are generally viewed as a sign of a healthy company, especially if the higher revenues are accompanied by increased income. Conversely, declining revenue may indicate a company is no longer competitive or that the firm's management is doing a poor job of promoting the company's products or services. Financial analysts are also interested in the accounting method by which a company arrives at the revenues and expenses that are reported. It is important to determine how a company determines the dollar amounts that are included as part of its financial statements.

You mean companies use different methods to calculate the financial information they report?

Companies must adhere to certain accounting standards when financial information is reported to the government and to the public. For example, rules exist regarding how and when sales should be recorded. Likewise, companies must follow approved methods by which long-term assets are reduced in value over time through depreciation. The Financial Accounting Standards Board, a group of professional accountants, developed these rules—called *generally accepted accounting principles*, or *GAAP*—so that financial information will have some degree of consistency, both among companies during the same year and for the same company over time. However, to account for differences among industries, the board permits some flexibility in reporting methods. For example, a regulated utility such as an electric company does not use exactly the same accounting methods as a computer manufacturer. The flexibility is designed to allow managers to use the accounting methods that best represent what is happening at their firms. The downside of this flexibility is it allows managers to use accounting techniques that may provide a misleading picture of a firm's financial condition. In addition, accounting practice includes gray areas in which a single transaction may be reported in more than one way. It is important to note that accounting standards change over time as the accounting profession attempts to make financial statements more representative of a company's financial position and performance.

Can you provide another example of a transaction that can be reported in more than one way?

Suppose a new auto supply company purchases 2000 oil filters at a cost of $1.50 each and another 3000 filters for $1.75 each. During the first month, the company sells 4000 filters at a price of $2.00 each. Total revenue for the first quarter is $8000, or 4000 times the selling price of $2.00, but how much in expenses should be recorded during the period? The company bought the filters at two different prices, so the expense it reports depends on which filters the firm assumes were sold. Did it sell 2000 of the $1.50 filters and 2000 of the $1.75 filters, or did it sell 1000 of the $1.50 filters and all 3000 of the filters that cost $1.75? Income is $1500 if the first method is used and $1250 if the second method is utilized. In the strange world of accounting, the firm can choose either method in accounting for the cost of the filters it sold. Thus, it could report either of two income amounts depending on the method used for reporting cost of goods sold.

You mentioned earnings as an important financial statistic. Can you provide an overview of the financial statement with this information?

The income statement reports a firm's revenues, expenses, and income, or profit, for a specified period of time, typically three months, six months, or a year. The numbers displayed on an income statement should be viewed as a series of flows, including the amount of money flowing into the company, the amount flowing out, and the amount that remains. If a company reports $10,000 in revenues and $7000 in expenses including interest and taxes, $3000 remains as income, or profit. An actual income statement is somewhat more complicated than this, of course, but this example conveys the general idea. The income that benefits the firm's owners, or stockholders, is the amount of money that remains after all the other individuals and organizations have been paid. These other parties typically include the firm's suppliers, employees, creditors, and various levels of government, all of whom must be paid prior to recording income for stockholders. If revenues exceed expenses, the company will report a profit. If expenses exceed revenues, the company will report a loss. Profit belongs to the firm's stockholders even though stockholders are unlikely to receive a check for the full amount of the profits.

Can you provide an example of an income statement?

Exhibit 2-1 illustrates a simplified corporate income statement. The firm's sales revenues and other income translate to $900,000 of net income after all expenses have been deducted. Notice that the claims of suppliers, employees, creditors, and tax authorities have been accounted for prior to any net income being reported for the firm's owners. Net income of $900,000 is split among 450,000 outstanding shares resulting in earnings per share of $2.00. The firm's directors voted to pay a dividend of $1.25 per share, which represents 62.5 percent of net income. In other words, the directors distributed more of the firm's earnings to stockholders than they retained for reinvestment or debt repayment.

Must profits be split among all of the firm's shareholders?

Net income is reported both in total and on a per-share basis. Investors attach more importance to *earnings per share* (eps) than to total income or profit. A very large company is likely to report a greater amount of net income than a small company with only a fraction of the larger firm's revenues, but the smaller company will have fewer shares of stock outstanding and may report higher earnings per share. Consider a firm that reports increased earnings, but during the past year issued additional shares of stock. The higher earnings must be split among more shares of

EXHIBIT 2-1

Example of a Corporate Income Statement

Net Sales	$7,284,000	(Sales less an allowance for returned goods)
Interest and Other Income	65,000	(Income from sources other than sales)
Less: Cost of Goods Sold	4,949,000	(Costs of raw materials, supplies, and labor)
Gross Profit	2,400,000	(Income prior to operating expenses such as depreciation)
Less: Selling and Administrative Expenses	1,397,000	(Expenses incurred for sales commisions, salaries, etc.)
Less: Depreciation	91,000	(Estimated cost of providing for wear and tear of fixed assets)
Net Operating Income	1,306,000	(Income prior to deducting expenses of financing the firm)
Less: Interest Expense	53,000	(Interest paid to lenders)
Income before Taxes	1,253,000	(Income prior to income taxes paid or incurred)
Less: Taxes	$ 900,000	(Income available to the firm's owners)
Average Shares Outstanding	450,000	(Outstanding shares of ownership)
Earnings per Common Share	$ 2.00	(Net income for each of the 450,000 ownership shares)
Dividends per Common Share	$ 1.25	(Dividend paid on each share of common stock)

ownership, and earnings per share may actually decline. Earnings per share are calculated by dividing the number of shares of ownership (shares outstanding) into a company's net income after taxes. If a company with 200,000 shares of stock outstanding reports $500,000 in net income, earnings per share are calculated as $500,000/200,000 shares, or $2.50. Earnings per share will increase to $3.00 if next year's profit increases to $600,000 while outstanding shares remain constant at 200,000. Changes in total income may be misleading for several reasons, including the possibility that the firm may have acquired another company during the year. The possibility of a change in shares outstanding is the reason why earnings per share are a more important statistic for shareholders than net income.

Does reported revenue represent cash the company collects during a period?

Companies are permitted to report revenues and expenses on an accrual rather than a cash basis. Accrual accounting allows companies to record sales for a particular period even though payment may not be received until a subsequent period. For example, a toy manufacturer is permitted to record as revenue fourth-quarter toy shipments even though most of its customers will not pay for their purchases until after the first of the year. The sales are recorded as revenue on the income statement although the toy manufacturer receives IOUs rather than cash from its customers. Likewise, the toy manufacturer records as an expense the plastic, wood, and other materials it purchases even though it may not pay its own suppliers until after the first of the year. Don't assume a company is flush with cash when the income statement indicates a high level of sales, because a large portion of sales may be on credit. Companies that report large increases in sales sometimes end up short of cash because their customers have not yet paid for the merchandise that has been shipped.

What happens to the earnings a company reports?

Several options are available for the earnings that are reported on the income statement. Some companies utilize all of their earnings for reinvestment. That is, earnings are used to pay for the purchase of additional assets such as machinery and warehouses that will hopefully produce even higher earnings down the road. Utilizing earnings for reinvestment means these same earnings are unavailable for the payment of dividends to the owners. The firm could acquire the additional assets without reinvesting income, but only by raising an equivalent amount of funds either through borrowing or by issuing new shares of stock. Financing additional assets with borrowed funds or with funds raised through a sale of stock both have drawbacks. Additional borrowing results in higher interest expense and greater risk for the firm. Additional shares of stock will dilute the ownership of shareholders and, perhaps, reduce earnings per share. Payment of a dividend causes a smaller amount of funds to be available for reinvestment. Companies that choose to pay all or a part of earnings in dividends to stockholders must reduce investments in new assets or rely on outside sources for additional capital to finance their investments

In what respects is a balance sheet different from an income statement?

The *balance sheet* is an accounting record of the assets, outstanding debts, and investments in the firm by its stockholders. Unlike the income statement that presents a company's flow of revenues and expenses during a period of time, the balance sheet presents the dollar amounts of assets, debts, and stockholders' investment at a particular point in time. A balance sheet should be viewed as a snapshot, while an income statement is more like a video. While an income statement may show sales, expenses, and income during the calendar year January through December, the balance sheet lists assets, debts, and shareholders' investment as of the last day of December. A balance sheet is a record of what a company owns and what it owes, while an income statement indicates how effectively the firm's managers are able to use the assets recorded on the balance sheet. The income statement shows how much profit a firm's managers can squeeze out of assets shown on the balance sheet.

Do dollar values on the balance sheet indicate the current value of the firm's assets?

Assets, things of value the firm owns, are valued on the balance sheet at the prices paid by the firm at the time the assets were purchased less any deduction for wear and tear (depreciation) that has occurred since the purchase date. In accounting lingo, assets are recorded on the balance sheet at *book value*. For example, land purchased years ago for $30,000 incurs no depreciation and will continue to be recorded on the balance sheet at a book value of $30,000 regardless of the current market value. Original cost continues to be used in valuing the asset on the balance sheet even though the land could possibly be sold currently for much more than the $30,000 purchase price. Land is unique, however, and most assets are subject to being depreciated, or reduced in value over time. A truck purchased two years ago for $50,000 will be valued on the balance sheet on the basis of the $50,000 purchase price less two years of depreciation. In practice, the truck will be listed at a book value equal to about half the purchase price. Likewise, a building is valued on the balance sheet at its purchase price less all of the depreciation that has been recorded subsequent to the purchase date. Assets listed on a company's balance sheet may have a market value that is much different from the dollar value indicated on the balance sheet.

Can you provide an example of a corporate balance sheet?

Exhibit 2-2 illustrates a simplified corporate balance sheet. The firm lists $4,844,000 in assets valued at historical cost (what the firm paid) less depreciation that has been recorded since the

EXHIBIT 2-2

Example of a Corporate Balance Sheet

Assets		
Cash	$ 24,000	(Currency held or deposits in financial institutions)
Marketable Securities	721,000	(Short-term debt securities such as U.S. Treasury bills)
Accounts Receivable	536,000	(Amount owned the firm by its customers)
Inventories	968,000	(Raw materials and products awaiting sale)
Prepaid Expenses	93,000	(Bills paid ahead of time)
Current Assets	$2,342,000	(Assets that will convert to cash within a year)
Plant and Equipment	2,830,000	(Purchase price of fixed assets that will eventually wear out)
Less: Accumulated Depreciation	880,000	(Estimated wear since acquired)
Net Plant and Equipment	1,950,000	(Fixed asset values after adjustment for wear)
Land	552,000	(Purchase price of land that is owned)
Total Assets	$4,844,000	(Assets owned by the firm valued at historical cost)
Liabilities and Owner's Equity		
Accounts Payable	$ 574,000	(Owed by the company to its suppliers)
Accrued Expenses	346,000	(Owed to employees, the government, and others)
Notes Payable	125,000	(Debt due within one year)
Current Liabilities	1,045,000	(Total debts that must be paid within the next year)
Long-Term Debt	814,000	(Loans not due for payment for over one year)
Total Liabilities	$1,859,000	(Claims of the firm's creditors)
Common Stock	95,000	(Funds invested by the firm's owners)

EXHIBIT 2-2

Concluded

Liabilities and Owner's Equity		
Additional Paid in Capital	185,000	(Funds invested by owners in excess of par value)
Retained Earnings	$2,705,000	(Earnings reinvested in the business)
Total Liabilities and Owners' Equity	$4,844,000	(Money invested in the firm by creditors and owners)

assets were acquired. Notice that the firm lists an unusually large amount of current assets that typically don't produce much income. The liabilities section of the balance sheet indicates that creditors to whom the firm owes a little less than $2 million are financing less than half of the firm's assets. The remainder of the assets are financed by owners, partly from the purchase of shares of stock that have been issued by the firm, but mostly from past income that has been reinvested, as indicated, by $2,705,000 of retained earnings.

How does a firm determine how much to deduct from an asset's value for wear and tear each period?

A company reduces the accounting value for each of its long-term assets according to a schedule established by the government. The schedule indicates the assumed life for different categories of assets and the rate at which these assets may be depreciated. For example, automobiles, light trucks, and most machinery are fully depreciated (depreciated to a value of zero) over a period of five years. Companies would generally prefer to deduct the entire cost of an asset in the year the asset is purchased. Large deductions reduce reported income and result in less taxes. However, the government requires that companies annually deduct a specified percentage of the initial cost. Thus, instead of deducting the full $50,000 cost of a truck in the year of purchase, a company will deduct only 20 percent, or $10,000, in the first year of use. Additional depreciation is deducted in the subsequent four years, until the asset is fully depreciated after five years.

Are you saying that assets on the balance sheet are valued at the price paid less the depreciation that has been recorded?

That is correct. In the above example, the truck would be valued at the end of the first year at $40,000 (initial cost of $50,000 less $10,000 in depreciation) on the firm's balance sheet. The recorded value following depreciation may or may not represent the true market value of the truck. Consider that this same method is used to value all of the other assets owned by the firm and it is easy to understand why the balance sheet is likely to provide a misleading dollar value for the assets a company owns. In some cases the balance sheet may grossly understate the true value of what a firm owns. In other instances the market value of a firm's assets may be overstated.

Are any assets recorded at their true market values?

Certainly. Cash is listed on the balance sheet at its current market value. Other short-lived assets (formally called *current assets*) are likely to be represented on the balance sheet at very close to their market values. For example, short-term loans to customers (called *accounts receivable*) for merchandise that has been shipped or services performed are likely to be listed at their true value. Even soon-to-be-paid debts can be misrepresented, however, when a company continues to list an amount to be received from a customer that is unlikely to fully repay its debt. Companies have been known to continue to list questionable assets at an inflated value because they don't want to penalize their earnings by declaring the debts as worthless. Still, accounts receivable are likely to be a fairly accurate representation of short-term debts likely to be paid to the firm within a year. Likewise, inventories, or goods being held for resale, are likely to be valued at current market value. Long-term assets such as buildings and real estate are most likely to have their value misrepresented on a firm's balance sheet. The misrepresentation is not generally intentional but a consequence of the accounting system that is employed.

Are the debts of a company likely to be misrepresented on the balance sheet?

Companies don't have much latitude in recording their own debts. A company that owes $50,000 to the bank must include the full amount of what is owed in the liability section of its balance sheet. As a result, liabilities are generally not subject to misrepresentation in the same manner as assets. Most individual debts included on the balance sheet will gradually decline as the debt is paid down over time. In other words, payments on a loan that exceed interest will reduce the principal of the loan and the amount shown as a liability on the balance sheet. A loan is removed from the liability section of the balance sheet once it has been fully repaid.

Are you saying that liabilities are stated at their true values?

Liabilities are indeed shown at their true values. However, the risk inherent in the liabilities must be interpreted in view of how soon the debts are to be repaid. Debts on the balance sheet are classified as either current liabilities or long-term liabilities. Debts due for repayment in under a year are considered current liabilities, while all other debts are recorded in the general liability section that follows current liabilities. The question is whether a given debt has the same implication regardless of when repayment is scheduled. Current liabilities, or short-term loans, are generally considered more burdensome because they must be paid fairly soon. Even debt classified as long-term can differ with regard to the burden it imposes on a business. For example, a $10,000 loan due in 5 years is recorded in the same manner as a $10,000 loan due in 25 years, even though the burden of the 25 year loan is probably less.

What does this mean for the stockholders' equity section of the balance sheet?

The *stockholders' equity* section of the balance sheet is a record of the money contributed by the firm's owners. The contributions consist both of reinvested earnings and money paid to the firm when shares of stock were issued. Keep in mind that the equity section of a firm's balance sheet includes only the money paid by stockholders who purchased stock when the shares were issued. It does not include entries for shares in the company that were purchased from other investors in subsequent trading. A million shares of stock originally issued a decade ago for $10 per share is recorded on the firm's balance sheet at $10 million even though the same shares may now trade for a much higher or lower price. Likewise, if a firm issued a million shares of stock for $10 per share 10 years ago and subsequently issued another million shares for $15 per share several years later, the stockholders' equity section of the balance sheet will include $25 million in common stock.

How is stockholders' equity related to a company's assets and liabilities?

By definition, stockholders' equity must equal a company's total assets less its total liabilities. Now that you understand how assets listed on the balance sheet are often overvalued or undervalued, it becomes easier to see why many financial analysts don't consider stockholders' equity to be a particularly important consideration in determining the actual value of a company. Consider the case of a software company that has developed several very popular computer programs whose sales bring in large amounts of revenue and income. The programs are likely to be recorded on the balance sheet at a relatively low value even though the software has considerable market value and could be sold to another firm for a large sum of money. Likewise, the market value of the firm's stock is likely to be much higher than the recorded value of stockholders' equity on the balance sheet. Just as assets are represented on the balance sheet according to their historical cost, shareholders' equity is recorded on the basis of the price at which the firm's stock was issued and the amount of profits the company has retained subsequent to the date it was incorporated. Shareholders' equity indicates little information about the earning power of the firm's assets and doesn't provide much useful information about the value of ownership.

Does each share of a company's stock receive equal treatment?

If a company has issued only a single class of stock, then each share of ownership has the same claim and the same rights. Some companies issue more than one class of common stock, while other companies issue both preferred stock and common stock. Preferred stock has a preference over common stock with respect to dividends and also with respect to asset distributions in the event the company is liquidated. Most companies have a single type of owner claim with one class of common stock and no preferred stock.

Doesn't stockholders' equity at the very least represent the minimum value of the stockholders' claims?

Not necessarily. Suppose a company owns several major assets that could not be sold for the values at which they are listed on the balance sheet. For example, a company might own a number of antiquated and inefficient manufacturing plants that would be difficult to sell at anywhere near the values at which they are recorded on the balance sheet. Suppose the company's directors decided for whatever reason to liquidate the firm by selling all the assets at their market values. Proceeds from the sale would be used to pay the company's creditors, who have a priority claim before remaining funds are distributed to the owners. With assets overvalued on the balance sheet, it is unlikely the stockholders will receive the amount indicated in owners' equity on the balance sheet. In this instance it is clear that owners' equity does not represent the minimum value of the shareholders' interest in the company.

Are other important financial measures related to the balance sheet?

Book value, mentioned previously, a term frequently used by financial analysts, is generally considered the same as shareholders' equity. In other words, the book value of a company is equal to assets minus liabilities. The equality of shareholders' equity and book value holds when a company has no outstanding preferred stock. Outstanding preferred stock is subtracted from shareholders' equity when calculating book value relevant to common stockholders. The par value, or face value, rather than the market value of the preferred stock, should be deducted in calculating book value. Book value is generally stated on a per-share basis in order to show the claim for each share of common stock. In other words, the common stockholders' claim on the company is equal to book value per share times the number of common shares outstanding. In theory, book value is the amount common stockholders would recover in the event the company is liquidated. However, as noted above, the liquidation of assets would have to occur at their accounting value, an unlikely event. In any case, investors seldom purchase common stock with the expectation that the company will be liquidated.

Can you provide an example of a book value calculation?

Suppose a firm lists $800,000 in total assets on its balance sheet. The assets include cash, debts owed the firm by its customers (accounts receivable), goods held for resale to its customers (inventories), buildings, and land. The buildings are valued after a deduction for accumulated depreciation. On the liability side, the company has $50,000 of short-term bank loans and $300,000 in long-term loans. With $800,000 of assets and $350,000 of total liabilities, stockholders' equity is equal to the difference, or $450,000. The stockholders' equity section of the balance sheet indicates $50,000 par value of preferred stock and 10,000 shares of common stock valued on the balance sheet at $100,000. Earnings of $300,000 have been retained and are included in the stockholders' equity section as retained earnings. Book value per common share is equal to total assets ($800,000) less total liabilities ($50,000 + $300,000) less preferred stock ($50,000), or $400,000, divided by common shares outstanding (10,000), or $40.

Can you calculate the book value for the business used in the earlier exhibits?

Exhibit 2-3 illustrates the book value calculation for the firm used in the previous exhibits. Subtracting total creditor claims of $1,859,000 from total assets of $4,844,000 produces a total book value for the firm of $2,985,000. Dividing this amount of shareholders' equity by 450,000 outstanding shares of stock results in a per-share book value of $6.63. This firm does not have any outstanding preferred stock that would be subtracted from shareholders' equity to calculate book value per common share.

EXHIBIT 2-3

Calculating a Firm's Book Value

Total Assets	$4,844,000
Less: Total Liabilities	1,859,000
Owners' Equity (Book Value)	$2,985,000
Common Shares Outstanding	450,000 shares
Book Value per Share ($2,985,000/450,000)	$6.63

How should shareholders interpret book value?

Financial analysts sometimes compare the market price of a firm's common stock to the company's book value per share. In other words, they compare the firm's market value with its accounting value. When the market value exceeds the book value, as is typical for successful companies, assets as presented on the balance sheet would appear as undervalued. On the other hand, if book value per share exceeds the stock price, investors must feel the company's assets are worth less than their accounting values. Some investors search for companies with book values that exceed the market price of the stock because they feel these firms are likely to be undervalued in the market. A company with undervalued assets may be more likely to become a buyout target of another company that is searching for a bargain acquisition. The company may also offer shareholders substantial stock price appreciation if management can squeeze more profitability from the existing assets.

How am I able to determine the number of shares a company has issued?

Information about the number of shares of ownership is included in the shareholders' equity section of the balance sheet. The balance sheet is likely to list both "shares authorized" and "shares outstanding" beside the entry for "common stock." Authorized shares indicates the maximum number of shares the corporate charter permits the directors to issue, while shares outstanding represents the number of authorized shares that have actually been issued and remain outstanding. When a company has issued all of the shares authorized by the corporate charter, directors must obtain the shareholders' approval before additional shares may be issued. Only outstanding shares are utilized in calculating earnings per share and book value per share. Likewise, only shares currently outstanding are entitled to dividend payments.

What if a company issues shares of stock and later repurchases some of the shares?

A company that repurchases a portion of its shares will reduce the number of shares outstanding at the same time that shares authorized will remain unchanged. The directors may later decide to reissue these shares. A reduction in outstanding shares results in fewer shares of ownership over which to divide income and pay dividends because a company does not include repurchased shares when it calculates earnings per share or when it pays dividends. Fewer shares outstanding means the remaining shares are likely to benefit from more earnings per share. Keep in mind that a company repurchases its shares with money that could be used for other purposes. For example, the firm could pay off a portion of its debt and reduce its interest expense or it could acquire new assets that would provide the company with additional revenues and income. Thus, the repurchase of stock entails a cost to the company and its shareholders.

What are some important relationships between the income statement and balance sheet?

Perhaps the most important relationship to understand is the flow of income from the income statement to the balance sheet.

Income after taxes that is not paid to stockholders in dividends flows into retained earnings in the stockholders' equity section of the balance sheet. An equal increase in an investment such as inventories, equipment, or cash or an equal decrease in a debt offsets this increase in retained earnings. In other words, income that a company retains will be used to acquire additional assets or to reduce liabilities. Either way, the company that chooses to retain income improves its financial condition.

Do retained earnings on the balance sheet represent a reservoir of cash?

The balance sheet entry for retained earnings does not represent a store of cash sitting idle while waiting for investment opportunities. The amount of cash available to a company is listed as cash in the asset section of the balance sheet. Retained earnings are a measure of income that has been retained from past operating periods. Retained earnings listed in the stockholders' equity section of the balance sheet represent funds that have already been committed to assets that are listed on the same balance sheet. Acquiring a new investment such as equipment or inventories does not increase or reduce the amount of retained earnings. Rather, the new asset is offset by a decrease in cash if the firm pays cash for the asset or an increase in debt if the purchase is financed with borrowed money. Income retained in the current period serves to increase the amount of retained earnings compared to retained earnings reported in the prior period.

Do any other important relationships exist?

Financial analysts evaluate a company's profitability by comparing income as shown on the income statement to both assets and to stockholders' equity, both of which are reported on the balance sheet. These calculations are similar to an individual investor determining the rate of return from owning an investment. Net income compared to assets illustrates the rate of return a firm's managers are able to earn on all of the firm's assets. Net income compared to stockholders' equity is a measure of the return the managers are able to earn on the investment of the firm's owners. High rates of return are desirable, of course, and so a high rate of return on assets and on stockholders' equity is considered a sign of effective management.

Will I earn the same return on my stock investment as the firm's managers earn on the company's assets?

The relationship between the return a company is able to earn on its assets and the return you earn on the stock isn't necessarily what you might expect. For example, a company may earn a relatively high return on its assets during a year when the stock price barely moves or even declines. Likewise, your stock may exhibit a large price gain during a period when the company's return on assets is relatively low. The reason, at least partially, is that investors price a stock on the basis of their expectations regarding the company's future operations. Current earnings are important, of course, but mostly to the extent they alter investor expectations regarding the firm's future. Suppose the company in which you own stock just posted relatively poor earnings. If investors had been expecting even worse results, you may well see an increase in the price of the stock. Conversely, if a company reports relatively good profits, but the profits are less than most investors anticipated, the stock price is likely to fall. Still, over time you can generally expect that a company's return on assets will directly affect its stockholders' return on their investment in the company's common stock.

Why is the statement of cash flows considered an important financial statement?

Many financial analysts consider *cash flows* to be more important than income in valuing a company and its stock. In fact, companies that report no earnings but generate large cash flows can be quite valuable. Remember, the income reported by a company is an accounting value and does not necessarily represent money that is available to spend. On the other hand, cash can be used to pay employees, buy assets, or pay down debt. A company's cash flow is particularly important when another firm may be considering the company as a potential acquisition.

What information does the statement of cash flows provide?

The statement of cash flows blends cash flows from the income statement with changes in various items on the balance sheet. The statement's purpose is to identify how the firm is generating cash and how cash is being used. For example, an increase in inventories (as shown by a change in balance sheet values from one period to the next) indicates the firm is devoting cash to building up its stock of goods available for resale. Likewise, an increase in long-term debt (also shown by a change in long-term liabilities on the balance sheet) shows the firm is relying on long-term borrowing to generate cash. The statement of cash flows allows you to determine if a firm is financing growth with earnings, borrowing, or new shares of stock. It also shows if more cash is coming in than going out.

How do I interpret the cash flow statement?

The statement of cash flows has three major sections: cash flows from operating activities, cash flows from investment activities, and cash flows from financing activities. Changes in the three sections taken together equal the change in the cash position of the firm. If operating activities and financing activities provide net cash inflows that exceed the cash outflows from investment activities, the firm experiences a positive cash flow for the period. Suppose a firm's operations for the year produce a cash inflow of $15 million. During the same year the company spends $20 million on new equipment that is financed, in part, with a $10 million long-term loan. Assuming no other investments or financing, cash flow for the year is a positive $5 million ($15 million − $20 million + $10 million).

Can a company with a negative cash flow still be successful?

A very successful company, especially a relatively young company lacking substantial ownership capital, may experience cash flow difficulties. The managers of a new company may feel a need to grow rapidly in order to establish the company's product or service before competitors can present a serious challenge. Thus, the firm may invest large amounts of money at a time when its small revenue base produces little cash flow from operations. The alternative is to borrow or issue additional shares of common stock in order to provide cash for investment spending. Substantial operating losses will require the firm's owners to seek outside capital in order to support the company's normal operations. Negative operating cash flows can only continue for a limited time before investors are likely to become disillusioned and refuse to supply additional capital.

Which of the financial statistics you mentioned is most important to me as a stockholder?

You are almost certain to find that the earnings reported by a company will have the greatest influence on the value of the stock you hold, at least in the short run. Keep in mind, however, that financial statements are filled with numbers from the past, and expectations of the future tend to drive a stock's market value. Still, viewing the past, especially the recent past, should provide insight for the future. Consider a company's financial performance over a period of time, not just the most recent year or quarter. Check the trend in dividends and earnings for the last five years. Evaluate the company's profitability over several years. Even poorly performing companies can turn around, especially under new management.

3

CHAPTER

HOW STOCK IS ISSUED

Chapter summary

Most companies use the services of investment bankers to assist in stock issues ... Investment bankers often buy stock from the issuer and resell shares to the public ... Pricing stock in an initial public offering is an art, and share prices may climb immediately following a new issue ... Some stock issues are unavailable to the general public ... Rights offerings are used when stockholders have a preemptive right ... Shares of foreign firms are generally traded indirectly with American Depositary Receipts ... Stock issues sometimes include already outstanding shares rather than new shares ... Participating in initial public offerings can prove very risky to investors ... Companies sometimes repurchase previously issued shares

Do companies issue stock directly to investors?

Companies that decide to issue shares of stock nearly always seek the assistance of specialized financial institutions, called *investment bankers*, to serve as an intermediary with the investment community. Very few companies have the time, expertise, or investor contacts to issue stock directly, and so they must rely on investment banking companies to perform this important task. Investment bankers specialize in the business of raising funds in the capital markets, and so they are familiar with the laws and paperwork required to bring a new issue of securities to market. In addition, established investment banking firms have ties with individuals and institutions with money to invest. A typical company requiring outside capital is in business to produce a product or service, not seek out investors and raise money in the capital markets. Lack of expertise and experience doesn't mean companies never directly issue stock to investors but that direct issues to investors are the exception rather than the rule.

Why is it so difficult for companies to issue their own stock?

A company desiring to issue shares of stock must identify investors who have adequate financial resources and are interested in becoming an owner of that particular firm. This, in itself, serves as a substantial roadblock for most companies, especially if a large amount of funds is required. In addition, issuing stock requires that a company adhere to state and federal regulations that tend to be detailed and complicated. The cost in both time and money of learning all the applicable regulations is very high, especially for a company that may issue securities only infrequently. A substantial portion of the fees earned by investment bankers results from their knowledge of the applicable regulations. A company deciding to issue stock without assistance is somewhat like a person who must learn plumbing in order to plumb a house. In each case, the time and expense of learning the ropes, along with the possibility of making a serious mistake, point toward using an expert.

What kinds of regulations apply to new securities issues?

Issuers and investment bankers must comply with regulations, many of which were enacted in the early 1930s to protect individual investors from being scammed. The regulations followed a stock market collapse in which many individual investors lost a large amount of their wealth. Companies wishing to issue securities must now file a registration statement with the Securities and Exchange Commission, the federal regulatory agency that handles most matters regarding financial securities. In addition, prospective buyers of new securities must be provided with relevant information about both the issuer and the securities being issued. The regulations are designed to provide full disclosure so investors can make an informed decision regarding the investment quality of the securities to be issued. The regulations do not require investors to pay attention to the information made available.

Can companies issue stock without meeting all these regulations?

Some stock issues are exempt from the complicated regulations included in federal securities laws. Stock issues that are placed with a single buyer or a small number of investors and do not involve a public distribution do not require a registration statement. Likewise, a security issue distributed within a single state is generally exempt from the federal regulations, although less restrictive state regulations are likely to apply. But most of the stock issues you come into contact with must complete the complicated registration process required by federal law.

Do investment bankers issue new shares through stock exchanges?

Stock exchanges are important markets for trading shares of stock that have already been issued, but exchanges do not normally serve as a conduit through which new shares are issued. Investment bankers seek out individual and institutional investors likely to be interested in purchasing the shares being offered for sale. In fact, investment banking firms attempt to locate and contact interested investors before the issue is brought to market. Thus, there is no need for them to go through the trading mechanism provided by securities exchanges. Stock exchanges and the secondary markets are discussed in Chapter 4.

How do companies needing funds connect with an investment banker?

Investment bankers earn their income by trolling the capital markets for large sums of money that can be made available to corporations in need of capital. As part of their business, they aggressively seek out businesses with a need for additional capital. Investment banking companies are continually in search of privately owned businesses that might benefit from access to the capital markets. These financial intermediaries even go so far as to try and convince reluctant company owners that it is in the owners' interest to take their companies public by issuing shares of stock to outside investors willing to provide the company with capital. Business owners who wish to issue stock but have not been approached by an investment banker can locate information about recent stock issues by reviewing financial publications such as the *Wall Street Journal*. Announcements include the names of the investment bankers that participated in the offerings.

Is the investment banker responsible only for locating investors who will buy the stock?

Investment bankers generally guarantee funds to the issuer by purchasing and then reselling to investors the shares that are being issued. In other words, the shares are bought by the investment banker, who immediately resells the stock to investors. Investment bankers who buy stock for resale act as underwriters and are said to *underwrite* the issue. This means the investment banker assumes the risk that the shares may be difficult to resell at the anticipated price. From the standpoint of the issuing company, a stock issue that is underwritten by an investment banker guarantees that the needed funds will be available. Most issuing companies choose to have their issues underwritten.

You mean the investment banker temporarily owns shares that are to be offered to investors?

Yes, for a short time the investment banker actually owns the newly issued shares that will soon find a home in investor portfolios. At least, the investment banker hopes the shares will find a home. As owner of the securities, the investment banking firm assumes the risk that part or all of the shares cannot be sold at the expected price. To help guarantee that this doesn't happen, the investment banker conducts substantial research prior to the issue in order to be reasonably confident it will not be stuck with the shares for a long period of time. The investment banker acting as an underwriter provides the issuer its money and is left to worry about locating buyers for the issue. Actually, most investment bankers will already have most or all of the buyers in place by the time the shares are issued. Many stock issues sell out almost immediately, while other issues may sell more slowly. In the latter instance, the investment banker may still be trying to sell shares several days or weeks after a stock issue is brought to market.

Are all new stock issues underwritten by investment bankers?

Investment bankers manage some stock issues on a *best efforts* basis. This type of offering commits the investment banker to making its best effort at selling the issue without actually guaranteeing a successful sale. The investment banker does not serve as an underwriter and purchase shares for resale when a best efforts offering is used. Rather, it acts as an agent and does its best to drum up interest from investors who agree to buy the shares. With a best efforts offering, the corporate issuer needing capital—not the investment banker—is at risk of the sale proving unsuccessful. The risk to the issuing firm is that the issue will not completely sell and the issuer will fail to obtain all of the needed money. A best efforts offering may occur over a period of time rather than on a single offering date. The relatively small amount of capital required of an investment banker means that smaller firms manage many best efforts offerings.

Do investment bankers assist with the sale of securities other than stock?

Investment bankers also underwrite bond issues. In fact, fees from bond issues are a major source of income for many investment bankers. These firms are also involved in secondary offerings when large blocks of outstanding securities are issued. For example, the founding family members of a publicly traded company may employ an investment banker to locate buyers for all or a portion of the owners' shares. The investment banker will underwrite the issue and offer the shares for resale. Keep in mind that a secondary offering does not involve newly created shares of stock but shares that were issued in the past and are being offered for resale. Thus, a secondary offering provides no additional funds to the company that initially issued the shares, because it involves the sale of stock from one investor group to another.

Do investment bankers perform other important functions?

Investment banking firms are active in mergers and acquisitions. For example, a firm's directors interested in seeking a merger partner are likely to enlist an investment banker who assists in the search. Investment bankers also assist firms that are attempting to thwart unwanted takeover attempts by other firms. Companies wishing to repurchase large amounts of their own shares will employ the services of an investment banker to assist with the repurchase. Basically, investment bankers are involved is just about every type of activity related to the capital markets.

Do investment bankers usually act alone when a stock issue is brought to market?

Several investment bankers often band together in a group, called a *syndicate*, when a stock issue is unusually large or particularly risky. The manager of the underwriting syndicate may then invite additional firms to assist in the sale. A syndicate facilitates the distribution of the shares because different investment banking firms have established contacts with different investors. In addition, a syndicate spreads the risk of being unable to sell a portion of the shares due to deteriorating market conditions. One firm that is unable to sell all of its allocation of shares may call on another member of the syndicate to locate buyers for the excess shares. The syndicate manager may choose to bring in additional firms as a selling group that will participate in selling shares without actually underwriting the issue.

Are some stock issues so large that several managers are required?

Stock issues sometimes involve more than a single manager. In some instances the issuer may request that a second firm serve as a co-manager of the deal. The investment banking firm that is chosen to serve as manager may feel the issue requires the financial resources and expertise of another firm that will only come into the deal as a co-manager. Keep in mind that a certain amount of prestige goes with being the manager or co-manager of a major stock issue. In addition, co-managers generally benefit from a larger allocation of the shares to be issued, which translates into more profit for the firm.

How do underwriters earn a profit?

The underwriter purchases shares of stock from the issuer for less than the price at which the shares are to be offered to investors. For example, an underwriter might pay the issuing company $25.00 for shares of stock that are to be sold to investors for $25.50. The 50-cent-per-share underwriting discount is known as the *gross spread*, a seemingly small fee that grows to a sizable sum when it is spread over millions or tens of millions of shares. For a stock issue of 40 million shares with a gross spread of 50 cents per share, for instance, the underwriting fee is $20 million. The amount of the gross spread is a function of the size of an issue and the expected difficulty in selling the issue. On a per-share basis, the spread tends to be larger when the issuing company is coming to market for the first time. These first-time sales, called *initial public offerings*, or *IPOs*, cause the investment banker greater difficulty in accurately judging an appropriate offering price for the stock. Likewise, a stock issue with a relatively small number of shares will result in a large gross spread for each share because the investment banker must cover its expenses with a smaller number of shares.

Are substantial financial resources required for investment banking firms that underwrite major stock issues?

Investment bankers generally don't possess the financial resources required to finance major stock issues. In other words, they don't have enough money to purchase outright all the shares that will be offered for resale to investors. With finite financial resources, investment banking firms are forced to take out short-term bridge loans that are repaid when the shares have been distributed and paid for by purchasers. Interest paid on the short-term loans is an expense investment bankers incur when they underwrite a stock issue.

Do all the syndicate members involved in an issue benefit from the same gross spread?

Members earn different spreads depending on their place in the pecking order of the underwriting syndicate. The manager assumes the greatest responsibility, does the most work, and receives the largest allocation of shares to sell. The extra responsibility and risk are accompanied by the largest gross spread. Members of the selling group who are not underwriters and do not commit their own money to the issue will incur the lowest risk and earn the smallest spread. While not all the members earn the same spread, all members are required to sell shares at the same price to investors. Thus, it doesn't matter from your point of view as an individual investor whether shares are purchased from the manager, from another member of the syndicate, or from a member of the selling group, at least from the standpoint of the price you will pay.

Are you saying it doesn't matter whether I purchase shares from the managing underwriter or a member of the selling group?

It doesn't matter with respect to the price you will pay to purchase the shares that are part of a new issue. However, it may matter a great deal from the standpoint of whether you will be able to buy the shares. You are likely to have a better chance of successfully acquiring shares when you go through the managing underwriter, who will have a larger allocation of shares to distribute. For example, a managing underwriter may retain 30 percent of the total shares for its own customers at the same time it allocates 15 percent to each of three other members of the syndicate, and 5 percent each to five members of the selling group. Members of a selling group sometimes end up with 1 percent or less of the shares in an issue. You are likely to have less success in buying new shares through a member of the selling group that has few shares to distribute. This difficulty is compounded for stock issues that enjoy large investor interest.

Can I buy shares in a new issue if I don't maintain an account with any of the members of the underwriting group?

You can contact a member of the underwriting syndicate to express your interest in purchasing shares even though you don't currently have an account with the firm. Shares are available to firms outside the underwriting syndicate only to the extent that members of the selling group are unable to locate investors to purchase all the shares they have been allocated. Members of the selling group earn more income by selling shares to their own customers and so are reluctant to turn over a portion of their allocation to an outside brokerage firm. If the stock issue is in great demand, you may find yourself unable to acquire shares even if you have an account with a member of the syndicate.

Can the shares of a new stock issue be offered in more than one country?

Although new stock issues are typically offered in only a single country, some issues are offered simultaneously in several countries. In addition, some stock issues take place entirely in countries outside the issuing firm's home country. Improved communications have caused the financial markets to become more global, and firms are always searching for investors who are willing to part with their money.

Do foreign companies issue shares in the United States?

Foreign companies often choose to raise debt and equity capital from investors in the United States. Although some foreign firms issue ordinary shares, most choose to issue *American Depositary Receipts* for the shares. These ADRs are claims on the actual shares that are held in trust by a financial institution. Think about the headaches of buying shares of a Japanese company and receiving dividend checks denominated in yen. The financial institution acting as trustee for the shares takes care of converting the foreign currency into dollars and issues dividend checks denominated in dollars. American Depositary Shares (ADSs) are similar to American Depositary Receipts.

Are ADRs issued on a one-for-one basis with the underlying stock?

American Depositary Receipts often represent multiple shares and even fractions of shares of the underlying stock. British Petroleum purchased U.S. oil giant Amoco Corporation in 1998 by swapping newly issued BP Amoco American Depositary Shares for the outstanding shares of Amoco. In other words, Amoco stockholders swapped their Amoco shares for newly issued share receipts of the combined company. Each of the BP Amoco American Depositary Shares received by Amoco shareholders represented six BP Amoco ordinary shares. The BP Amoco depositary shares denominated in U.S. dollars now trade in the United States on the New York Stock Exchange, while the BP Amoco ordinary shares denominated in sterling continue to trade in London.

Do I have the ability to exchange ADRs bought as part of a new issue for ordinary shares of the issuing company?

American Depositary Receipts can be exchanged for the underlying shares, although there is no reason to believe that you would benefit from swapping the shares. ADRs represent the ordinary shares and thus assume the value of the shares for which they can be converted, so no financial gain should result from a conversion. An investor who exchanges ADRs for ordinary shares of a foreign company will face the very difficulties American Depositary Receipts were designed to avoid.

How do companies determine the price at which shares are issued?

Establishing a price for new shares is a relatively easy task if shares of the company are already publicly traded. New shares cannot be issued for more than the price at which outstanding shares already trade. A company whose stock is currently trading for $27 per share will be unable to issue new shares for more than $27. Investors would not pay for $27.25 for new shares when they could purchase identical shares for $27.00. The company will establish the issue price for new shares at equal to or just below the current price of the existing shares. For example, a company with shares trading for $45.00 might issue new shares at a price of $44.87. Remember, once new shares have been issued and begin trading in the secondary market, investors are unable to differentiate between the new shares and the old shares. Thus, an investor would be unwilling to pay extra for shares that are part of a new issue.

Why would I want to purchase shares from an underwriter if identical shares trade at the same price?

Purchasing shares that are part of a new issue allows you to avoid a brokerage commission, which is usually charged when shares are purchased in the secondary market. The selling cost of new shares is included in the underwriting spread that is absorbed by the issuing company. In recent years online brokerage firms have lowered the transaction cost of buying stocks to the point that commissions are not much of a consideration as to whether to buy shares that are part of a new issue rather than buying shares that trade in the secondary market.

How does a firm issuing stock for the first time determine the price at which its shares are issued?

Pricing shares that are part of an initial public offering is tricky and entails additional risk for the underwriter, who may overestimate the value of the stock and the price at which shares can be sold to investors. The issuing company in consultation with an investment banker will consider a number of factors in pricing an initial public offering. Investment bankers are familiar with the current condition of financial markets and will take into account revenues, earnings, cash flow, assets, and many other factors. Perhaps most important is the current enthusiasm of investors for new stock issues and the success of recent stock issues. The issuing company benefits from obtaining as high a price as possible for the shares of stock it issues. A higher price for the stock means fewer shares must be issued to raise a specific sum of money.

Doesn't the overall value of the company become an important factor in pricing a stock issue?

The value of the company is very important to the overall value of a stock issue, and it certainly influences the price of the stock to be issued. However, a very valuable company does not always issue high-priced shares. A company valued at $20 million (a subjective evaluation on the part of the underwriter, the owners, and investors) could decide to issue 1 million shares for $20 each or 20 million shares for $1 each. The issuing company and investment banker decide on an issue price they believe will attract the most investor interest. New shares are sometimes issued at a relatively low price when the issuer wishes to attract speculators who tend to be drawn to low-priced stocks. The investment banker will utilize its knowledge of the capital markets in an attempt to arrive at the optimal combination of price and number of shares.

When will shares of an initial public offering begin trading?

Shares that are part of a new issue begin trading once the issue is released from the underwriting syndicate. At this point shares will trade at whatever price buyers and sellers are able to negotiate, which is likely to be different than the offering price. The release generally occurs when all of the shares in the issue have found a home with investors, although it may come earlier if the issue moves slowly because it is difficult to sell. A secondary market for the shares will develop immediately, as investors who were unable to obtain stock issued as part of the original offering attempt to buy shares from investors who were successful. Investors who purchase shares in an initial public offering sometimes try to earn a quick profit by immediately reselling these shares in the secondary market.

Why do newly issued shares often skyrocket in price immediately after they are issued?

Both the investment banker and the issuing company desire some increase in the price of newly issued shares so that investors participating in the issue will be pleased with their investment. Happy investors are more likely to purchase shares in subsequent stock issues underwritten by the same investment banking firm. Investors who purchase shares of a new issue only to see the shares immediately drop in value are not good candidates for future stock offerings. With a vested interest in having the shares increase in price, the investment banker will attempt to establish an offering price that is somewhat below the level it believes investors are willing to pay. Choosing a slightly lower price also provides some protection in the event investor demand for the issue has been overestimated. Again, selecting an appropriate issue price is as much an art as a science, and underwriters sometimes overestimate or underestimate the price that investors will pay for new shares. You may have read accounts of newly issued shares that doubled or tripled in price on the day of issue. This is overdoing a good thing, because the issuing firm could have obtained a much higher price for the shares that were issued.

Are all new stock issues made available to individual investors?

Some new issues are sold to a single buyer or small group of buyers. Called *private placements*, these issues are not available to the general public, so you would be unable to purchase shares included in these issues. Private placements generally entail less expense for the issuer and are frequently used for debt issues. One major advantage to the issuer of a private placement is that shares do not have to be registered. The buyer can also benefit from being able to purchase a large amount of stock at a fixed price. In other words, an institutional buyer such as a mutual fund can avoid bidding to buy shares in the open market, with the risk of running up the market price. Many companies hesitate to sell a large quantity of new shares of common stock to a single buyer for fear the buyer might decide to use its substantial voting power to influence management decisions of the issuing firm.

A friend told me he used rights to purchase new shares of stock. What are rights?

Publicly traded companies sometimes issue new shares of stock through a *rights* offering. Rights sent without charge to existing stockholders allow stockholders to purchase new shares that will be issued. Recipients can use the rights plus cash to purchase shares, usually at a bargain price. Stockholders who do not wish to purchase additional shares of stock can allow the rights to expire (a bad idea, because rights usually have a monetary value) or sell the rights to other investors who wish to purchase the new shares. As noted earlier, to entice existing shareholders to purchase additional stock, new shares are generally issued at a price slightly below the current market price of outstanding shares. In order to purchase shares through a rights offering, you must either receive rights as an existing stockholder or acquire rights from someone who wishes to sell. You cannot purchase shares in one of these issues without rights.

Why do companies go through such a cumbersome process?

Chapter 1 mentioned that corporate charters of some firms require that new shares first be offered to existing shareholders in proportion to the shares they already own. Shareholders of these firms are said to have a *preemptive right*. For example, if you own 5 percent of a company's outstanding shares, you will be offered an opportunity to purchase 5 percent of any new shares of stock the company issues. The preemptive right allows you to maintain your proportional ownership of the company. Stockholders with a preemptive right are not required to purchase new shares, but they must be offered the right to purchase new shares.

How do I find information about upcoming stock issues?

One way to find out about upcoming stock issues is to inform a broker of your interest in new issues. Brokers earn their income by selling financial products, and you can be certain that your request for information about new stock issues will not go unheeded. Financial publications are providing increased coverage of new issues as public interest in these offerings has boomed. For example, each Monday's *Wall Street Journal* publishes a partial listing of the week's upcoming issues of securities. Online brokerage firms often provide their customers with information about new securities issues. You can also learn about upcoming stock issues by reading the financial section of major newspapers and financial periodicals.

How can I learn about the company that will be issuing new shares to the public?

Companies planning an issue of stock are required to file an offering statement with the Securities and Exchange Commission. An abbreviated form of this called a *prospectus* is made available to investors who are considering an investment in the issue. The prospectus is available from syndicate members underwriting the issue and can often be found online. It will include details of how many shares are to be issued and the firm's plans for the funds that are raised. The prospectus will also include financial statements of the issuer and a discussion of the risks buyers face.

Do investment banking firms advertise upcoming issues?

The Securities and Exchange Commission imposes strict regulations regarding what companies are permitted to say and do before and during a stock issue. Prior to the issue, the investment banker who is managing an issue will often embark on a "road show" to drum up interest by soliciting institutional buyers and informing brokers of the offering. Unfortunately, individual investors are not likely to be included in this marketing plan, although it may alert brokers, who will then begin soliciting customer orders.

EXHIBIT 3-1

Cover of a Prospectus

Prospectus
August 9, 2000

3,000,000 Shares of Common Stock

Millennium Cell Inc.:

- We are an emerging technology company engaged in the development of a patented alternative energy source based on boron chemistry.

- Millennium Cell Inc.
  1 Industrial Way West
  Eatontown, New Jersey 07724
  (732) 542-4000'

Symbol and Market:

- MCEL/Nasdaq National Market

The Offering:

- We are offering 3,000,000 shares of our common stock.

- We have granted the underwriters an option to purchase an additional 450,000 shares of common stock to cover over-allotments.

- This is our initial public offering, and no public market currently exists for our shares.

- We plan to use the net proceeds from this offering to expand our research and product development efforts, including the construction of a pilot plant to manufacture sodium borohydride and a prototype battery manufacturing line, and for working capital and general corporate purposes.

- Closing: August 14, 2000.

	Per Share	Total
Public offering price	$ 10.00	$30,000,000
Underwriting fees	0.70	2,100,000
Proceeds to Millennium Cell[1]	9.30	27,900,000

[1] Excludes offering expenses estimated to be $1,000,000.

This investment involves risk. See "Risk Factors" beginning on page 4.

Neither the SEC nor any state securities commission has approved or disapproved of these securities or determined if this prospectus is truthful or complete. Any representation to the contrary is a criminal offense.

Morgan Keegan & Company, Inc.
The Robinson-Humphrey Company

Are public notices in financial publications a good place to learn about upcoming stock issues?

Announcements of new stock issues in publications such as the *Wall Street Journal* and the business sections of major newspapers are generally published after a new issue has been distributed. Thus, these advertisements, called *tombstones*, are not announcements of upcoming stock issues but paid notices for stock issues that have already been sold. By the time you see one of these notices, it will be too late to participate as an investor. In fact, the tombstones usually include a note that the notice is not an offer to sell the securities.

Are new issues ever announced and later withdrawn before the issue date?

Companies will sometimes withdraw an announced stock issue, generally because of a weak stock market. For example, a company needing capital may retain the services of an investment banker and settle on the price and the number of shares to be issued. They may even settle on a specific date for the issue. If the stock market suddenly takes a dive and the investment banker believes the issue will receive a chilly reception, the offering may be postponed until the climate for new issues improves.

Will I be able to resell the shares I purchase as part of a new issue?

Trading in newly issued shares can range from very active to very limited. Some new issues immediately enjoy an active secondary market and are easy to resell. An active market already exists for many publicly traded companies that issue new shares to raise additional capital. Privately owned companies with a widely recognized name are likely to enjoy an active secondary market for shares issued in an IPO. For example, the stock of Lucent Technologies, formerly part of AT&T, enjoyed a very active secondary market once it was divested from its parent and shares were available for trading. On the other hand, relatively small companies may issue shares that trade only sporadically after the original issue date. The extent to which newly issued shares will trade after the issue date should be an important consideration in deciding whether to invest in the shares. Shares that are expected to experience light trading should be acquired only if you are willing to accept substantial risk or to hold the shares for a lengthy period.

Are shares purchased as part of an IPO a risky investment?

Businesses with a short operating history tend to be risky enterprises because of the difficulty in projecting their future. Companies can begin with a great idea or an innovative product and subsequently be run out of business by bigger, better-financed competitors. History also indicates that individuals who are geniuses at innovating are often not adept at managing a business. In other words, a company can come out of the starting gate like a rocket, only to sputter down the road. Because most companies issuing shares for the first time have short or nonexistent operating histories, the shares of these companies tend to be very risky investments. In addition, new companies often have high startup expenses and fail to earn a profit for many years. The difficulty of earning a profit was especially evident in the many Internet-related stocks that went public during the 1990s. On the bright side, the shares of these companies also offer the potential of very large returns.

Are all initial public offerings risky?

Not all shares purchased as part of an IPO are risky investments. Some firms have a long operating history as privately held companies prior to going public with an initial public

offering. For example, United Parcel Service operated successfully for many years before offering $5.5 billion of common
stock to the public for the first time in November 1999. Likewise, several mutual insurance companies with a long history
of operating under the ownership of their policyholders converted to stock companies and offered shares in initial public
offerings. Not only did these companies operate in a mature
industry, they enjoyed operating histories that allowed investors
to have a fairly good idea of what the future might hold.

Why would mutual insurance companies decide to convert to stock companies?

The management of these firms felt the companies needed access
to additional capital in order to grow and remain competitive
in an industry that was likely to be dominated by giant, well-
financed corporations. Unlike regular corporations, mutual companies are unable to raise capital by issuing new shares of stock.
Insurance companies were being threatened by competition from
commercial banks, brokerage companies, and firms selling insurance over the Internet. The mutual form of organization restricts
a company's ability to raise capital and thus to grow.

Do the initial owners of a company that goes public pay the same price for their shares as investors who buy shares at the offering?

Are you kidding? The owners of a firm going public generally
purchase shares for a nominal price compared to the price other
investors are required to pay. For example, the original owners
might pay a dime a share for stock offered to the public for
$25 a share. A successful public offering is likely to result in
the original owners gaining instant wealth. Immense wealth
accrued to many of the entrepreneurs of technology companies
who took their companies public in the late 1990s. Many of

these individuals became instant multimillionaires. Some of these same firms later went out of business, causing the initial owners to lose most or all of their wealth gained from the initial public offering.

Can the owners of a firm that goes public sell all of their shares immediately after the initial public offering?

The Securities and Exchange Commission imposes limitations on when the owners of a firm can sell their shares after the firm goes public. In general, the owners must wait 180 days following an initial public offering to sell their shares. Exceptions exist, and some owners are able to dispose of their shares after a shorter wait. The sale of some shares by a firm's owners is not always a sign the owners consider the shares overpriced. The owners may have all their financial assets in the company's stock and wish to sell shares in order to diversify their personal investment portfolio.

Can you discuss share repurchases more fully?

Companies, especially mature firms with limited investment options, sometimes decide to repurchase shares of their own stock. A repurchase generally occurs when the directors of a company consider the market price of the stock too low. The directors may employ the services of an investment banker to gradually purchase shares in the open market, or the company may make an offer to existing stockholders to sell a portion of their shares back to the company. A public statement that a firm will be repurchasing its own shares is considered by some investors as a sign that directors feel the market price does not reflect the stock's true value. Although this may be correct, share repurchases often result in only a temporary increase in the price of the stock. Fewer outstanding shares are likely to result in higher earnings per share, but it will reduce the firm's dividend payouts.

4

CHAPTER

HOW MARKETS ARE MADE IN STOCKS

Chapter summary

Dealers in stocks act as market makers by quoting prices at which they are willing to buy and sell ... Each market maker specializes in a limited number of stocks ... The bid is the price offered to buy shares of stock and the ask is the price at which shares are offered for sale ... Bid and ask prices for a stock are changed by the market maker in response to fluctuations in supply and demand ... The spread between the bid and ask is greater for inactive stocks ... Market makers execute many transactions by matching buyers and sellers ... Specific rules determine the priority in which orders are executed ... Investors can specify several restrictions to orders placed with brokers ... Electronic communications networks that eliminate the need for dealers and organized exchanges are capturing an increasing share stock trades

How are stocks traded?

Privately owned firms that profit by facilitating the buying and selling of stocks comprise the framework in which securities are traded. The market in which securities are traded following their initial issue is called the *secondary market*. At the core of the secondary market are market makers who stand ready to buy shares from investors who wish to sell, and who are ready to sell shares to investors who wish to buy. To a degree, market makers are similar to used car dealers (no offense intended), except that market makers trade previously owned shares of stock rather than previously owned vehicles. In addition to traditional market makers, electronic communications networks (ECNs) provide computerized trading without the need for a middleman. ECNs are nothing more than computer bulletin boards that allow investors to post orders to buy and sell stock.

How can used car dealers be compared with market makers for stocks?

Market makers are individuals or companies who buy and sell a particular good. Very simply, market makers make a market in something that other people wish to buy and sell. Markets exist for baseball cards, jewelry, residential houses, and vehicles. It's just that market makers in stocks deal in a different line of goods compared to market makers for these other products. Used car dealers buy vehicles from people who want to sell, and sell vehicles to people who want to buy. The fundamentals of conducting business as a used car dealer are much the same for a market maker in the securities business who buys and sells shares of stock. Also, market makers sometimes bring buyers and sellers together, with the market maker's place of business serving as a meeting place for transactions. The analogy would be a car dealer who accepts vehicles on consignment. You have a car you want to sell, and agree to pay a fee to a dealer who can locate a buyer. The market maker, similarly, serves as an intermediary between the two parties without actually taking possession of the vehicle. Market makers for stocks perform the same function for investors who leave their orders to buy shares or to sell shares of stock for execution.

Are market makers involved in every trade in the secondary market?

The buying and selling of securities in the secondary market is increasingly being automated not only by the market makers themselves, but also by new electronic communications systems that replace the people, companies, and trading floors that have historically dominated stock trading in the secondary market. Electronic communications networks offer computerized trading in stocks by matching buy orders and sell orders that have been entered electronically by investors. Orders that cannot be matched and executed immediately are posted so other investors can view the prices asked by sellers and the prices offered by buyers.

Is my broker a market maker?

The firm that employs your broker may serve as a market maker for a limited number of stocks. Large brokerage firms often make markets for a sizable number of stocks, although some of these firms have recently reduced the market-making part of their business. As a market maker, your brokerage firm may buy the shares you sell or sell to you the shares you purchase. In all likelihood, however, your broker will place the order with another firm, which serves as a market maker for the stock you wish to buy or sell. The market maker who receives your order may conduct business on one of the organized securities exchanges, such as the New York Stock Exchange, or in the over-the-counter market, depending on where the stock is traded.

Are computers replacing market makers?

Computers are replacing much of the work historically performed by the individuals who serve as market makers. Market makers already utilize computers, of course, but the equipment is used primarily in a supporting role to facilitate their work. However, increased computing power and improvements in communications have allowed computerized trading by institutional investors who are able to bypass the normal channels controlled by market makers on the stock exchanges and in the over-the-counter market. Many academics and professionals believe computerized trading will eventually replace the market maker system that has long dominated securities trading in the secondary market.

Where are the market makers located?

At one time most market makers were located in New York City, which served as America's only major financial center. Firms that serve as market makers are now located across the globe in cities such as Atlanta, Chicago, Los Angeles, Toronto, Tokyo, London, Madrid, Stockholm, and, of course, New York. These are only a few of the many cities in which market makers operate. Vast improvements in communications allow market makers to operate from virtually any location. Buyers and sellers of stocks are not required to get together in person, only electronically, so there is no need for market makers to congregate at any particular location convenient to the investors who place orders. Just as you can now utilize your home computer to access information that was formerly available only at a library, participants in the financial markets can trade stocks without a physical presence at any particular location.

Are all markets for stocks made on stock exchanges?

Some market makers conduct their business on the stock exchanges, while others operate in the over-the-counter market.

Market makers on a stock exchange are called *specialists*, while those in the over-the-counter market are known as *dealers*. Both specialists and dealers operate as market makers even though their titles are different. In fact, specialists often act as dealers while executing orders for their own account. Prices quoted by market makers for stocks traded in both markets are determined by supply and demand from investors who place orders to buy and sell stock. Keep in mind that there are many stock exchanges in the United States and around the world.

How do the different exchanges decide which stocks to trade?

Companies that issue the stocks have a major say in determining where their shares are traded. Some firms wish to have their shares traded on one or more of the organized stock exchanges, while other companies prefer that their shares trade in the over-the-counter market. Firms that wish to have their shares traded on an exchange must meet the standards established by the exchange. For example, the New York Stock Exchange—the oldest, largest, and most active exchange in the United States—has minimum requirements for earnings, assets, number of shareholders, shares outstanding, and the market value of publicly held shares. Likewise, stocks and the companies that issue the stocks must meet certain standards in order to be included in the best known and most active segments of the over-the-counter market. Many companies have chosen to have their stocks traded in the over-the-counter market even though the firms meet all of the standards for a listing on the New York Stock Exchange.

Do substantial differences exist between transactions on the stock exchanges and in the over-the-counter market?

One of the main differences between the over-the-counter (OTC) market and exchanges is the number of market makers for each stock. A stock exchange has one designated market maker for each stock that is listed for trading on the exchange. For example, a single New York Stock Exchange specialist firm makes a market in the common stock of General Electric. Likewise, a single specialist firm handles all trading on the exchange for Union Pacific common stock. Although each stock listed for trading on an exchange has a single market maker, the same specialist firm is likely to make markets in several other stocks. On the other hand, multiple dealers often act as market makers in stocks traded in the over-the-counter market. The number of market makers for a stock depends primarily on the amount of trading activity. A very active stock may have a dozen market makers, all competing for the business of trading the stock. Unlike the stock exchanges that designate a single market maker for each stock, no restrictions exist for the number of firms that can act as dealers for a stock in the over-the-counter market.

Is the over-the-counter market primarily a market for the stocks of small companies?

The stocks of most small companies are traded in the over-the-counter market. Small firms that don't meet the minimum requirements established by the various exchanges don't have a choice other than to have their stocks traded over the counter. A relatively small firm may have too few shares outstanding or too few shareholders to meet established standards for listing on the New York Stock Exchange or one of the regional exchanges. The stock of these firms, if publicly traded, will trade over the counter. However, the directors of many large companies that meet the requirements for listing on an exchange choose to have their securities traded in the over-the-counter market. The stocks of Dell Computer, Intel, Microsoft, and Cisco Systems all trade in the over-the-counter market even though they meet listing requirements of the New York Stock Exchange.

Are minimum standards required for stocks traded over the counter?

The best known and most active OTC stocks are included in Nasdaq, a centralized quotation system in which market makers post firm bid and ask quotations they are required to honor. Nasdaq actually includes two components: the National Market System and regular issues. Stricter requirements regarding assets, income, number of shares available for trading, and number of shareholders apply to companies that wish to have their stock included in the National Market System. Stocks not included in the National Market System tend to be less actively traded and more risky to own.

How do investors make contact with market makers?

Individual investors must normally utilize the services of a retail brokerage firm to have an order entered with a market maker. The brokerage firm serves as an agent and transmits a customer's order to the appropriate market maker who provides the execution. As mentioned previously, the brokerage firm you employ will sometimes take the opposite side of the transaction for the order you place. For example, the brokerage firm may buy the shares of stock you are selling or sell the shares of stock you are buying. In most cases, however, the brokerage firm will transmit the order to an appropriate market maker or electronic communications network, where it will be filled.

Does each stock have a different market maker?

A single specialist firm acts as the market maker for each stock on a securities exchange. The number of market makers in the over-the-counter market for a particular stock will depend on the stock's trading activity. Actively traded stocks have several market makers, while a stock that seldom trades or a stock that was only recently issued is likely to have only a single market

maker. A firm will begin making a market in a stock if sufficient trading volume exists to make a profit. Some stocks trade
so actively that many firms can profitably make a market by
buying and selling shares. If many people in a community
enjoy Mexican food, then sufficient business will be available
to support several of these specialized restaurants. Likewise, if
many investors want to buy and sell a particular stock, several
market makers will be willing to participate in the trades.

Does the market maker set a stock's market price?

The market maker establishes a price in accordance with the
supply of and demand for the stock. A flood of investor orders
to buy a stock accompanied by few orders to sell the stock will
result in the market maker increasing the price in order to more
closely match buy and sell orders. Likewise, a large volume of
orders to sell a particular stock will cause the market maker to
decrease the price in order to reduce the number of sellers and
attract additional buyers. A market maker must constantly
adjust a stock's price in an attempt to equalize buying and selling pressures. Suppose a company's directors unexpectedly
announce news of accounting irregularities within the firm.
Concerned at the news, many of the firm's shareholders are
likely to phone their brokers with instructions to sell their holdings of the stock. At the same time, the bad news is unlikely to
attract the buyers necessary to absorb all the additional shares
being sold. The resulting imbalance between sell orders and
buy orders will force the market makers to lower the price of
the stock. Without lowering the price to attract more buyers, the
market maker will have to absorb all the shares being sold.

Will good news cause the opposite reaction?

Unexpected good news is likely to cause the market maker to
increase price quotations for the stock. Suppose a computer chip

maker announces a major innovation that allows the company to manufacture a more powerful memory chip at much lower cost. If the news is unexpected, buy orders for the stock will pour in to the market makers, thereby causing them to raise their price quotations for the stock. A higher price for the stock should act to reduce the number of buy orders at the same time it brings in more sellers. Demand and supply from institutional and individual investors drive stock prices by forcing market makers to change the prices at which they will buy and sell stocks.

Why does a stock's price change when no news is announced specific to the company?

Investors are constantly reevaluating what they feel a stock is worth. Individuals may become more optimistic or pessimistic about the economy or about interest rates. They may be concerned about political unrest in a foreign country. Perhaps pension funds have experienced large inflows of cash they need to invest. Many factors interact to cause stock prices to increase and decrease. Stock prices sometimes seem to change randomly and for no particular reason.

How do market makers quote a stock's price?

A market maker quotes a bid price and ask price (sometimes called an *offering price*) for each stock in which the firm makes a market. The bid is the price at which the market maker is willing to buy shares of the stock, and the ask is the price at which the market maker agrees to sell shares of the stock. For example, a bid of $25 and an ask of $25.25 means the market maker will buy stock at $25.00 per share and sell stock at $25.25 per share. The difference between the bid and ask, 25 cents in this instance, is known as the *spread*. The spread becomes the investor's main cost of doing business with a market maker. The stock you just bought for $25.25 per share could be immediately resold to the same market maker for only $25.00, a 25 cent loss. The market maker is no different than any retail business that tries to sell merchandise at a price that is higher than its cost. However, while most businesses are free to mark up merchandise as much as they wish, certain restrictions apply to the amount by which market makers are permitted to mark up stock prices.

So bid and ask prices for a stock change in response to investor orders?

Suppose a market maker for a particular stock is quoting a bid price of $20.00 and an ask price of $20.25. In other words, the market maker will buy the stock from investors for $20.00 per share and sell the stock to investors for $20.25 per share. A surge in orders to buy the stock is likely to cause the market maker to raise both the bid price and the ask price. An increase in the ask price (asking more for the stock) should reduce demand to purchase shares, and an increase in the bid price (paying more for the stock) should cause investors to offer more shares for sale. The bottom line is that investor supply and demand drive a stock's price by forcing the market maker to change the bid and ask prices that are quoted. But investor supply and demand being the most important factors in pricing a stock doesn't preclude that some pricing hanky-panky may sometimes occur.

Do market makers limit the number of shares they will buy at the bid price or sell at the ask price?

A market maker will include the number of shares, or *size*, with each quotation. For example, 1000 shares may be offered at the quoted ask price while the quoted bid is limited to 1500 shares. This quoted size means the market maker agrees to buy up to 1500 shares at the bid and sell up to 1000 at the ask. The size of the bid and ask will depend on a variety of factors, including trading activity in the stock and the market maker's desire to increase or decrease its holdings of this stock. A market maker wishing to decrease inventory of a stock, for instance, is likely to offer a large number of shares at the ask. A very active stock may have bid and ask quotes for thousands or even tens of thousands of shares, while an inactive stock may show a size of several hundred shares.

What determines the size of the spread for a stock?

The spread between the bid price and the ask price is a function of several factors, including trading activity and competition among market makers. A very active stock is likely to enjoy a relatively small spread. For example, an active stock may be quoted at $31.03 bid and $31.07 asked, or a spread of only 4 cents. On the other hand, an inactive stock may have a bid price of $22.20 and an ask price of $22.50, or a spread of 30 cents per share. The active stock is quoted with only 4 cents separating the price at which stock can be purchased and sold, while the inactive stock has a spread of 30 cents per share. A larger spread between the bid price and the ask price causes an investor to incur a higher cost of doing business. The spread for any particular stock varies in size during the trading day.

What about the competition you mentioned?

The greater the number of market makers who compete for the orders in a particular stock, the smaller the spread that is likely to exist between the bid and ask. Market makers compete with one another for business, and the highest quoted bid and the lowest quoted ask will attract most of the trading volume. Undercutting competitors' quotations will allow a market maker to capture a bigger share of the orders for a stock. Thus, competing market makers closely monitor one another's quotes. A market maker with a lower bid than competing market makers is unlikely to acquire many shares from sellers. Likewise, a market maker with a higher ask than competing market makers cannot expect to sell many shares. At the other extreme, a stock with only a single market maker will generally have a larger spread, simply because individual investors and their brokers have nowhere else to go in order to buy or sell shares. Residents of a town with only a single gas station are likely to pay a higher price for gasoline than residents of a town with a large number of stations. The same is true for investors who wish to buy or sell shares of stock. Investors are likely to get a better deal when multiple market makers compete for the business.

Do spreads represent a substantial cost for investors?

Consider the spread that is likely to exist for most other assets. How much do you suppose a jeweler paid for a diamond that is offered to you for $1200? How much would you receive if you tried to sell the same diamond several weeks after your purchase? Likewise, how about the markup on furniture, cosmetics, and nearly any other item you will find in a retail store? Most merchants mark up their merchandise much more than the markups on stocks by market makers. On the other hand, stocks tend to be relatively liquid and market makers don't anticipate a lengthy holding period for the stocks they purchase. A market maker can earn substantial profits on a small spread as long as volume is high.

Do market makers always buy the shares that investors sell?

Actually, these firms serve two functions in their role as market makers. In some trades the market maker will actually buy the stock that is offered for sale. The shares that are purchased become the property of the market maker, who will subsequently offer them for sale to another investor or, perhaps, another market maker. A market maker purchasing shares in this manner is said to be acting as a *dealer*. When operating on the opposite side of a trade, a market maker that sells shares from its own portfolio in order to satisfy an investor order to buy stock is also acting as a dealer. A dealer buys stock for and sells shares from its own portfolio. In acting as dealers, market makers take a direct position in the stocks in which they make a market. In other words, shares actually pass through their hands on the way from one investor to another.

How do market makers become involved in transactions without acting as dealers?

In many trades, a stock's market maker will match a buy order from one investor with a sell order from another investor. By matching orders from two investors, the market maker is not required to take possession of the shares included in the transaction. The market maker acts as a broker, rather than a dealer, when performing the role of connecting investors by matching orders. Matching transactions are less risky for market makers who don't have to worry about losing money because of a falling stock price during the time the shares are being held. Of course, the market maker acting as a broker also doesn't have an opportunity to earn income from an advancing stock price and doesn't benefit from the spread between the bid and the ask.

If matching orders are less risky to handle, why do market makers sometimes buy and sell for their own accounts?

A market maker often doesn't have offsetting orders to match. For example, an investor order to buy shares may reach the market maker at a time when no matching orders to sell are available. In this instance, the market maker would sell shares from its own portfolio. Conversely, if an order to sell shares reaches the market maker when no offsetting investor orders to buy are available, the market maker will buy the shares for later resale. In both these examples the market maker is acting as a dealer. Consider the consequences for the marketability of stocks if market makers failed to take positions in the securities they trade. Investors might be unable to sell a stock until another investor was ready to buy the same shares at an agreed upon price. Likewise, an investor would be unable to buy shares of a particular stock until some other investor decided to sell the same stock. Without market makers acting as dealers, liquidity in many stocks would disappear and the securities would become much less desirable to own.

What do you mean by liquidity?

Liquidity is the ability to convert an asset to cash at or near its last price, a desirable attribute for any investment. Many investors avoid assets that lack liquidity because they are concerned about being required to sell the asset at a reduced price or, even worse, not being able to sell the asset at all. Stock prices would suffer if investors believed they couldn't count on being able to sell their shares when they wanted. Thus, market makers who trade stocks provide a valuable service to investors, who are able to buy and sell shares pretty much at will. Having said this, keep in mind that not all stocks are equally liquid. Some stocks trade millions or even tens of millions of shares each day, while other stocks typically trade hundreds of shares and on some days don't trade at all. Stocks that seldom trade lack liquidity.

Do a stock's market makers trade with one another?

The bid and ask quotations from a market maker are applicable to other market makers in the same stock as well as to firms executing customer orders. A West Coast market maker in a particular stock may decide to reduce its holdings and sell shares to an East Coast market maker in the same stock. Likewise, a market maker may decide to increase its holdings by purchasing shares from another market maker. This kind of trading occurs only when a stock has multiple market makers.

Will a market maker accept stock orders at a specific price?

Market makers accept orders that specify a price at which execution can take place. Suppose you are interested in purchasing 200 shares of a particular stock currently trading for $38.50, but only if shares can be acquired for $36.00 or less. At the time your order reaches the market maker, the price quotation for the stock may be $38.25 bid and $38.50 asked. The market maker will not sell you shares for $36.00 when the current offering price is $38.50. With your order specifying a purchase at a price lower than current market conditions allow, the market maker will hold your order for later execution in the event the stock price falls to $36.00. Of course, you may decide to cancel the order prior to an execution. Suppose you enter the order, only to see the stock price climb to $46.00 within several months. At some point you may decide to throw in the towel and cancel the order to buy 200 shares at $36.00 because the price you specified is so far away from the price at which the stock is trading.

Can I also specify a price at which to sell stock?

Market makers accept both orders to buy and orders to sell with a price specified by the investor. Orders to buy at a specific price or lower, and to sell at a specific price or higher, are called *limit orders*. As an example of a limit order to sell, suppose you place an order to sell shares of a stock you own if you can obtain a price of $45.00 per share or higher. If the current price is $39.50, the market maker will hold the order until it can be executed or is later cancelled by you. You can specify if the order is to automatically expire at the end of the trading day it is placed. You can also specify that the order is to remain in effect until you rescind it at some unspecified date. A limit order without an expiration date is termed an *open order* or a *good-till-cancelled order*. Limit orders automatically cancelled at the end of the trading day are called *day orders*.

Does a market maker hold many unexecuted limit orders?

Limit orders often comprise a major part of a market maker's business. At any time, the market maker is likely to be holding orders for tens or hundreds of thousands of shares that can only be executed if the price of a stock achieves price targets specified by investors who entered the orders. These held orders will include limit orders to buy stock at prices below the current market price and limit orders to sell shares at prices above the current market price. As the market price of the stock moves upward, limit orders to sell will be executed and the orders will disappear from the market maker's order book. Conversely, as the market price of the stock declines, limit orders to buy stock will find sellers.

Is a limit order certain to be executed if the stock reaches the specified limit price?

In fact, a limit order may not be executed even though the stock reaches the specified limit price. Suppose you instruct a broker to sell 400 shares of IXT stock, but specify a price of $14.50 or better. In this case, better means a price higher than $14.50. The next morning you turn to the stock tables in the newspaper and see that the stock did indeed hit your limit price, which also turned out to be the high price of the day. You feel great until a call to your broker indicates the limit order was not executed and you still own the stock. In this instance another investor's order was executed at the price you specified. Perhaps only 100 shares were traded at $14.50. Maybe someone else entered a limit order at the same price but prior to the time your order was placed. The trade may have occurred between two other investors, neither of which attached a specified price their orders.

Do market makers have a short-term investment outlook?

Unlike individual and institutional investors who often buy stock they intend to hold for several years, market makers often buy shares of stock to hold for several minutes or hours. The job of making a market and creating liquidity for other investors necessitates a very short-term outlook. Just as retailers buy inventories that are intended for quick resale, market makers don't buy stock to keep, but rather, to sell. Inventory turnover is the name of the game with stocks as well as with produce.

Does a market maker consider market movements when trading stocks?

Consider that a market maker holding a large portfolio of stocks can lose a great deal of money in a short period of time. Large holdings of stocks will produce significant losses during a period of price declines, just as a large portfolio of stocks results in substantial profits during price advances. Thus, a market maker will anticipate short-term stock price movements in determining how many shares to hold. A market maker expecting price declines in the stocks being traded is likely to pare down the portfolio, while a market maker expecting prices to advance will increase its portfolio holdings. It is important to remember that market makers earn profits and suffer losses on stocks being held in their portfolio, so adjusting portfolio size for expected stock price movements is a normal part of making a market.

Does a market maker always hold a large inventory of the stocks in which it makes a market?

A market maker's inventory of a particular stock will depend on a variety of factors, including recent market activity in the stock. A substantial market decline may result in a market maker having a large inventory, while a strong upward movement may deplete a market maker's inventory for a particular stock. Market makers sometimes actually owe rather than own shares of a stock in which they make a market. In other words, a market maker may have sold more shares than were owned. A market decline in a stock would produce a profit for a market maker with a negative position in the stock.

Are market makers bound by rules that specify how orders are to be executed?

Pages of rules exist on how market makers are to conduct their activities. The New York Stock Exchange, the American Stock Exchange, and the regional stock exchanges each have their own rules for how orders are to be executed by market makers. Likewise, the National Association of Securities Dealers (NASD) has rules on how dealers are to make markets in the over-the-counter market. Some rules are universal; the highest bid and the lowest ask should receive priority, for example. Very simply, this means an order from the person offering the highest price to buy a stock should move to the head of the line. Likewise, an order from an investor offering the lowest price to sell a stock should receive precedence. In general, market makers are not allowed to buy or sell ahead of their customers. In other words, a market maker can't purchase stock for its own account prior to executing your order if you have offered to pay the same price.

Do stock prices always move in an orderly manner?

The price of a stock can take a sudden jump upward or downward when a particularly large order or a large number of orders to buy or to sell create an imbalance of supply and demand. For example, several large orders to sell may cause a sudden decline in the price of a stock as the market maker reduces the price to attract additional buyers. In the meantime the market maker will accumulate shares until sufficient buyers can be attracted to absorb the shares being sold. An imbalance of buy and sell orders can result in an unruly market for stock, at least temporarily.

Are large price movements more likely for a stock with low volume?

Stocks with low trading volume tend to rise and fall sharply with relatively modest order imbalances. A market maker will encounter more difficulty attracting investors to the stock of a lightly traded and little known company. Thus, an unusually large order or group of orders can have an inordinate effect on the stock price of a stock with little trading activity. Large and sudden price movements are not limited to stocks with low volume, however. Unexpected news can cause large price movements in stocks with substantial volume.

Can the market maker quit buying a stock?

Market makers in different markets are governed by different rules. In general, market makers can be expected to provide a continuous market even in the face of unusually heavy demand or supply for a stock. The rules of the New York Stock Exchange require its market makers to provide a continuous market in their assigned securities. Having said that, consider that some market makers in the over-the-counter market were heavily criticized for dropping out of the market and not offering bid and ask quotations during the sudden market decline in October 1987.

Are there any other rules that apply to transactions?

In general, competing orders entered at the same price are executed on a first-come, first-served basis. Suppose you enter a limit order with your broker to buy 300 shares of a particular stock for $55.00 when the current market price is $55.75. You have specified a price below the current market price, and so the order is considered a limit order and will not be immediately executed when it gets to the market maker. Shortly, another order reaches the market maker to buy 500 shares of the same stock at the same $55.00 price that you specified for your order. If 200 shares are subsequently offered for sale at $55.00, which of the two orders receives precedence? On the basis of first come, first served, your order should receive precedence and be executed first. Hundreds of other possible conflicts must be resolved daily by each market maker. For example, orders without a specified price generally receive precedence over limit orders.

Can I specify that all the shares in my order be bought or sold at one time?

Brokers will accept a special *all-or-none order* that requires all the shares in your order be executed in one trade or else no execution will occur. This type of order makes it more likely your order will not be executed. Without the restriction being included as part of your order, a portion, but not all of the order, might be executed. Perhaps the remainder of the order would be executed on the same day or a following day. You are permitted to specify all-or-none orders both to purchase and sell stock. All-or-none orders are generally used when an investor enters a good-till-cancelled order to ensure additional commissions are not incurred as pieces of the order are executed over several days.

Do market makers accept other special types of orders?

Several types of orders are available to individual investors. For example, you can specify that the order be executed at the moment it is received by the market maker or else it should be cancelled. Another restrictive order also includes a price at which you would like to buy stock or sell stock. This differs from a limit order, discussed earlier, in that this type of order restricts a sell order to a specified price or lower and a buy order to a specified price or higher. Called a *stop order*, it will be executed only if your price target (called the *stop price*) is reached. A *stop sell order* would be entered if you want to sell shares only when the price falls to a specific level or lower. For example, you might enter an order to sell 500 shares of Union Pacific with a stop price of $43.00. The order would be executed only if the price of the stock falls to $43.00 or less. A *stop buy order* specifies that the market maker buy stock if the price reaches a specific price or higher. Stop orders are not as popular as limit orders but they do have their uses.

Why would I want to sell my shares at less than the current market price?

Suppose you purchased shares of Microsoft several years ago when the price was much lower than today's price. You enjoy a substantial paper profit and would like to continue holding the stock but are concerned that the price may be due for a major decline. To protect yourself against a large fall in price, you place a stop sell order at a price lower than the current market price. How much lower to set the stop price is your decision, of course, but the closer you set the stop price to the market price, the more likely your shares will be sold. The negative aspect to this type order is the price may fall, your shares are sold, and then the stock subsequently bounces back to an even higher level. Unfortunately, there is no sure thing, even with specialized orders.

Will I pay a higher commission for a special order?

The brokerage firm you choose to handle an order establishes the commission you will be required to pay. Some brokerage firms charge extra for limit orders and stop orders, while other firms do not. In general, online brokerage firms with very low commissions charge extra for specialized orders, although you are likely to find that these restricted orders are often worth the extra charge. Brokerage commissions are discussed in Chapter 5.

How do electronic communications networks differ from a system of market makers?

Electronic communications networks are computerized networks that display investor orders to buy and sell securities. The networks are connecting points where investors who are interested in buying or selling stocks can view orders that have been posted by other investors. Investors who find an attractive price can buy from or sell to the investor who posted the price. Likewise, investors can enter their own orders to buy stock and sell stock at specified prices. Unlike the market maker system in effect on the exchanges and in the over-the-counter market, the ECNs do not have a market maker that acts as a middleman to buy and sell. Essentially, the electronic communications networks are a substitute for the market maker system.

Why are ECNs becoming so popular?

Proponents of ECNs argue that computerized trading not only provides executions at a much lower cost, it also makes information immediately available to all the interested parties, who are then better able to make informed investment decisions. In stock market jargon, electronic communications networks offer more "transparency." Investors are able to view limit and stop orders that have been placed away from the current market price by other investors. For example, an investor considering the purchase of a stock is able to view all other investor orders for the same stock. In contrast, market makers in the over-the-counter market and on the organized exchanges have privileged information that gives them a major advantage over the public.

What are the arguments for continuing the current system of market makers?

Market makers add liquidity by standing ready to take care of imbalances between buyers and sellers. These firms buy shares of stock when sellers outnumber buyers, and they sell shares of stock when buyers outnumber sellers. The market for a stock should never dry up completely if the market maker properly does its job. Electronic commerce networks do not provide this same service because they have no buyer or seller of last resort. Try to sell shares when no buyer is available, and you are out of luck.

Are all these trading systems connected?

Unfortunately, the trading systems are not formally connected, which means investor orders may not always be executed at the best possible price. That is, investor orders to buy stock may not be executed at the lowest available price, and investor orders to sell stock may not be executed at the highest price offered. For example, an investor order to buy stock may be executed at the lowest available price on an exchange at the same time that an even lower price is available on one of the electronic communications networks. Likewise, an investor order to sell stock may be executed at the highest posted price on an ECN at the same time an even higher price is available on an exchange. The lack of connection between the competing markets is called *fragmentation*. The Securities and Exchange Commission has been pressuring the different markets to interconnect in order to guarantee investors the best price for the stocks they trade.

5

CHAPTER

CHOOSING A BROKER FOR YOUR STOCK INVESTMENTS

Chapter summary

Products and services offered by brokerage firms ... Considerations in selecting a brokerage firm ... Differences among brokerage firms ... Online, discount, and full-service firms ... Decisions you will be required to make when opening an account ... Comparing margin and cash accounts ... Safekeeping of securities ... What you should expect from a broker ... Transferring an account to a different brokerage firm.

Do I need a brokerage account in order to buy and sell stocks?

In general, you will need to employ the services of a brokerage firm in order to buy and sell stocks as well as other kinds of securities. It is possible to purchase and sell shares of stock without having a brokerage account, but the process is inconvenient and generally restrictive, so a brokerage account is a necessity rather than a convenience for most individual investors. Brokerage firms have direct access to the secondary markets in which outstanding stocks are bought and sold, and to the primary market in which new issues of stock are offered to investors.

How can I purchase shares of stock without having a brokerage account?

A limited number of companies have implemented direct purchase programs that allow individuals to purchase shares directly from the companies. Rather than using a broker to assist in buying shares from other investors in the secondary market, direct purchase allows you to avoid an intermediary (the broker) and purchase shares directly from the issuer, often without paying a fee. Another method for avoiding use of a broker is to enroll in a company's dividend reinvestment program. These programs utilize cash dividends to pay for the purchase of additional shares of stock. Of course, you must already be a stockholder in a company in order to participate in the firm's dividend reinvestment program. Companies offering dividend reinvestment plans nearly always permit participants to purchase additional shares of stock, often without paying a fee. In other words, you are permitted to submit additional funds, which are added to the cash dividends to buy additional shares of stock.

Can I use these plans as a substitute for investing through a brokerage firm?

Both direct investment and dividend reinvestment are excellent methods for acquiring shares of stock, but both plans have limitations and tend to lack flexibility. For example, the amount of money you are permitted to submit in any one plan is generally capped, so you can only invest up to a certain maximum amount at any one time. Actually, this is probably a benefit because it keeps you from investing too much at once. Still, it reduces flexibility. Another problem is that several days elapse between when money is sent and when shares are actually purchased. Thus, you have more difficulty timing the purchase or sale than would be the case if a brokerage firm were utilized. In addition, these plans don't allow you to specify a price at which to buy or sell shares, as you can when placing an order through a broker. The bottom line is, you probably need a brokerage account in order to invest in stocks and bonds.

Can I buy mutual funds without using a broker?

Some mutual funds distribute their shares through brokerage firms, and other mutual funds distribute their shares directly to investors. You do not need a brokerage account in order to purchase shares from mutual funds that distribute shares directly. Shares in other funds can only be acquired by using an intermediary such as a broker or financial planner. There are certainly enough mutual funds of sufficient variety that it is possible to bypass a broker in the purchase of mutual fund shares.

Are all brokerage firms pretty much alike?

Substantial differences exist among brokerage firms with regard to the fees they charge, the services they provide, the products they offer, and the personal attention received by customers. Some large national and regional firms offer every product or service you could possibly desire. Other firms specialize in particular categories of products or offer very low fees and reduced services. Some brokerage firms accept orders 24 hours a day, seven days a week, while other firms operate mostly during hours when the security markets are open. Some firms cater only to investors who wish to buy and sell securities online using personal computers, while other firms offer a traditional brick-and-mortar operation where brokers personally interact with their customers.

Should I spend some time and effort selecting a brokerage firm?

You should definitely undertake some research on the fees and services offered by several brokerage firms prior to opening an account. You can always change firms if you become unhappy, of course, but the process is sometimes frustratingly slow. It is better to choose the appropriate firm initially so you won't need to move your account. Brokerage firms are generally helpful in explaining the products and services they offer and the fees they charge. It is not in their interest to spend their time and money opening accounts for individuals who are likely to become dissatisfied and move their accounts to competing firms.

What is the first thing to consider when selecting a brokerage firm?

First, determine which services you require, so you will know the type of brokerage firm to use. Will you be making your own financial decisions or are you likely to seek assistance in determining what stocks to buy and sell? If you are comfortable making your own decisions, you may want to shop for a brokerage firm on the basis of the fees you will be charged, both to maintain the account and to trade securities. However, many firms offer relatively low fees, so commissions alone can't be your only consideration. For example, do you wish to trade online with your personal computer or would you rather use the telephone to place orders? Maybe you are a novice investor who is just becoming interested in investing, in which case you need financial counseling. As a novice investor, you probably want a full-service brokerage firm that provides the assistance you desire even if it involves relatively high fees. Individuals sometimes tend to overrate their investment knowledge, especially when times are good and the stock market has been booming. These investors discover too late that they should have sought advice from an experienced and knowledgeable financial counselor, even at the cost of increased commissions.

Are online brokerage firms a good choice?

Online firms generally charge very low commissions, and most offer a wide variety of products. Some online firms charge as little as $5 or $10 for buying or selling several thousand shares of stock, a small fraction of the commission you will be charged by a full-service brokerage firm for the same trade. Online firms generally do a good job of providing order executions at low cost. These firms often provide free access to extensive online research, financial data, historical stock price data, and current stock and bond price quotations. The price quotations are real time, not delayed, meaning your computer provides access to current bid and ask prices. With an online account there is no need to deal with a broker and no one is looking over your shoulder to observe potentially bad trades that produce financial losses. There is a downside, however, because you are on your own in deciding which securities to buy and sell and when to buy and sell them. No one cautions you against engaging in excessive trading or concentrating too much money in a single stock.

Can I place an order by phone if I have an online account?

Online brokerage firms generally accept orders by telephone, but they often charge a slightly higher commission. A firm that charges $15 for an order entered online might charge $20 or $25 if the same order is placed by phone. Most online firms also offer account assistance by telephone, so you can reach a company representative, for instance, if you have a technical question about how an order is to be executed. Assistance is also available in the event you have a question about your account.

How do I choose among similar brokerage firms?

Many brokerage firms offer essentially the same services and fees, so you may want to seek personal recommendations from friends or colleagues at work. A brokerage firm that provides a high level of service, good execution, and a quick resolution of customer concerns should have satisfied clients who will sing its praises. Be certain to consider the investment experience and knowledge of the people who provide the recommendations. More than a few disreputable and greedy brokers have fleeced investors who, for at least a period of time, were seemingly satisfied, or they wouldn't have been fleeced. You might also want to research financial publications that periodically provide rankings of brokerage firms based on a variety of factors, including fees, customer service, and product offerings. Financial publications and newspapers often publish advertisements

EXHIBIT 5-1

Select List of Online Brokerage Firms

Brokerage Firm	Web Site
Ameritrade	www.ameritrade.com
Brown & Company	www.browncomcom
Datek Online	www.datek.com
E-Trade	www.etrade.com
Fidelity Investments	www.fidelity.com
Merrill Lynch	www.ml.com
Morgan Stanley Dean Witter Online	www.online.msdw.com
Charles Schwab	www.charlesschwab.com
Muriel Siebert & Company	www.siebertnet.com
TD Waterhouse	www.tdwaterhouse.com

from brokerage firms so you can call or send for information concerning commissions, products, and services offered by each firm. The telephone yellow pages generally include listings for all the local brokerage firms and also sometimes for larger national firms that can be reached via a toll-free number. Brokerage firms are generally listed in the yellow pages under the category *Stocks and Bonds.*

Will a broker advise me on which stocks to buy and sell?

The availability of advice will depend on the type of brokerage firm you choose, the broker who handles your account, and the size and trading activity of your account. Some firms specialize in research and advice they provide to their customers. The quantity and quality of advice can vary from broker to broker within a firm. Your needs are likely to enjoy increased attention if you have a relatively large and active account, compared to another investor who has a relatively small account and rarely buys and sells stocks. Of course, you are unlikely to require much attention if you have a small account and seldom trade stocks.

A friend deals with a financial consultant, not a broker. Is there a difference?

Part of the difference in titles is perception and part is real. Full-service brokerage firms have evolved from mainly providing for the execution of orders to buy and sell stocks, bonds, and mutual funds, to offering a wide range of financial products and services. Likewise, employees once known as brokers because they provided advice and took customer orders for stocks, now go by more chic names such as financial consultants or financial counselors. Both the brokerage companies and their employees want investors to know that they offer far more than just accepting orders to buy and sell securities. Brokers at many firms must now demonstrate knowledge of a variety of financial products.

What about brokers I don't know who call me at home with stock recommendations?

Don't be enticed by someone representing an obscure firm who tells you about a stock that offers unbelievable potential. Many individuals have been scammed out of substantial amounts of money by being either too trustworthy or too greedy. Stick with reputable firms that have a track record. Even this doesn't provide complete protection, of course, because disreputable brokers sometimes work for well-known firms. Still, reputable firms attempt to weed out unscrupulous brokers. Disreputable brokerage firms tend to rely on unscrupulous brokers.

What services do brokerage firms provide?

First and foremost, brokerage firms facilitate the execution of customer orders to buy and sell securities. Most brokerage firms will also assist with the transfer of securities, arrange for loans using securities as collateral, take care of bond redemptions, and collect dividend and interest payments on securities held in an account. They will also invest your funds in short-term investments similar to financial products offered by commercial banks and savings and loan associations. Brokerage firms have expanded the services they offer their customers as the companies seek to become one-stop financial centers that compete against commercial banks, savings and loan associations, and insurance companies. Basically, most major brokerage firms attempt to corral as much of your financial assets as possible.

What brokerage commissions can I expect to pay to buy and sell shares of stock?

Commissions vary a great deal among brokerage firms. Full-service firms tend to establish their commission schedules on the basis of the market value of the securities being bought or sold. These firms consider both the number of shares in a trade and the price per share, so that a larger commission is charged for trades involving securities with a greater market value. Most discount brokerage firms, including online firms, typically charge a flat fee per trade regardless of market value. These firms charge the same commission for buying 100 shares of a $15 stock as for buying 800 shares of a $70 stock. Fees typically range from zero to $30 per trade, although a limitation of from 1000 to 3000 shares is generally imposed. The upper limit varies by firm. Trades above the limitation incur a larger fee.

How can a brokerage firm afford to execute orders for such a small commission?

First, online firms tend to operate with lower expenses than full-service brokerage firms. In addition, brokerage firms are sometimes paid for order flow. That is, the firm is paid to send customer orders to a particular market maker. Thus, the brokerage firm earns an income from your order even though you may be charged a very low commission. The downside to this practice is that the order may not be executed at the most favorable price. "Payment for order flow" is too complicated a topic to fully explain in this book, but you should know that the procedure is controversial. You may want to ask your brokerage firm if it receives payment for order flow.

When am I required to pay for shares of stock that I buy?

Stock transactions settle three business days following a transaction. Thus, you will be required to have the appropriate amount of cash to your broker within three business days of purchasing stock. Remember, settlement is in three business days, so weekends and market holidays don't count. The three-day period also applies to the time you must wait to receive payment following the sale of stock. Sell stock on Tuesday, and you will receive payment three days later on Friday. Buy stock on Thursday, and you must come up with the money by the following Tuesday.

What financial products besides stocks do these firms offer?

Brokerage firms offer virtually any financial product your heart desires including stocks, bonds, certificates of deposit, mutual funds, Treasury bills, stock options, warrants, futures contracts, life insurance, partnerships, Treasury bonds, and more. Not every brokerage firm offers every product, of course. In fact, differences in product offerings should be a major consideration when you are selecting a brokerage firm. Some firms are more active in assisting corporations to raise funds in the capital markets. Participating in new stock and bond issues allows these firms to make new issues of securities available to their customers. Participating in new stock issues should be an important consideration if you are interested in investing in initial public offerings. Likewise, some brokerage firms offer low-cost, streamlined execution of orders to buy and sell stocks and bonds, but little else. Stock and bond executions are the only service that some individuals desire, and the low fees charged by many of these firms are often quite attractive, especially compared to full-service firms. Other individuals may need financial counseling or more complex investment alternatives, and so a bare-bones brokerage operation that offers only online accounts is probably not the best choice.

What other considerations are important in choosing a brokerage firm?

Accessibility of the firm's office may be an important consideration. Doing business with a local brokerage firm means you can easily deliver certificates for securities you sell, deposit checks, pick up research reports, or visit with your broker. Some individuals find it much more beneficial to talk with a broker in person rather than by telephone. Perhaps you are holding a stock certificate that needs to be exchanged in a merger or takeover. An account at a local brokerage firm allows you to deliver the certificate in person to your broker, who will take care of the paperwork. Sell shares of stock, and you can stop by the firm to pick up the proceeds rather than wait for the mail. Brokerage firms often offer investment information and maintain an in-house library that is made available for use by their customers. There are definitely advantages to having an account at a local brokerage firm.

Are there disadvantages to using a local brokerage firm?

The major disadvantage is the fees you are likely to be charged. Commissions at most local brokerage firms are often significantly higher than those charged by discount brokerage firms and, especially, by firms providing online access. Local offices tend to be expensive for a company to maintain, so you can expect to pay higher commissions to buy and sell stocks at one of these firms. Also, if the local firm is relatively small, you may find that it does not offer the wide range of products and services that are available from many large national brokers. Another consideration is knowledge of your assets and investment activity. Perhaps you don't want anyone in the local community to be privy to the state of your finances or to know about the success or failure of your investment decisions. Having an account in a distant city solves this problem.

Is it smart to have accounts at more than one brokerage firm?

Many individuals have accounts at more than a single brokerage firm. You may desire the convenience of an account at a local firm and also want to benefit from the low fees available from having an account at an online firm. Maintaining several accounts will also provide access to additional sources of research and recommendations. Don't expect to utilize your local broker's time to gain information you put to use in trades through your online account, at least not for long. This is not only unethical, but you will discover that the effort your local broker exerts on your behalf will depend in large part on the amount of business you send his or her way. Divert most of your business to your online account, and advice from the local broker will diminish accordingly.

Are there other advantages to having more than one brokerage account?

Multiple brokerage accounts can be advantageous if you are interested in participating in new stock issues. Firms that underwrite new stock issues give preference to their own customers, so having several accounts will offer more opportunities for you to participate in the market for new stock issues. You will also find that different brokerage firms hold different inventories of bonds, so you will have a better choice of debt securities if you are interested in adding bonds to your portfolio.

Is there a downside to having multiple brokerage accounts?

Multiple accounts may complicate your financial life. You will have more monthly statements to file and more telephone calls from brokers trying to sell you something. There will be additional entries on your federal income tax return (if dividend-paying stocks are kept in your accounts), and you will have to remember which transactions occurred in which account. Think of the complications you are likely to encounter if you simultaneously have several checking accounts. Multiple brokerage accounts mean you will present each of your brokers with an incomplete picture of your investment portfolio, which can be an important consideration if you rely on a broker for financial advice. Such a broker must have a complete picture of your financial assets and investment goals; a partial view can result in faulty investment advice. Of course, there may be reasons you would prefer your brokers to have a less than complete picture of your financial life.

Are there other disadvantages to having multiple accounts?

You may discover that multiple accounts result in higher account maintenance fees. Many brokerage firms charge an annual fee in addition to the brokerage commissions you will pay to buy and sell securities. Thus, opening more than one account may result in additional fees. Brokerage firms will sometimes waive the annual account fee for relatively large accounts or for investors who generate substantial commissions. Thus, consolidating all your assets in a single account may allow you to avoid an annual fee altogether. Even brokerage firms that have no written policy of waiving fees for large accounts may rebate your annual fee if you ask. A fee waiver is unlikely if you maintain a small or a relatively inactive account.

How do I go about opening a brokerage account?

Opening an account at a brokerage firm isn't any more difficult than opening a checking account at a commercial bank. Everything can be accomplished by mail, online, or in person. It is best to visit the firm and fill out the paperwork in person if you plan to open an account at a local firm. You not only want to open the account, you also want to meet the people you will be dealing with, especially the broker who will handle your account. It may be worthwhile to visit each brokerage firm when several are available. Choosing a firm is an important decision, and you shouldn't hurry the process.

What can I expect if I visit a local brokerage firm?

The office will have a receptionist who assists individuals who wish to open an account or talk with a broker. Tell the receptionist that you would like to meet the office manager. Actually, it is best to call ahead and schedule an appointment with the manager so your time isn't wasted when the manager is out of the office or busy with another customer. The office manager will be well-acquainted with each of the firm's brokers. The manager will ask you some basic questions to assist in identifying a broker with whom you would be compatible. Would you rather work with a new broker or an experienced broker? New brokers, especially young ones, often suggest a more aggressive investment strategy. Are you interested in a particular type of investment such as options, bonds, or commodities? Brokers often specialize in particular types of investments, and understanding your interests will assist the manager in identifying a compatible broker.

Once my account is assigned to a particular broker, can I later change to a different broker?

You can request that your account be assigned to a different broker in the event you become disenchanted with your existing broker. Perhaps you feel you have not been receiving sufficient attention or you have become unhappy with your broker's stock recommendations. Personalities sometimes clash such that a parting of the ways is mutually beneficial. Regardless, if you wish to stay with the same firm and the same office (maybe it is the only brokerage firm in town), talk with the office manager, who will assist with the transfer. Transferring an account between brokers in the same office is no big deal and requires no paperwork on your part.

What about changing to a different brokerage firm?

Changing to a different firm can be as simple as opening an account at the new firm in the event you have possession of all your securities. You may want to close your existing account if it incurs an annual maintenance fee. Some firms charge only for an inactive account, so you may want to check on this even if you haven't been charged a fee in the past. The process of moving an account becomes somewhat more complicated in the event your securities are being held in street name by your existing brokerage firm. One method for changing firms is to ask for delivery of all the securities being held in your current account and then personally deliver those securities to the new firm you have selected. Delivery requires some time, and you should keep in mind that your current firm may charge a fee for each security it is asked to deliver. Another method is to open an account at a new firm and then request that the new firm take care of having all of your securities transferred to your new account. A broker-to-broker transfer will require that you complete all the paperwork for a new account plus an additional form that requests the transfer. This type of transfer is also likely to take at least several weeks.

What information is required when opening a brokerage account?

You will be asked to supply standard information, such as your name, address, phone number, and Social Security number. The brokerage firm will also ask you to identify your investment objectives, such as growth in value, current income, speculation, etc. Your selection of one or more investment objectives will assist your broker in suggesting recommendations. You will also be asked about the amount of your net worth and annual income, and you can reveal whatever information you think appropriate. You will need to make some important decisions, such as whether the account will be in your name only or in joint name with another person such as your spouse, parent, or child. You must also decide whether you want a cash account in which case purchases of all securities must be paid in full, or a margin account that allows you

to buy securities with a combination of cash and borrowed
money.

Is it better to have an account in joint name or in my name only?

The decision on whether to add someone else's name to your
account depends on individual circumstances. Being married
means you are likely to want to include your spouse's name on
the account. In general, assets held in an account in joint name
will pass to the joint account owner in the event of the death of
one party. An account in your name only will pass, on your
death, to your estate that will then be distributed according to
your will. The decision on how to title an account becomes
fairly complicated if you are relatively wealthy and concerned
about estate taxes. Keep in mind that a joint owner has equal
access and ownership of a joint account. You may or may not
find this to be desirable. If you are married, two individual
accounts may result in higher annual fees if you are required to
pay maintenance charges on two accounts rather than on one
joint account. Two accounts also mean you will receive twice
as many monthly reports and annual account summaries to file.
You should consider how you will register an account before
meeting with a broker so you will be prepared to ask any questions you have regarding this issue. A meeting with a tax attor-
ney or tax accountant is advisable if you expect to have a
relatively large account.

Should I choose a cash account or a margin account?

A margin account offers more flexibility than a cash account
because it enables you to purchase securities with the proceeds
of a loan arranged by your broker. You may view credit availability as an advantage or a disadvantage depending on your
self-control. Buying securities using borrowed money can sub-

stantially increase the risk you face as an investor. A margin account also provides the opportunity to borrow money at relatively low cost by utilizing securities held in the account as collateral. The borrowed funds from a margin loan can be used for any purpose, including buying a vehicle, taking a vacation, or paying down another loan.

What interest rate will be charged on a margin loan?

The interest rate on margin loans is based on a short-term rate, generally the broker call loan rate or the prime rate. The rate you will be charged depends both on the amount you borrow and the brokerage firm holding your account. Different brokerage firms charge different rates, which generally decrease with the amount of money that is borrowed. In other words, the more you borrow, the lower the interest rate you will be charged. If there is some possibility that you will be borrowing money in a margin account, you should ask about a firm's margin loan policy before opening an account. The difference in interest rates on a relatively large balance can more than offset differences in commissions.

Will a margin loan require payments like my car loan?

Margin loans do not have a required payment schedule, and you can pay down the balance whenever it is convenient. The entire loan can be paid off in a few days or weeks, or you can allow the loan to remain outstanding for a year or more. Of course, the greater the balance, and the longer the balance remains outstanding, the more interest you will be charged. Your brokerage firm will be happy to allow you to leave the entire loan balance unpaid so long as the value of the securities held in your account provides sufficient collateral. Margin loans are an important source of income for many brokerage firms.

Does a margin account entail a higher annual maintenance fee?

A margin account and a cash account incur the same fees except for the interest expense that results from borrowing money in a margin account. Many firms don't levy an annual fee for either type account. Firms that do levy an annual maintenance fee generally charge the same for either a cash or margin account. The danger is that a margin account makes available a new source of credit that may be abused. If you have difficulty controlling use of your credit cards, you may want to opt for a conservative cash account rather than a margin account. Choosing a cash account forces you to pay in full for the securities you purchase.

Are any special types of brokerage accounts available?

Many of the major brokerage houses offer an all-in-one brokerage account that includes a credit or debit card, free check writing, margin access, security safekeeping, and the automatic sweep of idle balances into a money market account. This type account, pioneered by Merrill Lynch as its trademarked Cash Management Account, is now offered by a number of brokerage houses under various names. The basic features at all the accounts are similar. Dividend and interest payments as well as proceeds from the sale of securities are automatically swept into a money market account. Customers can generally choose among several different money market accounts, both taxable and tax exempt. The credit or debit card and checks both provide access to funds in the money market account and to margin loans, using as collateral securities held in the account. Shares in the money market account are sold in order to satisfy checks that are presented for payment. The checks and credit card can also be used for borrowing money. In other words, you can write a check or use the credit card for an amount that exceeds the balance in your money market account. Any check in excess of the money market account balance is treated as a margin loan on which interest is charged. One nice feature of these accounts is that you receive a single monthly statement containing all your activity, including checks, credit or debit card purchases, and security sales or purchases. The account statements are typically more detailed than statements sent to regular clients.

Is there a charge for these special accounts?

Most firms levy an annual fee of approximately $100 for these accounts. The accounts usually include unlimited check writing (with free checks) and use of the debit or credit card, so the annual fee isn't unreasonable. Some firms waive the annual fee for accounts with assets above a specified amount. Also, you may be able to convince your broker to waive the fee if you are a good customer. Comprehensive brokerage accounts do not eliminate the need for a local bank account.

Will the brokerage firm send me certificates for stocks that I purchase?

Another choice you will have to make when opening an account is whether to ask for delivery of securities that are purchased. The alternative is to have securities held in street name by the brokerage firm. Most investors choose to leave the securities with their broker. Leaving securities in street name eliminates a variety of problems with taking delivery, including arranging for the safekeeping of certificates. Lose a certificate and you will encounter paperwork and a stiff fee in order to have a replacement certificate issued. The cost will generally amount to 2 percent of the market value of the shares represented by the lost certificate. The more valuable the stock represented by the certificate, the more the replacement will cost. Another headache caused by taking delivery of certificates is that you must be able to present the appropriate certificate in the event you subsequently sell the stock. Holding certificates in a safe deposit box means a trip to the bank and then a trip to the brokerage firm. If the firm is out of town, you should strongly consider sending the certificate via registered mail, another expense not incurred if you leave certificates in care of your brokerage firm. To top it off, many brokerage firms now charge customers to deliver a certificate.

Are there any disadvantages to leaving securities in care of my brokerage firm?

The main disadvantage to leaving securities in your account is that you are unable to sell the security through a different brokerage firm until the certificate is transferred to another firm or delivered to you. The transfer and delivery process can consume weeks, which means you are likely to be stuck selling the shares through the same brokerage firm where the shares where purchased. This is not a major disadvantage, but it does reduce your flexibility somewhat. If you normally purchase securities through a full-service brokerage firm, you may wish to sell some shares at a lower commission through a discount broker. Still, the advantages are compelling for leaving securities in the care of your brokerage firm.

What happens to dividends paid on shares of stock held in my account?

Dividends paid on stock held in your account will most likely be rolled into a money market account. Some firms require a minimum amount of cash in an account before funds are moved to a money market fund. This policy means there is some possibility that dividends will sit idle as cash until the minimum balance is accumulated. The policy varies among brokerage firms, so you will have to ask your broker about the firm's policy regarding cash balances in your account.

What happens to annual reports and other information sent by companies in which I own shares?

As odd as it sounds, companies that issue the shares being held in your brokerage firm will not be able to identify you as one of their shareholders. As a result, the reports will be sent by the company to the brokerage firm and subsequently forwarded to you. You will eventually receive everything, but you will receive it a little later than shareholders who hold their certificates in their own names.

How safe are securities and cash kept in my account?

The assets held in your brokerage account are as safe as the money you keep in a commercial bank. Brokerage firms are members of the Securities Investor Protection Corporation (SIPC), a government-sponsored organization that insures individual brokerage accounts to a total value of $500,000, including cash to a maximum of $100,000. SIPC insurance is designed to protect the assets being held in your account in the event the brokerage company goes out of business and your assets cannot be recovered. The coverage does not provide protection against loss of value because of market fluctuations. In other words, don't expect the insurance to cover losses caused by a decline in market value. Most large brokerage firms purchase additional coverage from private insurers. For example, a brokerage firm might purchase private insurance so your account is covered for $2 million in losses above the $500,000 SIPC coverage. The additional insurance may or may not be an important consideration, depending on the size of your account. Regardless, it doesn't cost you anything.

6
CHAPTER

FUNDAMENTAL ANALYSIS FOR VALUING STOCKS

Chapter summary

How investments are valued … The importance of cash flows in valuing a business … Why future cash flows are discounted … Valuing stock as a business … Dividends vs. earnings in determining stock values … The effect of interest rates on stock prices … The relationship of stock and bond values … How stock values are affected by stock dividends and splits … The effect of inflation on stock values … The importance of a stock's price-earnings ratio … Taxes and stock values … Does a stock tend to trade at its true value?

How are investments valued?

Financial theory holds that investments should be valued on the basis of the cash flows the investments are expected to produce for their owners. In short, an asset's value is determined by cash flows to be received by all of the owners, present and future. The value of a particular asset is a function not only of the dollar amounts of the future cash flows, but also the timing and certainty of the cash flows to be received by the asset's owners. According to this theory, an asset has greater value (1) the larger the amount of the cash flows to be received, (2) the sooner the cash flows are expected to occur, and (3) the greater the certainty that the expected cash flows will actually be realized. This relationship between current value and cash flows is relevant to any investment, including real estate, certificates of deposit, gold coins, U.S. government bonds, and, of course, shares of stock.

Can you provide an example of how an investment's value is influenced by cash flows?

The relationship between the current value of an asset and the asset's expected cash flows is easiest to understand when a single future cash flow is promised. For example, what is today's value of a specified lump sum payment to be received on a specific date in the future? First, the greater the size of the cash flow expected, the more valuable the investment. It is not difficult to understand that a promised payment of $10,000 one year from today has a greater current value than a promised payment of $7000 on the same date. All things equal, it is better to receive $10,000 than $7000. Second, an asset is more valuable the sooner the cash is to be received. Ten thousand dollars to be received next year has a greater current value than the same amount of cash to be received in five years. Even if you don't think you will need the money when it is to be received in a year, the cash can always be reinvested and grow to more than $10,000 in another four years.

Third, the greater the certainty the expected payment will occur on time and in full, the more valuable the asset. A $10,000 payment to be received in five years and guaranteed by the U.S. Treasury is more valuable than a $10,000 payment on the same date when the promise is from a financially strapped corporation. Size, timing, and certainty of expected cash flows are important factors in determining the value of an investment asset.

You mentioned that future cash flows should be discounted. How is discounting accomplished?

Money has a present value. That is, a dollar today is worth more than a dollar tomorrow. Likewise, a dollar tomorrow is worth more than a dollar next week. Calculating the current value of a future cash payment or a series of future cash payments requires that the future payments be discounted, or reduced in value, to account for the delay in receiving the cash. The longer the delay before a cash payment is to be received, the more the payment should be discounted in order to establish the payment's current value. The objective of discounting is to determine a current value that makes you and other investors indifferent in choosing between the discounted amount today and the full amount of the future cash flows. Suppose I owe you a total of $5000 that is to be paid in five annual installments of $1000 each. The first payment is scheduled to occur one year from today. Attempting to get a better deal, I ask how much money you will accept today in order to forgive the entire debt. In other words, I am asking how much you will take in a lump sum payment today to forgive the five annual $1000 payments. In formulating an answer, you must determine the current value of the five cash payments you are scheduled to receive under the existing loan agreement. The current value is calculated by discounting each of the $1000 payments by an appropriate rate.

Can you explain this problem more clearly?

Exhibit 6-1 illustrates how the five $1000 payments are discounted. Suppose you decide that 8 percent is an appropriate discount rate for the payment stream because you feel you could earn an 8 percent return on money you invest during the next five years. The first payment of $1000 scheduled one year from today and discounted at 8 percent has a present value of $925.93. In other words, $925.93 today is equivalent to $1000 in one year when the discount rate is 8 percent. The $1000 payment to be received in two years has a present value of $859.11. The second payment has less current value than the first payment because you must wait a year more. Overall, you should be willing to forgive the loan and its five $1000 payments in return for a single payment today of $3994.50. The present value of each payment would decline with a higher rate of discount and increase with a lower rate of discount.

What is an appropriate rate to use in discounting an investment's cash flows?

The starting point (e.g., lowest possible discount rate) is the rate of return currently available to buyers of U.S. government securities on which there is no risk of not being paid. The rate of interest on these securities, called the *risk-free rate,* should be used to discount a series of cash flows when the promised payments are certain to be received in full and on schedule. For example, interest payments and principal of an insured certificate of deposit are certain to be paid and should be discounted by the risk-free rate. Cash flows that are in any way uncertain should be discounted at a rate higher than the risk-free rate. The rate at which to discount risky cash flows is adjusted upward from the risk-free rate to account for the possibility that you may not receive the expected cash, or the payments may be late or less than promised. The less the certainty of the projected cash flows, the higher the rate that should be used to discount the cash flows in order to calculate the current value. The ratio-

EXHIBIT 6-1

Calculating the Current Value of a Series of Payments

You are promised payments of $1000 per year for the next five years with the first payment scheduled one year from today. You expect to be able to earn an annual return of 8 percent over the same five-year period. In other words, you could earn a return of 8 percent on any funds that are available for investment. The 8 percent return is your opportunity cost of funds (the return you could earn on funds during the next five years) and is used to determine the value of the five-payment stream.

$$\text{Current Value} = \frac{\$1,000}{(1+.08)^1} + \frac{\$1,000}{(1+.08)^2} + \frac{\$1,000}{(1+.08)^3} + \frac{\$1,000}{(1+.08)^4} + \frac{\$1,000}{(1+.08)^5}$$

$$= \frac{\$1,000}{1.0800} + \frac{\$1,000}{1.1640} + \frac{\$1,000}{1.2597} + \frac{\$1,000}{1.3605} + \frac{\$1,000}{1.4693}$$

$$= \$925.93 + \$859.11 + \$793.84 + \$735.02 + \$680.60$$

$$= \$3,994.50$$

Thus, the five $1000 payments when discounted at 8 percent have a current value of less than $4000. The current value of $3994.50 means you should be willing to cancel the debt if I offer you a lump sum payment of $4000 or more. A $4000 or greater payment today has a greater current value than the five scheduled annual loan payments of $1000.

nale of a higher discount rate is that you should expect to earn a higher return on an investment that entails a higher risk of not being paid. Wouldn't you expect to earn a higher return on a loan to your neighbor than you are able to earn on the same money placed in an insured savings account?

Can the same theory of discounted cash flows be used to value a business?

In a financial sense, a business can be viewed as a machine that spits out a series of cash flows. Cash flows produced by a business vary from month to month and from year to year and may actually be negative (more cash being consumed than produced) during some particularly bad economic periods. The technique for valuing a business is the same as illustrated in Exhibit 6-1, even though the typical business is certainly more difficult to value than are certificates of deposit or U.S. government securities. Cash flows to be received from owning a certificate of deposit are easy to determine in comparison with the cash flows you will receive as the owner of a business. In addition, businesses are able to choose one of several applicable methods to account for transactions or to take account of wear and tear on assets. The accounting method chosen influences reported income, taxes, and cash flows. Still, the same rules of valuation apply to a business as apply to any other investment. A business is more valuable the greater the cash it is expected to generate for its owners, the sooner the cash will be available to the owners, and the greater the certainty the business will produce the expected cash flows. A change in the forecast for any of these variables will affect the value of the business.

Can you provide examples of how the value for a business might change?

Suppose a company announces that sales for the upcoming year are likely to exceed current forecasts. The higher revenues should translate into increased future cash flows compared to the flows previously expected. Larger cash flows should result in a greater current value for the business. Now suppose a group of legislators propose a law to limit how much petroleum companies can increase the wholesale price of crude oil. Uncertainty as to whether the legislation will become law makes future earnings and cash flows of companies involved in the petroleum business more difficult to forecast. Increased uncertainty means projected cash flows of these companies should be discounted at a higher rate, thereby reducing the current value of the cash flows and the current value of the companies.

Are current cash flows or future cash flows most important in valuing a business?

The cash flows a business can expect during its many years (hopefully) of operations are more important than the cash flow of any single year, even the current year. However, a firm's current cash flow is important because of the influence it has on investor expectations for the firm's future cash flows. A better-than-expected cash flow in the current year is likely to signal both the firm's managers and the investment community that future cash flows will also be better than previously anticipated. Current information influences expectations for the future, which is the reason current news about a company can result in such a large change in the firm's market value. A 10 percent fall in a firm's current earnings may signal to investors a potentially much larger decline in future earnings.

Are cash flows more important than earnings in valuing a company?

Reported earnings are certainly important and will have an impact on a company's stock price. However, continuing cash flows are the lifeblood of any business. Large cash inflows present a company's managers with the financial means to undertake new investment opportunities, pay employees and suppliers, take care of debts that come due, repurchase shares of the firm's stock, or distribute cash dividends to shareholders. A company that enjoys large cash flows can also become an attractive takeover target for acquisition-minded companies. Cash flows are crucial to valuing a company, especially over a long period of time during which managers can utilize the cash to improve the financial and strategic position of the company. In the short run, however, investors seem to pay more attention to reported earnings than cash flows.

How is valuation theory applied to shares of stock?

Shares of stock represent ownership of a business. The total value of all a firm's shares of stock is equal to the ownership value of the business. An increase in the value of a business means an increase in the total value of the firm's stock. A firm with an ownership valued at $1 million will have $1 million worth of outstanding stock. The stock is the ownership. The value of each share of ownership depends on two factors: the total ownership value of the business represented by the shares, and the number of shares of stock that are outstanding. If the firm valued at $1 million has 100,000 ownership shares outstanding, each share is worth $1 million/100,000 shares, or $10. If 200,000 shares of stock of the same company are outstanding, the value of each share is worth $1 million/200,000, or $5 per share. Twice as many shares means each share is worth half as much. Some relatively small companies have so many shares outstanding that individual shares are worth very little. A company with 2 million shares outstanding and an ownership valued at $1 million will have its shares valued at 50 cents each.

What about shares of stock a company's owners have authorized but the company has not issued?

Only shares of stock actually outstanding are relevant for valuation purposes. Shares the owners have authorized but directors have not yet issued are not entitled to dividends and are not utilized in calculating earnings per share. Likewise, shares that were once outstanding but have subsequently been repurchased are not included in calculating earnings or paying dividends.

Only shares that have been issued and remain in investors' hands are included in per-share calculations.

Why would a company's stockholders authorize shares that the company doesn't issue?

Corporate management must normally obtain shareholder permission to authorize additional shares of stock. Rather than ask the shareholders every couple of years to authorize additional shares, directors generally prefer to seek authorization for more shares than the firm currently plans to issue so that a reserve of authorized shares is available for issue down the road. Having more shares authorized than issued provides a company's directors with the flexibility to issue additional shares without going back to the owners for permission. Most corporations have more shares authorized than outstanding, but only the outstanding shares are used for valuation purposes.

How are individual shares valued?

Conventional financial theory holds that a share of stock should sell for the discounted value of all expected future dividend payments. In practice, most investors think of stock values in terms of the two kinds of cash flows a stockholder will receive, dividend payments and cash received when shares are eventually sold. The greater the amount of the dividends to be received, and the higher the price at which shares are expected to sell on a future date, the more the stock should be worth today. These two concepts are not at odds, because the price an investor receives when shares are sold should equal the discounted value of all future dividend payments from that date forward. In other words, the investor who buys stock in the future will be valuing the stock on the basis of dividends to be received beyond the purchase date.

Why use dividends rather than earnings in valuing stock?

Dividends flow from earnings, so the two variables are not incompatible. Earnings represent the potential to pay dividends, so future earnings should benefit when a firm's directors choose to reinvest current earnings in additional assets. More assets should produce higher earnings, which in turn result in the potential for higher future dividends compared to when more current earnings are paid in dividends. Thus, directors can pay dividends now or they can forego current dividends for the possibility of paying higher dividends in future years.

What causes changes in the value of a stock?

Any event that alters investor expectations regarding either dividends or a stock's future price will affect the current value of the stock. News that an important corporate executive has met an untimely death is likely to depress a stock's price, as investors worry that the firm's financial results may suffer under new leadership. Unexpected news that a firm's earnings will fail to meet expectations is likely to result in a decline in the firm's stock price, as investors act on lower expectations for future dividends and the likelihood that the future price of the stock will be less than previously expected. Conversely, unexpected good news regarding higher sales or reduced expenses is likely to cause a stock's price to increase, as investors raise their expectations for both dividends and the future stock price. A stock's price is in constant flux as investors and stock analysts continuously alter their estimates of future dividends and the future stock price.

A stock I own didn't change in price when a higher dividend was announced. Why?

Investors often anticipate an event, so the event is already incorporated in the stock price. For example, a stock's current price already reflects investor expectations of a series of future earnings and dividend payments. The stock price remains unaffected so long as dividends meet investor expectations. In the case of your stock, the investment community evidently anticipated the higher dividend that was announced, so the stock price didn't change when the announced dividend was as expected. The price of your stock would likely have increased if the dividend increase had been more than anticipated. On the other hand, the stock price would probably have declined if the dividend had remained unchanged or had increased less than anticipated. Stock values are about the anticipated future.

Does the same theory hold for earnings announcements?

You have probably noticed that stock prices sometimes fall when companies announce higher earnings, and they sometimes increase when companies announce lower earnings. The current price of a stock includes earnings projections. The current stock price may anticipate a decline in reported earnings compared to the same period in the prior year. The price is likely to change little if the lower earnings are reported, so long as the earnings are not lower than expected. Likewise, a stock price is unlikely to rise when a company announces increased earnings that were already expected by investors. Only if the earnings increase is higher than expected is the stock price likely to rise. In fact, a company can announce higher earnings only to see its stock price fall dramatically if the earnings increase is smaller than expected.

Why do stocks that don't pay dividends often sell at such high prices?

Remember that dividends are only one part of the valuation equation. The other part, which many investors consider more important, is the future stock price. A firm's directors may decide it is in the stockholders' interest for the company to retain most or all of its earnings, to be used for reinvestment in additional assets. The new assets should provide a base to increase future earnings and boost the stock price. The directors evidently feel the firm's stockholders will gain more benefit from the increased stock price that should accompany higher earnings than from dividend payments. Directors of young companies often choose not to pay a dividend to their stockholders and instead reinvest all of their earnings in additional assets. In terms of future cash flows, the companies are asking their stockholders to forego current dividend cash flows in return for the expectation of a much higher cash flow when the stock is eventually sold at a higher price. The higher price is only likely to be realized if the additional assets prove to be profitable.

Does the opposite hold true for stocks with relatively large dividend payments?

Companies that pay a large part of their earnings in dividends typically have limited growth potential. A company that pays all of its earnings in dividends isn't reinvesting in new assets that help make the firm more productive and more profitable. Investors buy stocks in these companies more for the cash flows from expected dividends than for the likelihood that the shares will produce major gains in value. High-dividend-paying stocks usually appeal to conservative investors who choose relatively certain dividend payments over uncertain gains in value. Future stock prices are very difficult to forecast compared to more predictable dividend payments. In addition, stocks with relatively high dividends tend to have a more stable market price, another factor that is likely to attract conservative investors.

Should I be wary of stocks that pay a high dividend?

The comparison of a stock's annual dividend and current stock price is called the *dividend yield*. A stock selling for $40.00 with an annual dividend of $1.20 per share has a dividend yield of $1.20/$40.00, or 3 percent. Dividend yield is the rate of return you would earn from the annual dividend if you bought the stock at the current price. This narrow measure of yield does not take into account a possible change in either the current dividend or the market price of the stock. It is for good reason that some stocks sell at a price to provide investors with a high dividend yield. One possible reason for a high dividend yield is that the annual dividend currently being paid is likely to be reduced in the near future. Thus, you may buy the stock and earn the indicated dividend for only a short period before the firm's directors cut the dividend to a lower level or, perhaps, eliminate it altogether. You can gain some insight on the likelihood of a dividend cut by checking on the firm's earnings per share during the last several years. A dividend is often likely if earnings per share have been declining to the point that current earnings barely cover the annual dividend. It is possible the current dividend is safe but likely to remain at the same level for many years. Mature companies that have experienced flat earnings sometimes pay the same dividend for many years. Continuing flat earnings make it unlikely that dividends will be increased. An unusually high dividend yield is likely to indicate a problem and should cause you to investigate the company more thoroughly.

How are stock values affected by interest rate changes?

Rising interest rates tend to be bad news for stock values. An earlier section of this chapter discussed why investment values are a function of discounted cash flows. In the example, a series of certain cash flows was discounted at a rate equal to that paid on U.S. government securities. The discount rate is adjusted upward depending on the uncertainty of the cash flows. Rising interest rates mean that even certain cash flows should be discounted by a higher rate, thereby resulting in lower investment values. The same relationship between interest rates and investment value

holds for stock prices. Higher interest rates cause future dividends and proceeds from stock sales to have a reduced current
value. In addition, higher interest rates are likely to result in
reduced cash flow estimates for many companies. Most corporations are big borrowers, meaning higher interest rates result in
increased interest expenses and reduced profits. Lower profits, in
turn, are likely to keep dividends lower than would be the case
with low interest rates. Thus, rising interest rates are likely to
decrease future cash flows at the same time they cause cash flows
to have a lower current value. Exhibit 6-2 illustrates the effect of
different discount rates on the same series of cash flows. In this
instance, the investment promises 10 annual end-of-year payments of $1000 each, or a total of $10,000. A 3 percent discount
rate results in a present value of $8530, while the higher discount
rate of 12 percent reduces the current value of the 10 payments to
$5650. The same type of analysis applies to a stream of rent pay-
ments, interest payments, or dividend payments.

Do declining interest rates help boost stock values?

Declining interest rates have exactly the opposite effect as
increasing interest rates. Lower interest rates result in lower
borrowing costs and reduced interest expenses. Increased profits and a likely increase in future cash flows from dividends
accompany lower interest expense. The expectation of higher
dividend payments should cause a stock price to increase.
Declining interest rates also result in reducing the rate at
which cash flows are discounted. The lower discount rate
should result in rising stock prices. The great bull market in
stocks that commenced in 1982 and continued on and off
through the end of the century is attributable in large part to a
major decline in interest rates during the same time period.
The historical relationship between stock values as measured
by the NYSE Composite Index and long-term interest rates is
illustrated in Exhibit 6-3.

EXHIBIT 6-2

Impact of the Discount Rate on the Value of an Investment

The investment: Ten annual end-of-year payments of $1000 each.

Total Funds to Be Received	Discount Rate	Current Value of the Investment
$10,000	2 percent	$ 8,983
10,000	3 percent	8,530
10,000	4 percent	8,111
10,000	5 percent	7,722
10,000	6 percent	7,360
10,000	7 percent	7,024
10,000	8 percent	6,710
10,000	9 percent	6,418
10,000	10 percent	6,145
10,000	12 percent	5,650
10,000	14 percent	5,216
10,000	16 percent	4,833

Are stock values and bond values related?

Stock and bond prices tend to move together because the values of both types of securities are strongly affected by interest rates. Both stock and bond values are negatively affected by rising interest rates. Conversely, falling interest rates cause upward price movements for both stocks and bonds. Although the values of the two securities tend to be directly related, changes in value are not proportional. In other words, bond prices shouldn't be expected to increase in value by 10 percent when stock prices increase in value by 10 percent. Even individual bond prices react differently to changing interest rates, depending primarily on the maturity length of the bonds. Stock values tend to move more closely in unison with bonds with long maturity lengths than with bonds having short maturities.

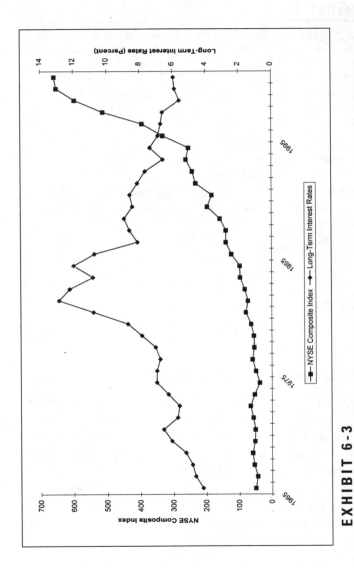

EXHIBIT 6-3

Relationship Between Long-Term Interest Rates and Stock Prices (1965–2000)

Are stock values affected by inflation?

Inflation and inflationary expectations have a major impact on stock values. In general, unanticipated inflation can be expected to cause most stock prices to decline. The worse the news about inflation, the bigger the negative impact on stock prices. On the other hand, favorable inflationary news and the expectation of stable consumer prices can be expected to have a positive influence on stock prices. There are several reasons why higher inflation is bad for stock prices. High inflation makes it more likely that the Federal Reserve will act to increase interest rates in an attempt to reduce economic growth and the inflationary pressures that accompany economic growth, especially when the economy is operating at near full employment. As previously discussed, rising interest rates are bad for stock prices. Inflation also makes it more likely that a company will have to pay higher wages to its employees and higher prices for the goods it buys, thereby hurting profits and cash flows. And a squeeze on profits and cash flows makes dividend increases less likely.

Does inflation affect all stock values to the same extent?

Different companies and their respective stock prices are affected differently both by interest rates and inflation. The stocks of some companies are likely to rise with higher inflationary expectations. Natural resource companies with operations in petroleum, timber, and mining often benefit from inflation because the firms are able to sell their products at higher prices. In addition, assets owned by these companies (e.g., land, mineral deposits, and so forth) are likely to increase in value during inflationary periods. Many companies can be hurt by inflation if they are unable to pass through cost increases in higher prices to their customers. Regulated utilities tend to fall into this category, although deregulation may produce greater pricing flexibility and allow these companies to adjust more quickly to inflationary conditions. Still, inflation and higher interest rates tend to penalize most stock prices, although to varying degrees depending on the industry in which a company operates and the methods of financing utilized by the firm.

What effect does a stock dividend or a stock split have on a stock's value?

Stock dividends and stock splits result in additional outstanding shares of stock without offsetting increases in the company's assets, earnings, or cash flows. With either a stock split or a stock dividend, a company with the same total assets, liabilities, and earnings is suddenly divided into more pieces, with each piece necessarily worth less than before the additional shares were issued. Thus, stock splits and dividends cause a decline in the price of a stock but will result in little or no change in the aggregate value of a company's stock. Stock splits are primarily intended to reduce the market price of a company's stock to a level investors find desirable. Stock dividends are infrequent and generally utilized as a substitute for a cash dividend. Having said that either of these actions will reduce the market price of a company's shares, some researchers believe that the announcement of a forthcoming stock dividend or stock split can have a positive effect on a stock's price, at least temporarily.

How is a stock's price-earnings ratio used in valuation?

The price-earnings ratio (PE), also called a stock's *multiple*, is the ratio of a company's stock price to its earnings per share. A company with 125,000 shares of outstanding common stock and annual earnings of $250,000 has earned $250,000/125,000 shares, or $2 per share. If its common stock trades at a price of $30, the stock's price-earnings ratio is $30/$2, or 15. In other words, the stock sells at a price of 15 times current earnings per share. Analysts sometimes use next year's expected earnings rather than current earnings to calculate the price-earnings ratio. A relatively high PE for a stock indicates that investors are paying a high price for a dollar of the firm's earnings. A high PE generally occurs when investors expect a company's earnings to grow rapidly in future years. Conversely, a relatively low PE ratio indicates investors are paying a low price for the company's earnings. A low PE generally indicates investors are pessimistic about earnings growth, and so are unwilling to pay a high price for a dollar of current earnings.

What size PE is judged to be relatively high or relatively low?

The average price-earnings ratio for stocks varies over time and between industries at any particular time. A PE ratio that is judged to be relatively high during one year may not be considered so high during a different year. The market PE is generally defined as the average price-earnings ratio of the 500 stocks used to calculate the Standard & Poor's 500 Index. If the PE for the S&P 500 is 25, a PE of 35 to 40 for an individual stock would be considered relatively high. On the other hand, if the market PE is 15, an individual stock PE of 25 would be considered relatively high. Regardless, a relatively high PE for a stock indicates investors expect higher earnings growth for that particular company than for business as a whole. Price-earnings ratios also vary by industry. The stocks of companies in mature industries offering little promise of rapid growth tend to sell at relatively low PE ratios. Stocks of companies with substantial growth potential, such as Merck and Corning, tend to trade at prices that result in relatively high PE ratios. On the other hand, the stocks of companies that operate in mature industries, such as Consolidated Edison and Sears, Roebuck, tend to trade at low price-earnings ratios. Exhibit 6-4 provides a snapshot of differences in price-earnings ratios among companies that operate in various industries.

EXHIBIT 6-4

Price-Earnings Ratios for Stocks Representing Different Industries (Early 2001)

	Stock Price	PE Ratio
Financial Companies		
Citigroup, Inc.	$55	21
Morgan Stanley Dean Witter & Co.	83	17
Schwab (Charles) Company	28	55
Suntrust Banks	65	17
Manufacturing Companies		
Alcoa Corporation	$35	19
Boeing Company	58	24
Ford Motor Company	28	12
Goodyear Tire & Rubber	25	25
Medical Related Companies		
Abbott Laboratories	$46	26
Merck & Co.	82	29
Pfizer, Inc.	44	75
Petroleum Companies		
BP Amoco	$52	18
Chevron Corporation	83	10
ExxonMobil	81	16
Royal Dutch Petroleum	59	18
Retail Companies		
Gap, Inc.	$32	27
Sears, Roebuck	37	10
Talbots, Inc.	49	32
Wal-Mart	54	39
Technology Companies		
Corning, Inc.	$55	61
Intel Corporation	36	24
Microsoft Corporation	64	36
Oracle Corporation	30	27
Sun Microsystems	31	50

EXHIBIT 6-4

Price-Earnings Ratios for Stocks Representing Different Industries (Early 2001) (*Continued*)

	Stock Price	PE Ratio
Transportation Companies		
AMR Corporation	$37	7
CSX Corporation	27	10
Roadway Express	22	8
Union Pacific	49	15
Utility Companies		
American Electric Power	$43	23
Consolidated Edison	35	11
Duke Energy	77	16
Southern Company	29	14

Are stocks with high PE ratios overvalued?

Stocks with high PE ratios are not necessarily overvalued, just as stocks with low PE ratios are not necessarily undervalued. Individual stocks have high PE ratios because investors are looking ahead and pricing the stocks on the basis of future earnings, not current earnings. If the outlook is especially bright for the future earnings of a business, the firm's stock is likely to sell at a price with a high price-earnings ratio. If future earnings growth actually pans out as anticipated, the current high PE may be justified. The current high PE may actually undervalue the stock if earnings grow even more rapidly than anticipated. Likewise, investors are unlikely to reward a stock with a high PE ratio if the company's earnings are expected to grow slowly or even decline. Even a low PE ratio can overvalue a company's stock if a pessimistic earnings outlook turns out to be too optimistic. In other words, actual results can sometimes be even worse than the poor results that are expected.

Does anything other than expectations of future earnings affect price-earnings ratios?

Price-earnings ratios are inversely related to long-term interest rates. Falling long-term interest rates generally result in a rising stock market and higher average PE ratios. Conversely, increasing long-term interest rates are generally accompanied by reduced PE ratios caused by a falling stock market. Interest rates have a powerful influence on the stock market, which causes professional stock analysts to devote considerable attention to economic variables such as consumer prices, growth in output, unemployment, and productivity. Analysts are also very interested in the actions and public statements of the Federal Reserve Board. Rising interest rates place downward pressure on corporate earnings and on the multiple that stock investors will pay for these earnings. The double whammy of falling earnings and a reduced PE ratio caused by rising interest rates can have a major impact on stock prices.

Can you provide an example of how a change in interest rates can impact a stock's price?

Suppose long-term interest rates increase from 6 percent to 7 percent during a 12-month period. Higher interest rates result in increased borrowing costs that reduce net income. The lower income caused by increased interest expenses is likely to result in reduced earnings estimates for future periods. Investors observe that the company is unable to meet earnings expectations, and they assume that future earnings are also likely to fall short of expectations. Because the value of an investment is directly related to the size of future cash flows, reduced earnings and dividend estimates caused by higher interest rates are likely to result in lower stock prices. To compound the problem, higher interest rates will result in higher rates of discount utilized to calculate current stock values. The higher discount rates result in an even greater decline in stock values. The combination of lower cash flow expectations and an increased rate of discount brought about by rising interest rates is bad news for stock values.

Is a company's book value an important consideration in valuing its stock?

Book value is the accounting value of a firm's assets minus any debts the company owes. If the company sells all of its assets at the values recorded on the balance sheet and utilizes the proceeds of the sale to pay all of its outstanding debts, the remaining cash will be available for distribution to the owners. The stockholders' claim against the company is also called the company's book value. A company with $600,000 in assets and $250,000 in debts has a book value of $350,000. Book value is usually stated on a per-share basis, in which a company's aggregate book value is divided by the number of outstanding shares of stock. If the firm with a book value of $350,000 has 10,000 shares outstanding, its book value will be $35 per share. Book value per share can also be calculated by dividing stockholders' equity by the number of outstanding shares. You may remember from an earlier chapter that the accounting value of assets on a firm's balance sheet is often understated because assets are recorded at historical cost, or the price paid by the firm when assets were acquired. Book value may have some relevancy to valuing a company that is likely to be liquidated. For valuing companies as going operations, however, analysts pay little attention to book value per share. Analysts and investors are interested in the earnings and cash flows a firm's assets are expected to generate, not the price the company paid to acquire the assets.

I have heard analysts discuss the importance of a company's stock price to sales ratio. How is this ratio calculated, and is it important in valuing a firm's stock?

The price-to-sales (P/S) ratio compares a company's stock price with the firm's sales for each outstanding share of stock.

Sales per share of stock is calculated by dividing the number of
shares outstanding into annual sales. This calculates the dollar
amount of sales for each outstanding share of ownership. The
price-to-sales ratio has gained increasing use in recent years as
analysts attempt to value companies that operated at a loss. The
price-earnings ratio discussed above serves as an important
stock valuation measure, but it has no meaning for a company
with no earnings. The theory of using the P/S ratio to value a
company is as follows: Earnings are derived from sales and so
a large amount of sales can translate into substantial profits
with even a small increase in profitability. In other words, a
company with a large amount of sales volume offers the possibility of substantial earnings in future periods. A low P/S ratio
indicates a potentially undervalued stock for which investors
are paying a relatively small price for the sales the company is
currently generating. A slight increase in the profitability of
these sales would produce a big increase in profits, which in
turn could result in a big increase in the stock price. Exhibit 6-
5 includes data for the price-to-sales, price-to-book, and price-
earnings ratios of a diverse group of companies. Notice the low
ratios for General Motors relative to the ratios for Coca-Cola
and Microsoft.

Are stock values affected by taxes?

An investment should be judged by the after-tax return, not the
before-tax return the investment is expected to provide. After-
tax return means the rate of return that is earned after taxes have
been paid on any income that is realized. A reduction in taxes
levied against income from stock investments should result in
higher stock prices because additional funds will flow into the
stock market. For example, a reduction in the tax on long-term
capital gains from the 20 percent to 10 percent would prove to
be a significant boost for all stock prices although the change
will affect the prices of some stocks more than others. Stocks

EXHIBIT 6-5

Price to Sales, Price to Book, and Price-Earnings Ratios for Select Companies (All figures are per share—early 2001)

Company	Price/ Sales	Price/ Book Value	Stock Price/Earnings
AOL Time Warner	17.1	19.0	101
AT&T Corp.	1.4	.8	13
Coca-Cola	6.8	14	76
Convergys	3.5	6.8	44
GenCorp	0.4	2.2	8
General Electric	3.6	9.7	35
General Motors	.2	.9	8
Microsoft	13.6	7.0	36
Qualcomm	16.6	9.5	95
Texas Instruments	7.8	6.9	26
Verizon Communications	3.0	4.4	14
Worldcom, Inc.	2.1	1.1	13

desirable primarily for the dividends they provide would not be helped much by a reduction in the capital gains tax because little capital gains are anticipated. A reduction in the tax rate on regular income would provide a major assist to these dividend-paying stocks. Imagine how the prices of high-dividend stocks would skyrocket if the U.S. Congress declared that dividend income was no longer taxable by the federal government.

Would stock values be hurt if taxes were raised?

An increase in the rate of taxation on capital gains would almost surely depress stock prices along with the values of most other investments. The greater the increase in the tax rate, the more stock prices would be hurt. If Congress repealed the special tax treatment of capital gains so that realized gains were taxed as regular income, the effect on stock prices would likely be dramatic. Tax laws play a major role in the valuation of investments. In fact, some investments owe their value primarily to the tax benefits reaped by the owners.

Does a stock's market price accurately reflect its value?

This is a very good question that has been studied endlessly by academicians. Unfortunately, there is no definitive answer. Economists and finance professors have spent considerable time and effort in an attempt to determine if a stock price accurately represent the stock's true, or intrinsic, value. Some financial analysts and theoreticians believe the market price of a stock is the best measure of the stock's true value. If General Motors common stock currently trades at a price of $67 per share, then $67 is the best estimate of how much each share of the stock is worth. Likewise, a high-flying stock that trades for $300 per share must have an intrinsic value of $300 or it wouldn't sell at that price. However, a majority of financial analysts believe that stocks often trade at prices that are more or less than the stocks are really worth. Thus, an analyst might argue that the stock of General Motors has an intrinsic value of $85, thereby making the stock a bargain at the current market price of $67. Brokerage research departments are in the business of identifying stocks that sell for less or more than the analysts believe they are worth. Financial analysts earn hefty salaries for this effort, but an analyst is unlikely to last long if he or she makes a series of recommendations that cause the firm's clients to lose money. Likewise, many long-time investors spend a great deal of their own time in independent research in an attempt to identify undervalued stocks.

What is the basis for believing that stocks trade at their true values?

The active buying and selling by large numbers of investors who constantly monitor financial, political, and economic data relevant to stock values are likely to cause stock prices to reflect the values justified by this information. Any deviation of a stock price from the stock's intrinsic value will immediately be met with buying or selling that causes the stock's market price to converge with its true value. The theory that stocks sell at their intrinsic values is based on the assumption that the financial markets are efficient and that relevant information is immediately and widely disseminated to members of the investment community. If stock prices depend on the facts that should be relevant to their values (earnings, interest rates, management quality, accounting method utilized, etc.), then stock prices should reflect these values so long as the relevant information is freely available. Dissemination of relevant information has certainly been hastened by availability of information on the Internet.

Does this mean I shouldn't expect to beat the market averages with my investments?

If the stock market is truly efficient and stocks are priced at or near their intrinsic values, you will be unable to beat the market on a risk-adjusted basis regardless of how much time and money you spend on research. This doesn't mean you can never beat the market, because you can, sometimes, just as you can occasionally flip a coin and have it come up heads four times in a row. You can also expect to beat the market if you choose to own stocks that have greater-than-average risk. Even though stocks may be priced at their intrinsic values, financial theorists believe that stocks with greater risk tend to provide higher returns over the long run.

7

CHAPTER

TECHNICAL ANALYSIS FOR EVALUATING STOCKS

Chapter summary

Adherents of technical analysis generally engage in short-term trading rather than long-term investing … Charting stock prices is a favorite activity of technical analysts … Price charts produce trends and formations that can be used to forecast stock price movements … Some investors utilize fundamental analysis to select stocks to buy or sell and use technical analysis to determine the timing … Trading volume is used to validate stock price movements … Many statistical studies cast doubt on the validity of technical analysis.

What is technical analysis?

Technical analysis is the use of market data for predicting movements in the stock market and in individual stock prices.

Whereas fundamental analysis makes use of variables such as assets, earnings, revenues, cash flow, management quality, inflation, and interest rates, technical analysis concentrates on market data such as trading volume and historical stock prices. Devotees of technical analysis, often called *technicians* or *technical analysts*, follow an entirely different road than that of fundamental analysts, who concentrate on economic and financial data.

How can volume and price information be used to make investment decisions?

Technical analysts generally believe that fundamental factors such as earnings and management quality are already embodied in a stock's price. In other words, current stock prices already take into account all relevant information regarding earnings, revenues, and economic factors that interest investors who pursue fundamental analysis. As a result, digging through piles of fundamental data will do little to assist an investor to determine whether a particular stock is undervalued or overvalued. Investors who practice technical analysis also believe that history tends to repeat itself, i.e., that trading volume and stock price movements follow familiar patterns that can be evaluated and used to make investment decisions.

Is technical analysis concerned with stocks being overvalued or undervalued?

Technical analysis is concerned more with supply and demand for stocks than with any kind of fundamental valuation that a stock is or isn't worth the current price at which it is selling. Technical analysts don't concern themselves with determining whether stocks are undervalued or overvalued in a fundamental sense. They leave that work for others to investigate. Technicians are worried about whether a stock is oversold (sells at too low a price) or overbought (sells at too high a price). Technical analysts tend to concentrate on price trends, not economic fundamentals. Price trends may result from investors buying and selling on the basis of fundamental analysis, but the "why" of a trend is not really important. It is the trend itself that is important, because the trend provides guidance with regard to the appropriate investment decision.

Do technical analysts believe fundamental information doesn't affect a stock's price?

Not at all. Technical analysts tend to agree that good fundamental analysis can produce superior investment results. Analysts who produce very good fundamental analysis and are able to put the analysis to use should be able to outperform the market on a risk-adjusted basis. The problem is that superior fundamental analysis is very difficult to achieve and act on, especially for individual investors who have limited resources and time. It is better that others with more resources and contacts are left to perform this rigorous work, while technical analysts spend their time evaluating price trends that will indicate what major investors are up to.

Does this mean that financial statement information isn't an important part of technical analysis?

Technical analysts are generally suspicious of the data presented in financial statements. Companies enjoy substantial flexibility regarding the information presented in their financial statements. Occasionally the data in financial statements are intentionally misleading. More frequently the data are merely massaged by managers in order to present the company's financial results in the most favorable light. Different methods for presenting identical information make it difficult for most individuals to evaluate corporate financial statements. Thus, these statements provide individual investors with little help in

making investment decisions. Again, technical analysts leave
the evaluation of financial statements to others who have the
time and qualifications to dig behind the numbers.

Are fundamental analysts also suspicious of technical information?

Some analysts who rely on financial analysis feel that much
technical analysis is little more than financial witchcraft. They
tend to categorize technicians as individuals who don't have the
time, the patience, or the knowledge to perform good fundamental analysis and choose instead to rely on the smoke and
mirrors of charts and graphs. On the other hand, individuals
who describe themselves as fundamental analysts may pay
attention to the technical analysis produced by their colleagues.
Many members of the financial community feel that the best
investment decisions make use of both technical and fundamental analysis.

How is historical stock price information evaluated?

Technical analysts generally utilize charts to investigate historical stock prices. The typical graph, known as a *bar chart* (see,
for example, Exhibit 12-3 in Chapter 12), illustrates stock
prices by means of vertical lines, or bars. Time in days, weeks,
or even months is measured along the horizontal axis, while the
stock's price (or, in the case of a stock market index, the value
of the index) is measured on the vertical axis. Each day, the
stock's high price and low price are connected with a vertical
line. A step, or notch, usually on the right side of the vertical
price line, indicates the closing price. New information is
posted daily to produce historical price trends or formations
that are used in forecasting future price movements. Bar charts
are sometimes drawn with weekly or monthly price data, rather
than daily price data. Stock and market indicator bar charts are

available on many Internet sites and in several financial publications, including *Investor's Business Daily* and the Money and
Investments section of the *Wall Street Journal*. The *Journal*
publishes charts for the four Dow Jones averages but not for
individual stocks. Each issue of *Investor's Business Daily*
includes bar charts for a select group of individual stocks.
Charts for stock market indicators and individual stocks are
drawn in the same manner, and many analysts chart stock market indicators as well as individual stocks.

How can price information be used to make investment decisions?

Successive stock price changes sometimes form identifiable
formations that provide guidance regarding future movements. For example, a stock may gradually decline in price at
a lesser and lesser rate over a long period of time until the
declines stop and are replaced by gradual increases that grow
larger over time. The "saucer" formation resulting from these
successive price changes is useful for forecasting future price
movements. At least, this is what technical analysts claim.
Technical analysts believe historical price movements such
as the "saucer" can be utilized to forecast future price movements. A saucer formation is bullish, and the stock should be
purchased soon after moving beyond the bottom of the
saucer. An upside down or inverted saucer formation is bearish, and the stock should be sold shortly after the price begins
to decline. Other popular price formations utilized by technical analysts include the head-and-shoulders, triple top,
ascending triangle, and descending triangle. These are only a
few of dozens of price formations used by technical analysts.
The name assigned to each is generally descriptive of its
appearance on the price chart. Exhibit 7-1 illustrates several
of the better-known price formations utilized by technical
analysts.

E X H I B I T   7-1

Selected Stock Price Formations

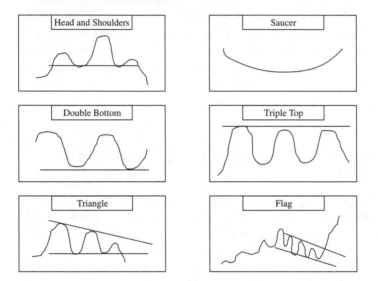

How do chart formations indicate whether stocks should be bought or sold?

Technical analysts believe stock price formations tend to repeat themselves. If a particular formation generally leads to a subsequent decline in price, the formation is a bearish sign and the stock should be sold. For example, a head-and-shoulders formation is thought to signal a major price decline and, as a result, is considered a signal to sell the stock. A triple top formed by three unsuccessful attempts by a stock to move above a particular price that serves as a resistance level is also considered a bearish signal. Just as a particular price may prove resistant to being penetrated on the upside, a support level may exist that resists penetration on the downside. Unfortunately, price movements do not always produce clear-cut formations, and so technical analysis also involves interpreting stock price movements to determine if an identifiable price formation has actually occurred. Thus, analyzing stock price formations is as much an art as it is a science. Two analysts might view the same group of successive stock price movements and reach different conclusions as to whether it is a signal to buy or to sell.

Is there anything else of importance regarding stock price movements?

Technical analysts believe stock prices tend to move in trends. The trends may be upward, downward, or sideways, but in each case the general direction of movement will continue until a significant price movement in the opposite direction ends the trend. Trends are generally displayed on charts as channels, or trend channels. A straight line connecting successive high prices forms the top of the channel, and a straight line connecting successive low prices forms the bottom of the channel. The lines run in the same direction but do not have to be exactly parallel. A stock can be expected to bounce up and down within the trend channel until a strong movement through one of the lines, usually on high volume, indicates the trend has ended. A breakout through the bottom line of an upward trend channel is a signal to sell the stock. A breakout through the top line of a downward trend channel is a signal to buy the stock. Exhibit 7-2 illustrates a stock's price movements in a downward trend channel and its subsequent breaking out and into an upward trend channel.

Does breaking through one of these lines represent a change in a stock's price trend?

A stock price breaking through a trend line is considered very important, especially if the breakout occurs on relatively high trading volume. "Relatively high" means the trading volume is above average for that particular stock. The line that is drawn to connect successive high prices is called a *resistance line*. The

E X H I B I T   7-2

Stock Price Trend Chart

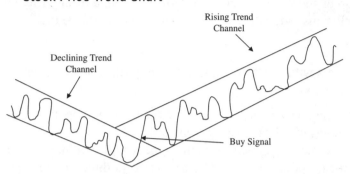

resistance line serves as a ceiling against which the stock price can be expected to keep bouncing back as buying slacks off and selling pressure intensifies. A new upward trend is likely if the stock can gain sufficient strength to actually break through the resistance line. Technicians consider an upside breakout to be very bullish and a sign that a stock should be purchased. The buy signal denoted in Exhibit 7-2 occurs where the stock price breaks above the resistance line of the downward trend channel.

What about a price break in a downward direction?

The support line that is drawn to connect successive low prices represents price levels at which investors can be expected to purchase shares and support the stock. The stock will likely bounce upward off the support line. A sell signal occurs when a stock breaks through its support line, especially if the movement is accompanied by relatively heavy trading volume. The heavier the relative trading volume when a stock's price breaks through a resistance line or a support line, the more confidence you can have in the buy or sell signal. Keep in mind that the support line may be upward sloping, downward sloping, or horizontal.

Aside from bar charts, are there other ways of graphing stock prices?

Line charts and point-and-figure charts are also used to record historical stock prices. Line charts are similar to bar charts in that time is measured across the horizontal axis and the stock price or indicator value is measured on the vertical axis. A line connects the closing prices or indicator values for each day, week, or month, depending upon the time measurement utilized. A line chart omits the vertical lines that represent the price range (the high and low price and associated connecting line) for each period, and thus it presents less data. Line charts are frequently used to present large amounts of price data over long periods of time.

What are candlesticks?

Bar graphs are sometimes drawn using candlesticks rather than simple vertical lines. The candlestick makes use of a stock's high price, low price, opening price, and closing price. In other words, the candlestick utilizes one extra piece of data: the opening price. The candlestick is designed to emphasize the difference between the opening and closing prices. A candlestick is drawn with a thin vertical line that connects the stock's high price and low price, the same as the line drawn in a regular bar chart. The main body of the entry connects the opening price with the closing price. The effect is the same as a rope hanging through an open barrel. The barrel is left clear if the closing price is higher than the opening price, indicating the stock price rose during the day. The barrel is filled in if the opening price is higher than the closing price, indicating the stock price fell during the day. A series of mostly dark candle-sticks is a bearish signal, while a series of mostly clear candle-sticks is a bullish sign.

How are point-and-figure charts constructed?

A point-and-figure (P&F) chart is not particularly difficult to construct but is quite difficult to explain. These charts are drawn on a grid with X's and O's used in place of dots or lines. The stock price (or stock indicator value) is measured on the vertical axis, the same as bar charts and line charts. However, time is not a concern with a point-and-figure chart, and the horizontal axis is not labeled. Stock price increases are recorded with a series of X's in a column of boxes on the grid, while stock price declines are recorded with a series of O's in an adjacent grid. X's or O's are recorded in a column of boxes so long as the stock price continues moving in the same direction. In other words, a series of X's continue upward in a column as the stock increases in price. O's begin in the next column only when a predetermined price reversal occurs and the stock value has started to decline. The O's are then recorded in a downward direction until an upward price reversal occurs. Point-and-figure charts are designed to emphasize major price trends by omitting small price changes.

How is a point-and-figure chart interpreted?

The same set of rules applies to a point-and-figure chart as to a bar chart. Support and resistance lines are drawn, trends are observed, and the price formations previously discussed are used to forecast future price movements. One difference is that point-and-figure charts can be used to forecast the extent as well as the direction of price movements. Exhibit 7-3 illustrates both bullish and bearish point-and-figure chart formations. The

E X H I B I T 7-3

Example of Point-and-Figure Chart

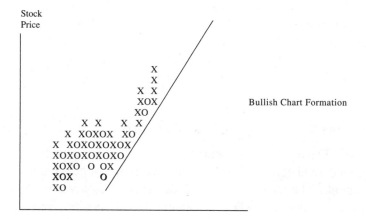

Bullish Chart Formation

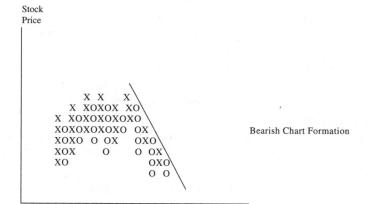

Bearish Chart Formation

diagonal line on each chart represents a trend line that is used to help make an investment decision to buy or sell the stock. The top chart is considered bullish because it projects an upward movement in the stock price. The bottom chart is bearish because it projects a downward move in the stock price. One column in a point-and-figure chart may represent price movements during a month or more because a significant price reversal is required to mark entries in the next column.

What is the Dow Theory and how is it used?

The Dow Theory, one of the earliest tools of technical analysts, is utilized to determine the direction of major stock market movements. The Dow Theory provides guidance on when you should buy stocks and when you should sell stocks, but for the long term, not the short term. The theory divides stock market movements into three categories: primary, secondary, and daily. According to the theory, daily movements are random and cannot be predicted. Day trading isn't in the cards for proponents of this theory. Secondary movements are temporary reversals of major trends. The secondary movements often fool investors into believing the major trend, or primary movement, has ended. It is primary market movements that are important. You should acquire stocks when the primary movement is upward, and sell stocks when the primary movement is downward.

How can I determine when a primary market movement has changed course?

During a full-fledged bull market, secondary declines terminate at higher and higher levels. Visualize climbing a mountain that has peaks and valleys along its side. Each peak and each valley is higher than the one that preceded it. The primary direction is upward on this side of the mountain. A secondary decline that takes the market to a level lower than the previous reversal provides a cautionary signal that the primary trend may have changed from upward to downward. In other words, the market has likely crossed the main peak, so the primary trend is downward. When this is the case, secondary increases will top out at ever lower levels. Only when a reversal moves to a level higher than the previous secondary movement is it a cautionary signal that the primary trend may have changed from downward to upward. The Dow Theory also holds that a corresponding movement in the Dow Jones Transportation Average must confirm a primary movement in the DJIA.

Do investors pay much attention to the Dow Theory?

The theory doesn't receive much attention today, even from technical analysts. Still, it is instructive to have some familiarity with it, since many consider the theory the granddaddy of technical indicators.

What is a moving average?

A moving average is a mathematical calculation of consecutive averages for a series of numbers. Each average is calculated for a predetermined amount of numbers. The moving average is typically displayed as a line or curve. In technical analysis, a trend line is drawn using average closing prices for a particular stock over a fixed period. For example, a 50-day moving average is calculated as the average closing price of a stock during the last 50 trading days. Each day's average is calculated by adding the most recent 50 closing prices and dividing the total by 50. The average is recalculated each day by including the most recent price and deleting the most distant price. Technical analysts often use a 200-day moving average to determine a stock's primary trend. Breaking above or below this trend is thought to provide guidance regarding future price movements. A stock price breaking above its 200-day moving average trend is considered a bullish sign. Conversely, a stock price that moves downward through its moving-average trend line is considered a bearish sign.

What is the advantage of using a moving average?

A moving average produces a relatively smooth trend line that makes it easier for a technical analyst to grasp the big picture. Short-term price swings disappear in a moving average. The longer the period included in calculating the average, the smoother the trend line that will result.

Do analysts ever use two moving average trend lines at once?

Yes, an analyst may plot two moving averages on the same chart. For example, a 200-day moving average may be used to show a stock's long-term price trend, while a 60-day moving average is more responsive to recent price changes. A change in the trend occurs when the 60-day moving average crosses the 200-day moving average on relatively heavy volume. This is a bullish sign. Conversely, a signal to sell occurs when the 60-day moving average crosses below the 200-day moving average. Exhibit 7-4 provides a short price history of Union Pacific common stock. The graph includes daily price movements along with a 60-day moving average trend line. Notice that the stock price penetrates the moving average trend on three occasions. An upward price movement through the moving-average line is considered bullish.

Can a moving average also be used as a technical tool for forecasting the overall market?

Moving average trend lines are used by technical analysts to determine the primary trend of the market as well for determining the price tend of individual securities. The trend of the overall

E X H I B I T 7-4

Example of a Moving Average Trend Line

Price

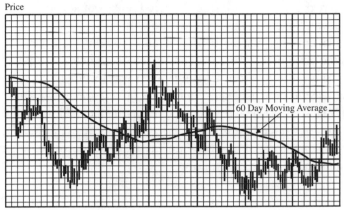

60 Day Moving Average

Time in Days

market provides guidance as to buying and selling opportunities. The moving average for a stock index is calculated in exactly the same manner as for a stock's price. The closing value of the index is averaged over a fixed period of time, often 200 trading days. The average is recalculated each day or week, depending on the desired time interval.

Can stock price trends be used to make profitable investment decisions?

Extensive statistical studies have been conducted to determine if historical stock price information can be used to earn above-average returns or "beat the market." As with many stock market theories, studies support both sides of the question, but with technical analysis it may be for a legitimate reason. When technical analysis is being heavily used, especially for a limited group of stocks, price expectations from using stock price charts are self-fulfilling, at least in the short run. That is, stock price movements forecasted by price charts will occur as expected when enough investors act in the same manner on the same information. A large number of investors charting the same stock will place buy orders when the stock's price breaks out above a resistance level. Sufficient buying pressure will cause the stock price to move upward, just as technical analysts expect. Likewise, when the price of a closely watched stock drops below a support level, heavy selling from investors who use technical analysis will at least temporarily cause the stock price to decline further. When investors are heavily engaged in buying and selling on the basis of stock price trends, stock prices tend to be very volatile, since large numbers of investors are buying or selling at the same time and on the same information.

Can I make good returns using technical analysis?

You can put this information to profitable use only if you are able to place orders before your fellow technical analysts. If everybody is watching the same charts, and everyone acts at approximately the same time, only investors who act first will get the best price. It's similar to musical chairs. Act a little late, and the price change projected by the analysis will already have taken place. In other words, you will miss the move.

What about studies that demonstrate the opposite results?

Nearly all studies indicate that stock price charts cannot be utilized to produce exceptional investment returns when these charts are not in vogue, or for stocks that are not closely followed by investors who buy and sell on price trends. In other words, unless you buy and sell stocks that are traded primarily by other investors who use stock price charts, price trends and formations are unlikely to provide information that is useful in forecasting future price movements.

Why do investors continue to use charts if evidence indicates the charts often aren't useful?

Many individual investors simply don't know or care about the studies that are buried in academic journals and often difficult to understand, even by other academicians. The average investor who attempts to read the results of one of these studies would quickly conclude that it is just more academic mumbo jumbo written by people who need to get a real job. On the other hand, some very intelligent and knowledgeable individuals continue to utilize charting despite the many studies that refute its usefulness. These investors must feel that the studies are unconvincing and that stock price charts are indeed useful. Using stock price trends is very appealing in no small part because the charts allow you make investment decisions without being required to learn a lot of economics, accounting, and financial analysis.

Does technical analysis involve more than stock price charts?

Stock price charts are only one segment of technical analysis. Many technical analysts follow a series of rules based on the premise that the majority of investors tend to make bad investment decisions. This group of technical analysts, sometimes called *contrarians*, attempt to determine what most investors are doing and then do the opposite. In other words, they buy stocks when most investors are selling stocks, and they sell stocks when most investors are buying stocks. Contrarians buy stocks of companies operating in industries that other investors avoid. The idea is to buy cheap and sell high rather than buy high and sell higher. This may seem unusual, but professionals who serve as market makers often take the same action. Market makers become buyers when no investors are willing to purchase shares from sellers, and market makers become sellers when insufficient investors are available to sell shares to other investors who wish to buy. Going against the market has generally served market makers very well.

How do contrarians judge investor sentiment?

Several indicators are utilized to judge investor sentiment. When the majority of investment advisory services (individuals and companies that provide investment advice) are bullish and recommending that stocks should be purchased, contrarian theory says it is time to sell stocks. This rule is based on the theory that investment advisors tend to be most bullish just before the end of a bull market. If the investment advisors are all predicting a rising stock market, contrarians assume the market has peaked. Conversely, contrarians feel that investment advisors tend to be most bearish just before a market bottom. When investment advisors are heavily bearish, it is time for contrarians to buy stocks. In other words, the professional advisors are generally wrong and you should act accordingly.

Is there another method for measuring investor sentiment?

Contrarians who watch investor advisory sentiment are also likely to monitor mutual fund cash balances. Mutual funds typically hold cash in order to be able to reimburse their shareholders who wish to redeem shares. Mutual funds do not normally maintain large cash balances for this purpose because cash inflows from new investors are generally adequate to cover redemptions, at least during normal periods when a fund is growing in size. Contrarians are interested in knowing if the cash balances are larger than normal. Fund managers who believe stocks are overpriced are likely to increase the size of their cash balances in order to take advantage of lower stock prices following an anticipated market decline. Conversely, mutual fund cash balances will be relatively small when fund managers want to be fully invested while expecting an upward move in the stock market. Contrarian investors believe mutual fund managers and other institutional investors tend to make the wrong investment decisions near market tops and market bottoms. That is, mutual fund managers who are expecting a market downturn will hold large cash balances, a signal to contrarians that it is time to buy stocks. Conversely, small mutual fund cash balances indicate the managers are bullish, a bearish sign for contrarians.

Are other technical indicators available to contrarian investors?

Technical analysts sometimes track the amount of credit balances held in customers' brokerage accounts. Credit balances accumulate when investors sell securities and leave the proceeds in their accounts with the expectation the funds will eventually be used to purchase additional securities. A large amount of credit balances is considered bullish because it represents buying power that will eventually be used to purchase securities. Large credit balances also indicate that investors may feel stock prices have not come down to an acceptable level. The larger the amount of credit balances, the more bullish the indicator. Conversely, small credit balances indicate investors are fully invested and relatively meager buying power is available. Relatively small credit balances are a bearish indicator.

Can stock options be used as a technical tool to forecast stock prices?

Put and call options are indeed used by contrarian investors to forecast stock price movements. Investors who expect a stock price to decline purchase put options, which allow them to sell shares of the stock at a fixed price. Investors who expect a stock price to increase purchase call options that give them the right

to buy shares of the stock at a fixed price. Heavy trading volume in put options indicates a large number of investors are
bearish, while heavy trading in call options is evidence that
many investors are bullish. A high ratio of trading volume in
put options to trading volume in call options provides technical
analysts with evidence that investors are relatively bearish
which, from a contrarian's point of view, is bullish. A low ratio
of trading in puts to trading in calls indicates investors are relatively bullish, which causes contrarians to be bearish. Remember, contrarians tend to measure investor sentiment and then do
the opposite.

When is trading volume utilized to make investment decisions?

Technical analysts judge speculative investment activity by
comparing the ratio of trading volume in the over-the-counter
market to trading volume on the New York Stock Exchange.
The theory is that a relatively high ratio of OTC trading volume
to NYSE trading volume signifies sizable speculative investing,
an indicator that a market top is approaching. A low ratio of
OTC volume to NYSE volume demonstrates less speculative
investing, a bullish sign. This ratio of OTC volume to NYSE
volume derives from the theory that speculative investing is
more prevalent in over-the-counter stocks than in New York
Stock Exchange stocks.

Does trading volume have any other use?

Trading volume is used to validate stock price movements. A
stock price that breaks out of a trading channel on relatively
high trading volume is more likely to provide an accurate buy
or sell signal. A price movement on relatively light trading volume is suspect. Technical analysts pay great attention to trading
volume.

Do technical analysts act on any other theories?

Technical analysts generally believe informed investors are able to invest more wisely and earn higher returns than uninformed investors. Informed investors include wealthy individuals and institutions that have the financial knowledge, monetary resources, and political clout to learn which stocks are undervalued and which are overvalued. The "smart money" invested by these informed individuals and institutions tends to flow into the undervalued stocks that offer the greatest opportunity for gains in value. On the opposite side of these trades are individual investors who operate at a major disadvantage that stems primarily from lack of knowledge.

How can I determine what the "smart money" is doing?

You can gain insight on what smart money is doing by observing the actions of small investors. If small investors are selling more stock than they are buying, the smart money must be accumulating stock from these small investors. Conversely, if small investors are buying more stocks than they are selling, the smart money must be moving out of stocks. The key is to determine whether small investors are net buyers or net sellers of stocks and then do the opposite. When small investors are net buyers, you should sell. When small investors are net sellers, you should buy.

How can you tell when small investors are selling?

Many small investors have limited financial resources that cause them to trade stock in odd lots – transactions of less than 100 shares. Small investors often buy 50 shares rather than 100 shares of stocks that sell for $40 or above. On the other hand, smart money often buys or sells thousands or even tens of thousands of shares at a time. If odd lot sales exceed odd lot purchases, then small investors are selling more shares than they are buying. If odd lot purchases exceed odd lot sales, then small investors are on balance buying stock. Following the smart money means you should do the opposite of the small investors. Odd lot purchases and sales are reported daily in the *Wall Street Journal*.

Is there another method for determining what smart money is doing?

Some technical analysts use Barron's Confidence Index to determine whether informed investors are bullish or bearish. This indicator compares yields on different grades of bonds and is based on the theory that major players representing smart money dominate the bond markets. Stocks should be purchased when the index indicates informed investors are bullish, and stocks should be sold when informed investors appear bearish. The Confidence Index compares *Barron's* average yield on 10 high-grade corporate bonds with the yield of the Dow Jones average of 40 corporate bonds. The smaller the spread in yields between high-grade bonds (the numerator) and a cross section of bonds (the denominator), the more bullish are bond investors. If only a small premium in yield is necessary to entice bond investors to acquire lower-yielding bonds, then bond investors must have great confidence, so it is time for the rest of us to buy stocks. However, if the spread is large (the Confidence Index is relatively low), institutional investors must be bearish because they are demanding a large premium to invest in bonds that are not considered high-grade.

Shouldn't investments made by a firm's directors be considered smart money?

A company's directors and officers should certainly be expected to have a better-than-average understanding of their firm's prospects. Thus, you could fairly say that investments by these individuals represent smart money. However, as insiders who have access to special information, a corporation's officers and directors are prohibited from using privileged information for personal gain. For example, the president of a company is not permitted to buy stock immediately ahead of a public announcement of higher, than, expected earnings. Insiders can purchase and sell the stock of their firms when the transactions are reported to the Securities and Exchange Commission. The SEC subsequently releases this information to the public. Technical analysts believe that substantial purchases by insiders indicate the stock is undervalued and should be bought. Conversely, a report of substantial sales by insiders signals that it is time to sell the stock. Keep in mind that insiders sell stock for many reasons. The president of a company may need funds to purchase a new house or pay an ex-spouse. Thus, insider purchase decisions may be a better indicator that insider decisions to sell.

Can stock price charts be used to monitor smart money?

Technical analysts use trading volume and stock price formations in an attempt to determine whether smart money is buying or selling a particular stock. The chart formations discussed above are all about accumulation and distribution of stocks. An accumulation of shares by smart money is a signal for a technical analyst to buy the stock. Conversely, a distribution of shares by large investors is a signal to sell the stock. The key, of course, is being able to determine whether a particular stock is being accumulated or distributed.

What are some other technical tools I can use?

Short interest—the cumulative total of shares sold short and not yet repurchased (a stock's *short interest*)—is a popular indicator for technical analysts. A large short interest in a particular stock indicates many investors believe the stock is overpriced and due for a decline. In other words, these investors are bearish. Technical analysts generally feel that a large short position is bullish because of the large number of shares that must eventually be repurchased in order to replace the borrowed shares and cover the short positions. Buying shares to replace shares sold short will result in substantial demand that should push a stock price higher. The relative importance of the short position depends on the volume of trading that typically occurs. This is true for an individual stock, and it is true for the market as a whole. Thus, the indicator is generally shown as the ratio of short interest compared to average daily trading volume. The higher the ratio, the more bullish you should be with regard to the stock. At least, this is the theory.

What is an advance-decline line?

The advance-decline line (also known as *breadth of the market*) measures the cumulative difference between the number of stocks that have advanced in price compared to the number of stocks that have declined in price. The difference between advancing issues and declining issues is calculated either daily or weekly and maintained as a running total. The cumulative total is displayed on a graph and compared with a market average, typically the Dow Jones Industrial Average. The market average and advance-decline line generally move together. If both are rising, the market is technically strong and additional advances can be expected. If the two are declining, the market is technically weak and further declines are likely to occur. If the two are moving in opposite directions, the market average is likely to reverse its direction. For example, if the advance-decline line begins to top out or decline while the market average continues upward, a signal is given that the average is likely to reverse course and begin declining. The opposite would be true during a bear market. That is, a turn upward in the advance-decline line signals the market average is likely to reverse its decline and begin moving upward.

What does relative strength mean?

Relative strength compares a stock price to a stock average or an industry average. The ratio is generally plotted on a graph over time. The graph shows whether the stock is gaining or losing strength relative to the market or relative to an industry average. Technical analysts tend to believe that trends persist, so that a stock that has been outperforming the market will continue to outperform the market. Conversely, a stock that has been underperforming the market will continue to underperform the market. Thus, a stock's relative strength can be used to determine whether the stock should be purchased or sold. Analysts sometimes calculate the relative strength of an industry by comparing an industry index to a market index.

8

CHAPTER

MUTUAL FUNDS AS MANAGED BASKETS OF STOCKS

Chapter summary

Advantages of investing in mutual funds ... The organizational structure of mutual funds ... Types of funds available to investors ... The importance of net asset value ... Sales fees you may be required to pay ... Other charges paid by mutual fund shareholders ... Income earned by mutual fund owners ... Taxes applicable to mutual fund investments ... Exchange-traded funds ... Closed-end investment companies ... Unit investment trusts

What is a mutual fund?

A mutual fund is a special type of investment company that pools funds contributed by individual investors. The investors' money is invested in a wide range of securities or other assets. While most companies own factories, equipment, office buildings, and land that is utilized to produce products or services offered for sale to consumers, an investment company acquires and manages a portfolio of financial assets for the benefit of its own shareholders. Rather than manufacture automobiles, toasters, or computers, an investment company might own shares of stock or hold debt securities of the companies that manufacture and sell these products. Investors who contribute funds by purchasing the shares of an investment company own a portion of the company's portfolio.

Why do individuals choose to buy shares of investment companies?

Investment companies employ the services of professional portfolio managers who presumably have the expertise and experience to make wise investment decisions. Buy shares of an investment company and you hitch your wagon to a company operated by someone who makes his or her living managing money. Your money is entrusted to the care of a professional investment manager who chooses your investments for you. Your hope in buying into an investment company is that the manager will be able to identify and invest in undervalued assets and avoid or dispose of overvalued assets. As with any type of business, the performance of an investment company is only as good as the managers chosen to run it. A successful portfolio manager who chooses profitable financial assets will make money for you and the other shareholders of the investment company. An unsuccessful manager will make bad investment decisions that are likely to cost you money.

Are there any other reasons to put my money in an investment company?

Investment companies provide individual investors with immediate diversification. Shares of an investment company represent a small ownership stake in each of the assets held in the investment company portfolio. In other words, a relatively modest investment allows you to acquire part of a ready-made portfolio. Purchase shares in an investment company that owns stock in 100 different companies, and you indirectly hold partial ownership in each of those companies. The diversification available from owning shares in an investment company is difficult if not impossible for most individual investors to achieve by purchasing individual stock and bond issues. Exhibit 8-1 illustrates the impressive growth in the number of mutual funds that have been made available for purchase by individual investors. The bottom section of each bar represents mutual funds that specialize in common stock investments, while the middle section illustrates the growth in the number of mutual funds that specialize in bond investments. The upper section of each bar represents the number of money market funds offered to investors. Investment companies are not all the same. They have different investment goals, charge different fees, and subject investors to different risks.

How is a mutual fund different from other investment companies?

Mutual funds enjoy a unique corporate structure in which they can continually issue new shares of their stock at the same time that they stand ready to redeem their outstanding shares from owners who wish to cash out their investment. As a mutual fund shareholder, you are permitted to submit all or a portion of your shares at any time for redemption by the fund. Guaranteed redemption by the issuing company contrasts to the more normal corporate structure in which companies issue a fixed number of shares that remain outstanding. Shareholders of a company that has a normal corporate structure can only liquidate their investment by selling shares to another investor, generally with the assistance of a brokerage firm. Likewise, the typical corporation issues new shares only infrequently, and then only with the permission of current

EXHIBIT 8-1

Growth in the Number of Mutual Funds

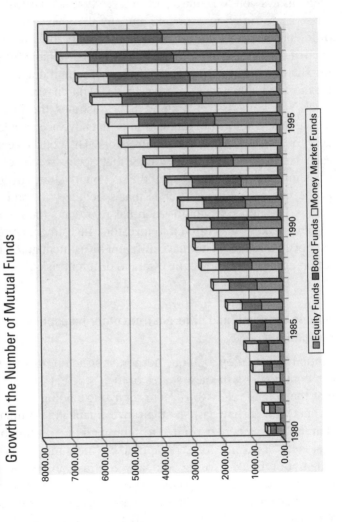

shareholders. A mutual fund can issue any number of new shares without receiving an okay from its shareholders.

Why aren't all corporations structured the same as mutual funds?

Most corporations issue shares of stock in order to raise long-term capital that is used to purchase equipment, buildings, and other long-term assets. These companies are unable to easily sell a portion of these assets in order to come up with the cash to pay for share redemptions. Can you imagine General Motors being required to sell one of its automobile plants because a large number of shareholders have decided to liquidate their ownership position by redeeming their shares? Not only would a factory or some other long-term asset have to be sold to raise funds to pay for the redemption, the asset would have to be liquidated immediately so that the redeeming shareholders would not be kept waiting for their money. The only way to avoid a fire sale of assets would be for the company to maintain huge amounts of unprofitable cash that could be used to pay for share redemptions. Guaranteed share redemption means the managers of a company would never know how long they could retain and use the assets they have acquired. Such a requirement would not work for most types of businesses.

How can mutual funds obtain the cash necessary to redeem their shares on demand?

Mutual funds mostly own securities that can be quickly sold in the financial markets to other investors. The liquidity of most of their assets allows mutual funds to quickly turn these assets into cash that is needed to pay for share redemptions. Likewise, additional assets can be readily acquired by a mutual fund in the event that investors purchase more shares of its stock. In other words, cash received by a mutual fund from issuing new shares of stock is soon invested in additional assets. It's not as if mutual funds must build new factories or locate new equipment to buy and operate. They just purchase additional stocks and bonds, assets that are readily available in the financial markets. You might view a mutual fund as a giant balloon full of liquid assets in which cash is continually flowing in and flowing out. The balloon expands with additional assets when more cash is flowing in than flowing out. On the other hand, the balloon contracts when more shares are being redeemed than issued. Every mutual fund goes through these expansions and contractions, depending on whether investors are in a buying mood or a selling mood. The expansion or contraction depends in large part on what kind of job the portfolio managers are doing for the fund's shareholders. A record of high returns to a fund's shareholders is likely to result in substantial amounts of additional cash pouring into the fund.

How do mutual funds differ from each other?

Mutual funds differ in several respects, the most important of which is the types of assets they buy and hold in their portfolios. Some mutual funds invest only in bonds, while others buy only stocks. Mutual funds that limit their holdings to stocks often specialize in the equities of companies that operate in a particular industry, or of companies located in a particular country or region of the world. For example, some mutual funds limit their holdings to the stocks of companies involved in energy production and distribution. Mutual funds that choose to specialize in bond investments may hold mostly bonds with long maturities, while other mutual funds limit their holdings to short-term debt securities. A large number of mutual funds invest only in municipal bonds that pay interest exempt from federal income taxes. Thus, mutual funds hold widely differing portfolios that, during the same time period, can produce widely differing returns for their shareholders.

Can you provide examples of broad categories of mutual funds?

Most mutual funds are classified as equity funds because they invest their shareholders' money in shares of stock. Equity funds are by far the most popular category of mutual fund, with several thousand different funds offering a wide variety of portfolios and investment philosophies. Some mutual funds invest their shareholders' funds in intermediate- and long-term debt securities and are called *bond funds*. Mutual funds that invest in both stocks and bonds are called *balanced funds*. Money market mutual funds, also called *money market funds*, are a very popular choice for investors who desire the ultimate in liquidity. Money market funds invest in very short-term and high-quality debt securities. Money market funds tend to provide investors with relatively low returns coupled with the ability to redeem shares of the funds at a fixed price of a dollar each. Money market funds won't make you rich, but it is unlikely that you will lose any of the principal you invest.

Do mutual fund managers alter the composition of the portfolios they manage?

A mutual fund tends to stick with a stated investment objective at the same time the managers continuously alter the portfolio in order to better achieve the objective. For example, the portfolio of a mutual fund with an investment objective of aggressive growth in asset value (a high-risk investment philosophy that is likely to produce unusually large returns or losses) is continually altered as the portfolio manager attempts to acquire stocks that are judged to be undervalued and to sell stocks that are judged to be overvalued. A stock that is considered a bargain at $20 per share may be judged overvalued and sold when it reaches $35 per share. Some mutual fund portfolio managers are very aggressive in buying and selling stocks, while other portfolio managers follow a conservative course and seldom trade the securities held by the mutual fund they manage. High portfolio turnover tends to increase the expense of managing a fund.

What are index funds?

Index funds are investment companies that hold portfolios
designed to duplicate as closely as possible the performance of
a particular market index. The index selected for duplication
may be a broad market measure or it may be an index designed
to measure a particular segment of the market. A fund that builds
and manages a portfolio that duplicates the S&P 500 Index will
produce investment results for its shareholders that are approximately the same as this popular market index. Buying an index
fund allows you to "buy the market" or a select segment of the
market depending on the particular fund you choose. Index
funds involve passive asset management in that the manager is
merely required to adjust the fund's portfolio in response to a
change in the composition of the index the fund is attempting to
duplicate. Index funds tend to have low expenses because of the
minimal amount of portfolio management and transactions that
are required.

Do mutual funds pay dividends?

Mutual funds pay dividends to their shareholders. In fact, a
mutual fund is generally required to pass through to its shareholders all the dividends and interest received from the assets
held in its portfolio. Mutual funds also distribute capital gains
that are realized when assets are sold for more than their cost. A
mutual fund can be viewed as a conduit through which pooled
funds are managed in order to earn income that is passed
through to the owners. Income that is realized from the receipt
of dividends and interest, and from the sale of assets, is passed
through to the mutual fund shareholders, who are required to
report the distributions as income on their tax returns. On the
plus side, the mutual funds themselves are not required to pay
taxes on the income that is earned and passed along to their
shareholders. In other words, interest, dividends, and capital
gains earned by a mutual fund are taxed only one time.

Is there a minimum amount of money required to open an account?

Each mutual fund establishes the minimum investment it requires to establish an account and the minimum amount that is required to buy additional shares once an account has been opened. For example, a particular mutual fund may require a minimum initial investment of $5000 and minimum subsequent investments of $500. Minimum requirements are established by managers of the individual funds and can vary quite a bit from firm to firm. From a mutual fund's point of view, high minimums reduce operating expenses at a cost of keeping some investors from becoming shareholders. Many funds have lower minimums for Individual Retirement Accounts than for regular accounts.

How are mutual fund shares priced?

Mutual fund shares are priced at their *net asset value* (NAV). The NAV is calculated as the market value of a mutual fund's portfolio of securities divided by the number of shares of the fund that are outstanding. Suppose a mutual fund holds $60 million of stocks and bonds valued at current market prices. In other words, securities held in the mutual fund portfolio could be sold for $60 million. If the mutual fund has 3 million of its own shares outstanding, each share has a net asset value of $60 million/3 million shares, or $20 per share. A mutual fund's net asset value is very important because it determines the price at which new shares are issued and the price at which shareholders of the fund can redeem their shares. Remember, the vast majority of mutual fund shares are not traded on an exchange or in the over-the-counter market, so no price is quoted for these shares in the secondary market. The net asset value of a mutual fund is the most important number to a mutual fund investor.

What causes a mutual fund's net asset value to change?

The net asset value of a mutual fund is influenced by the value of the assets held in its portfolio. An increase in the value of securities in its portfolio will cause a mutual fund's net asset value to increase, assuming no additional shares are issued. Suppose the portfolio value of the mutual fund mentioned in the prior answer increases by 10 percent over a six-month period from $60 million to $66 million. If the number of shares outstanding remains unchanged at 3 million shares, the net asset value of the fund will have increased from $20 per share to $66 million/3 million shares, or $22 per share. A gain of $2 per share would have been realized if you purchased the fund's shares at the beginning of the period for $20 each and had the same shares that could each be redeemed for $22 at the end of six months. Just as you were permitted to redeem your shares at the higher net asset value of $22, new investors could have purchased shares at this same price. Issuing and redeeming shares at net asset value does not affect the net asset value even though the change in outstanding shares causes a change in the size of the mutual fund's portfolio.

How can a mutual fund issue and redeem shares without altering the net asset value?

Changes in the portfolio value caused by issuing and redeeming shares at net asset value are offset by the change in shares outstanding. Suppose a mutual fund with $20 million in assets has 2 million shares outstanding for a net asset value of $10 per share. If an additional 1 million shares are each issued at the net asset value of $10, the mutual fund's portfolio will grow in value by $10 million, to $30 million. The new shares will cause shares outstanding to grow by 1 million shares to a total of 3 million shares, so that the net asset value of $10 remains unaffected. Issuing and redeeming shares at net asset value has no impact on a mutual fund's net asset value. A mutual fund's shareholders will not see the value of their shares change because new shares are issued or because other owners redeem their shares. Only changes in the market values of the portfolio's assets will cause a change in a mutual fund's net asset value.

Why is a mutual fund always valued at its net asset value?

Investors are able to purchase shares at net asset value from the fund, an option that caps the price of the shares, because no one should be willing to pay more than this price. Likewise, stockholders of a mutual fund can have their shares redeemed at net asset value, which becomes the minimum share value, because no owner of the fund should be willing to accept a lower price. Basically, each mutual fund fixes the price of its own shares at net asset value by agreeing to issue new shares and redeem existing shares at net asset value. Keep in mind that mutual fund shareholders are guaranteed to be able to redeem their shares at net asset value, but the fund does not guarantee the size of the net asset value. If the assets held in a mutual fund's portfolio decrease in value because of a decline in the market, the net asset value of the mutual fund's shares will also decline and the fund's shareholders will lose money.

How do I make a profit from investing in a mutual fund?

You stand a chance to make money from two sources: distributions made by the fund and increases in the net asset value of the shares that you own. Distributions and increases in share value are the same two sources of income that allow you to profit from owning any stock. It's just that a mutual fund is a ready-made portfolio of stocks and bonds that distributes the income it realizes. If securities in the fund's portfolio increase in market value but are not sold, you will profit from an increase in the net asset value of the mutual fund shares you own. In other words, you will be able to sell your shares at a higher price than you paid. In addition, if the mutual fund earns any dividends or interest and if it realizes any gains from selling securities, you will receive dividends and capital gains distributions from the fund.

Do mutual fund distributions affect the fund's net asset value?

Dividends and capital gain distributions directly reduce a mutual fund's total assets and net asset value. Consider that a distribution comes directly from a mutual fund's assets that are used to calculate the fund's net asset value. A decrease in the amount of assets without a corresponding reduction in outstanding shares results in a smaller net asset value. Receive a $1 per share distribution, and the fund's shares will drop in net asset value by $1. The distribution you receive is exactly offset by a reduction in the market value of the shares you own. The bad side is that the distribution will result in a tax liability even though the overall value of your investment (share value plus distribution) has not changed. Many investors prefer to purchase mutual fund shares after rather than before a distribution.

How are mutual fund shares issued?

Mutual funds distribute shares through an underwriter. The underwriter markets shares to individual investors either directly from the firm or indirectly through an agent who acts on behalf of the underwriter. With direct distribution, you must generally contact the firm yourself, either through the mail, by phone, over the Internet, or in person at a company office. Mutual funds that sell shares directly typically market themselves through advertisements in newspapers or financial publications. These advertisements include a toll-free telephone number you can call for information and an account application. You must make the effort to contact a mutual fund that distributes shares directly.

How are shares distributed through agents?

About half the mutual funds distribute their shares using salespersons who act as agents for the underwriter. Agents include brokerage firms, financial planners, and insurance agents who are paid a commission to sell and redeem the shares. Some funds use a captive sales force that sells only mutual funds operated by a single fund group. For example, insurance agents sometimes offer mutual funds that are sponsored by the same company that underwrites the life and casualty policies they sell. Many brokers sell mutual funds sponsored by their own brokerage firm, as well as mutual funds sponsored by outside distributors. An agent takes care of buying and redeeming your mutual fund shares and also often offers advice on which funds are most compatible with your investment goals.

Why do some brokerage firms advertise that they don't charge a commission for the mutual funds they sell?

Some large brokerage firms act as financial supermarkets in that they sell mutual funds of many different sponsors. These brokerage firms are able to sell mutual funds without charging investors a sales commission because the mutual fund sponsors provide compensation in the form of splitting their management fee. Individual investors who buy mutual fund shares through these brokerage firms will not pay a sales commission but are likely to end up paying a somewhat higher annual management fee compared to funds purchased directly from the sponsor. The best known mutual fund supermarket is the One-Source program offered by Charles Schwab. Fidelity, America's largest mutual fund distributor, also sells funds from other sponsors through its FundsNetwork. These fund supermarkets have become very popular and offer several advantages for investors.

Should I purchase mutual fund shares directly or through an agent?

Count on paying some type of commission or extra fee if you buy a mutual fund through an agent such as a broker or insurance agent. The commission may be added to the net asset value when shares are purchased, subtracted from the proceeds when the shares are presented for redemption, or buried as an annual expense. Somehow, the salesperson will be compensated for selling you shares of a mutual fund. The fee may be a bargain if you are a novice investor who requires advice on which funds are best suited to meet your investment needs. Perhaps you require assistance in determining your investment needs. On the downside, advice provided by mutual fund salespersons is sometimes of questionable value, and in some cases outright misleading. Of course, the same is true of investment advice from virtually any source that benefits financially from your investments. Keep in mind that a salesperson offers a limited group of products that are presented to you in their best light. You may be better served by purchasing shares directly if you feel comfortable evaluating the wide array of mutual fund offerings. Investment assistance is available via a toll-free number from some of these firms. However, you must be the ultimate judge of your own knowledge and abilities in evaluating the advantages and disadvantages of the thousands of mutual funds available for purchase.

What commission can I expect to be charged?

The sales charge or commission to buy mutual fund shares is known as the fund's *load*. Depending on the fund you choose, the load will vary from zero to up to 6 percent of the amount you invest. Many funds distributed directly levy no sales charge and are referred to as *no-load funds*. With no sales fee, you are able to purchase shares of no-load funds at the net asset value. Other funds tack a sales charge of up to 6 percent on top of the net asset value. Some funds charge a relatively modest sales charge of 2 to 3 percent and are called *low-load funds*. A mutual fund distributor or its agent will provide a prospectus that details each fund's investment goal and the fees involved in buying, owning, and selling shares of the fund. A prospectus offers boring reading but presents some very important information. Exhibit 8-2 provides an illustration of the fee information that is provided in a mutual fund prospectus. This particular fund offers two types of shares, Class A and Class B. Class A shares have a 5 percent sales commission but no redemption charge. Buyers of Class B shares incur a deferred sales charge in place of an initial sales charge. Notice that the Class B shares have higher annual operating charges.

How is a redemption fee assessed?

A redemption fee, also called a *back-end load*, or *contingent deferred sales charge*, is charged when shares of some mutual funds are redeemed. Redemption fees typically start at 6 or 5 percent of the net asset value of the shares being redeemed, with a reduction of 1 percent for each year the shares have been owned. The longer you own the shares being redeemed, the lower the fee you will be charged when the shares are sold back to the fund. For example, the redemption fee might be 5 percent if you redeem shares purchased within the last year but only 3 percent if the shares had been purchased two and a half years ago. Funds with a sales charge generally either levy a load when shares are purchased or a back-end load when shares are redeemed, but not both. Of course, many funds do not charge either a load or a back-end load.

Is a declining back-end load preferable to a front-end load?

The declining redemption charge in place of a front-end sales charge sounds more advantageous to investors than it actually

EXHIBIT 8-2

Fee Information from a Mutual Fund Prospectus

The following fee information is fairly typical for an equity fund that offers two classes of shares.

Shareholder Fees	Class A	Class B
Maximum sales charge (load) as a percentage of offering price	5.00%	none
Maximum deferred sales charge (load) as a percentage of redemption value	none	5.00%[*]
Annual Fund Operating Expenses		
Management fee	0.80%	0.80%
Distribution and service (12b-1) fees	0.25	1.00
Other expenses	<u>0.13</u>	<u>0.20</u>
Total annual fund operating expenses	1.18%	2.00%

[*] The deferred sales charge for Class B shares is reduced over time and is zero after shares have been held six years.

Example of ownership expenses over several years:
Expenses assume an initial investment of $10,000 with an annual investment return of 5 percent. All distributions are reinvested in additional shares.

	1 Year	3 Years	5 Years	10 Years
Class A	$614	$856	$1,117	$1,860
Class B	$703	$927	$1,178	$2,116
(with redemption)				

is. Redemption charges are frequently accompanied by an added annual expense known as a *12b-1 fee.* An increasing number of mutual funds are charging an annual 12b-1 fee to pay for distribution expenses such as annual reports, advertising, promotional literature, and commissions paid to salespeople. This fee is an ongoing operating expense charged each year, so the longer shares are held, the greater the cost of this fee to the shareholders. The fee can range up to 1 percent of assets but is usually in the range of 0.25 to 0.50 of assets. Although a 12b-1 fee is also sometimes charged by mutual funds with front-end loads, it is more frequently levied, or is levied at a higher percentage, by funds that impose back-end loads. Mutual funds that charge this extra annual fee can afford to reduce the redemption fee for shares that are held over a longer period of time because the funds will receive additional annual reimbursement from the 12b-1 fee.

Will I be charged any other fees as a mutual fund shareholder?

All mutual funds charge shareholders a fee to cover operating expenses, including advisory fees paid to the portfolio manager, administrative expenses, and miscellaneous costs of operating the fund and its portfolio. A mutual fund's charge for operating expenses is calculated as a percentage of assets and is periodically deducted from assets. Like the 12b-1 fee, the charge for operating expenses has the effect of reducing the return earned by a mutual fund's shareholders. The Class A shares of Exhibit 8-2 have an annual 12b-1 fee of 0.25 percent (one-quarter of 1 percent each year the shares are held), while the Class B shares without an initial sales charge have an annual 12b-1 fee of 1 percent.

My broker told me I could choose whether to pay a sales load or redemption fee. How does this work?

Some mutual funds offer two classes of shares, with each class based on the same portfolio of assets. One class, typically called *Class A*, is sold with a load of 4 to 6 percent of funds invested. A second class of stock, generally called *Class B*, has a combination 12b-1 fee and a redemption charge but no front-end load. Some funds even have Class C shares that impose a higher 12b-1 fee but no redemption fee, and Class D shares that have a front load and a relatively small 12b-1 fee. In general, the longer you plan to hold mutual fund shares the more you should try to avoid a fund that has a 12b-1 fee because of its continuing nature. As complicated as all this sounds, keep in mind that you can choose to invest in mutual funds that don't levy any of these fees.

Can you summarize the fees I am likely to pay as a mutual fund shareholder?

You can count on being charged a periodic fee to cover the fund's operating expenses. This fee can vary from less than a quarter of 1 percent to well over 1 percent of a fund's assets, depending on a variety of factors, including the type of fund, the size of the fund, and the distributor of the fund. You cannot avoid this fee but you can choose to invest in a fund that levies a fee that is at the low end of the range. Index funds require little management effort and typically have low operating costs. You may or may not be charged a 12b-1 distribution fee depending on the mutual fund you choose. This fee reduces the return you will earn, and it can be avoided by choosing a mutual fund that does not impose a 12b-1 charge. Sales charges and redemption fees can also be avoided by choosing to invest in a fund that doesn't impose either of these fees.

Should I expect to earn better returns from a mutual fund that charges higher fees?

Front-end loads and redemption fees compensate a salesperson, not a portfolio manager, so there is no reason to believe that paying either of these fees will improve a mutual fund's investment performance. Likewise, a 12b-1 fee is used to cover distribution charges, including compensation of a salesperson. Thus, this fee should have no bearing on the returns you can expect to earn. In fact, a 12b-1 fee is charged against the fund's assets and will decrease, not increase, the return of the fund's shareholders. The annual operating expense is partially used to compensate the portfolio manager, but even here it is uncertain that a higher charge will result in better investment returns. You are more likely to benefit from investing in funds with low fees than in funds with high fees.

What about mutual fund investment goals?

Each mutual fund has a stated investment goal. The goal provides insight into the investment strategy of a mutual fund's portfolio manager. Some funds aggressively seek capital gains for their shareholders, while others are geared to providing their shareholders with current income. Still other funds choose their investments in an attempt to balance current income and capital gains. It is in your interest as an investor, of course, to select a fund compatible with your personal investment goals. Choose one of the many fixed-income funds if you are primarily interested in maximizing your current income. On the other hand, a mutual fund that seeks capital growth is more likely to suit your needs when you are investing for retirement. You may have two or more investment goals and find it desirable to buy shares of several mutual funds.

Can I move money from one mutual fund to another?

You certainly can move your money to a different mutual fund. Your investment objective might change since the time of your original investment, and you may decide that a different mutual fund will be more in sync with your new objective. For example, as you move closer to retirement you may want to transfer money from a mutual fund with an investment goal of capital growth to a fixed-income fund. Or you may become dissatisfied with the investment performance of your mutual fund and decide to move to a different fund with a similar investment objective but a different portfolio manager. In other words, you are looking for better performance from the same type of fund. Perhaps you feel that your current fund is charging fees that are too high and you wish to move your money to a fund with lower operating expenses.

Is it difficult to move money between different funds?

In order to move your money from one fund to another, you must sell shares in one fund and use the proceeds to purchase shares in another fund. Each mutual fund sponsor is likely to oversee many different funds with a wide variety of investment objectives. Owning shares in a mutual fund that is part of a family of funds makes it easier to move your investment to a different fund because the firm already has your completed paperwork. In addition, most of these firms charge only a nominal fee to move your money among their funds. You may end up paying another sales commission if you move your money to a fund from a different distributor. Regardless, you will be required to sell shares in one mutual fund in order to move your money into another fund. Exhibit 8-3 provides a partial list of large mutual fund distributors that offer funds with a variety of investment objectives.

Will I be taxed if I move my money between funds?

Unfortunately, selling shares in a mutual fund is considered a taxable event, even if the proceeds are reinvested in a different fund sponsored by the same company. The Internal Revenue Service doesn't care what you do with the proceeds from the sale of mutual fund shares; it only wants to know if the proceeds from the sale amount to more than the cost basis. Did you receive more or less than you paid? Your tax

EXHIBIT 8-3

Select List of Large Mutual Fund Distributors

Aim Management Funds www.aimfunds.com 800-347-4246	American Century Investments www.americancentury.com 800-345-2021
Dreyfus Service Corporation www.dreyfus.com 800-782-6620	Fidelity Investments www.fidelity.com 800-544-6660
Franklin Templeton Investments www.franklintempleton.com 800-342-5236	Lord, Abbett & Co. www.lordabbett.com 800-874-3733
Putnam Investments www.putnaminvestments.com 888-478-8626800-842-2776	TIAA-CREF www.tiaa-cref.org
T. Rowe Price www.troweprice.com 800-225-5132	The Vanguard Group www.vanguard.com 800-523-0790
Van Kampen Investments www.vankampen.com 800-341-2911	

liability will depend on whether you realize a gain, and if so, how much. The tax you are required to pay will also depend on how long you held the shares that were sold. Shares held over a year qualify as long-term assets and receive favorable tax treatment in a sale. The gain or loss you report will depend on the change in the fund's net asset value between the dates the shares were purchased and sold. A loss will be realized and a tax benefit will result if your shares are sold for less than you paid.

Do I have to sell all of my shares?

You can sell all or part of any mutual fund shares that you own. Suppose you purchased 500 shares of a particular mutual fund, all on the same date. You can sell 10 shares, all 500 shares, or any number of shares between these two extremes. Likewise, you can sell all or part of the shares you purchased on several different dates. Perhaps you purchased 100 shares each year for the past 10 years, so that you currently own 1000 shares of a particular mutual fund. You can decide to sell any number of the shares you own.

How do I determine the gain to report when the shares have been purchased on several different dates at different prices?

Determining the appropriate cost basis can be a headache when you have acquired shares in a fund on different dates at many different prices. This complication is most likely if you have chosen to reinvest all dividends and capital gains distributions in additional shares of the fund. Calculating the cost basis of shares you sell will not be a problem if all your shares are sold. You need only determine the cost basis for all the shares you purchased and subtract this total from the proceeds of the sale. Suppose at different times over the past several years you purchased 100 shares of a fund for $10 per share, another 150 shares of the fund for $15 per share, and 300 shares of the fund for $20 per share. Your cost basis is $1000 plus $2250 plus $6000, or $9250. If all 550 shares are sold for $30 per share your capital gain is equal to the proceeds of $16,500 less the cost basis of $9250, or $7250. This is the gain on which you will be taxed if all your shares are sold for $30 each.

What if I sell only a portion of the shares I own?

If you decide to sell 400 of the 550 above-mentioned shares, you will need to determine which shares have been sold in order to determine your cost basis and the resulting gain to report to the

IRS. Did you sell the first 400 shares or the last 400 shares you purchased? Unless otherwise indicated, the Internal Revenue Service assumes the first shares bought are the first shares sold. In this example your cost basis for the sale of 400 shares is $6250 (100 shares at $10 each, plus 150 shares at $15 each, plus 150 shares at $20 each), for a gain of $12,000 less $6250, or $5750. This gain must be reported for tax purposes as a capital gain on IRS Schedule D. You can also choose to use the average cost of the shares you own in calculating the cost basis of the 400 shares that have been sold. The average cost is calculated as the total cost of the shares owned divided by the number of shares that are owned. In this case, the average cost is $9250/550 shares, or $16.82 per share for a total cost basis on 400 shares of $6728. Using average cost produces a gain of $12,000 less $6728, or $3272. Utilizing the average-cost method will increase your cost basis and reduce the gain and tax liability because the shares were purchased at increasingly higher prices. A third alternative is for you to identify which shares you wish to sell and then use the cost of those particular shares to calculate the capital gain. The lowest tax liability on these shares would result if you identify the last shares acquired as the shares being sold. The last shares acquired have the highest cost and, as a result, produce the highest cost basis, the smallest realized gain in value, and the lowest tax liability. Keep in mind that using the highest-cost shares as a cost basis reduces current taxes but will cause future taxes to be greater when the remaining shares are sold. Exhibit 8-4 illustrates the three methods of calculating gains for a series of share purchases. Shares of the mutual fund have been purchased on nine different dates at different prices. As with the above example, the realized gain and tax liability will depend on which shares are selected for sale.

What are exchange-traded funds?

Exchange-traded funds are baskets of stocks that trade like individual securities on an organized exchange. Unlike shares of a

EXHIBIT 8-4

Three Methods for Determining a Cost Basis When Calculating Capital Gains

The following is a complete record of your share purchases in the Green Acres Growth Fund.

Date Purchased	Amount Invested	Price	Shares Bought	Shares Owned
3/07/00	$ 5,000.00	$15.00	333.333	333.333
6/15/00	3,000.00	14.50	206.897	540.230
8/20/00	2,500.00	15.10	165.563	705.793
11/10/00	2,800.00	15.30	183.007	888.800
12/15/00*	844.36	16.25	51.961	940.761
2/09/01	2,000.00	16.12	124.069	1,064.830
6/28/01	2,500.00	15.75	158.730	1,223.560
7/10/01	600.00	16.50	36.364	1,259.924
10/12/01	3,000.00	16.75	179.104	1,439.028
	$22,244.36		1,439.028	

* Reinvestment of a 95 cents per share distribution paid by the fund at the end of the year

Total amount invested = $22,244.36

Average cost per share is $22,244.36/1,439.028 shares, or $15.45 per share

A. Sale of all shares

Suppose on 12/1/01 you sell all of the shares at a price of $17.00 per share. The total gain on the sale equals the gain per share ($17.00 sale price minus an average cost of $15.45, or $1.55) times the number of shares sold (1439.028), or $2230.49. Gains from the sale of 888.800 shares held over one year (888.800 × $1.55, or $1377.64) qualify as long-term. The remaining portion of the gain is considered short-term. An alternative is to compute the average cost for shares held over a year ($13,300/888.800 shares, or $14.96) and use this as the cost basis for calculating the long-term gain. A second cost basis would then be calculated for shares held a year or less.

EXHIBIT 8-4

Three Methods for Determining a Cost Basis When Calculating Capital Gains (*Continued*)

B. Sale of 800 shares

Suppose you sell only 800 of your 1439.028 shares at a price of $17.00 per share. Selling part of your holdings means you must determine which of the shares have been sold in order to be able to calculate the gain and the tax liability.

1. *Average price*—The total gain equals the sale price minus the average cost ($17.00 – $15.45, or $1.55) times the 800 shares sold, or $1240.00.

2. *First bought, first sold*—Calculate the gain for each group of shares to a total of 800 shares, beginning with the first shares purchased. Using the information from the table, you have a gain of $2.00 per share ($17.00 – $15.00) on the first 333.333 shares, $2.50 per share ($17.00 – $14.50) on the next 206.897 shares, $1.90 per share ($17.00 – $15.10) on the next 165.563 shares, and $1.70 ($17.00 – $15.30) on 94.207 of the 183.007 shares purchased on 11/10/00. The total gain of $1,658.63 is classified as long-term because all of the shares sold have been held over a year.

3. *Selected shares*—If you intend to minimize the gain reported to tax authorities, request that the mutual fund sell shares with the highest cost. Request that the fund sell 179.104 shares bought at $16.75, 36.364 shares bought at $16.50, 51,961 shares purchased at $16.25, 124.069 shares purchased at $16.12, 158.730 shares purchased for $15.75, 183.007 shares purchased at $15.30 each, and 66.765 of the 165.563 shares bought at $15.10. The total gain using this approach is $852.49, about half the gain realized from the first bought, first sold method. Keep in mind that some of these gains will be short-term.

regular mutual fund, which are continually issued and redeemed by the fund, individual investors must use a brokerage firm to buy or sell shares of exchange-traded funds. These funds are structured so they trade at or very near their net asset value. This is accomplished by allowing investors with substantial financial resources to buy or redeem shares directly from the company in 50,000-share blocks. Most exchange-traded funds are designed to track a particular index, such as the Dow Jones Industrial Average, the Nasdaq 100 Index, or the S&P 500 Index. Exchange-traded funds allow you to invest in an overall segment of the market in much the same manner as an index fund. However, unlike mutual fund shares that are priced only at the end of each day, shares of exchange-traded funds vary constantly in price with the value of their underlying securities. Also, exchange-traded funds can be sold short and purchased on margin.

What other types of investment companies are available for purchase?

Mutual funds are classified as open-end investment companies because of their ability to continuously issue and redeem shares of ownership. Closed-end investment companies offer an alternative investment for individuals who desire professional money management. Closed-end investment companies are organized with a fixed number of outstanding shares. These shares are issued in an identical manner to most other corporations. That is, the fund employs the services of an investment banking firm to assist with an initial public offering of the company's shares. Unlike mutual funds, a closed-end investment company does not agree to redeem its shares at net asset value and it generally has no plans to issue additional shares of stock. A professional portfolio manager who attempts to identify undervalued stocks and/or bonds invests funds that are raised through the initial stock offering. The portfolio is subsequently managed according to an established investment objective.

How can I dispose of my shares if the fund doesn't accept redemptions?

Shares in a closed-end investment company are sold in the same manner as shares of most other corporations. That is, you must employ the services of a broker who will take care of having your shares sold on an exchange or in the over-the-counter market. Being required to identify another investor to buy your shares means you may get more or less than net asset value. Shares of closed-end investment companies are priced according to supply and demand, which is influenced but not totally determined by net asset value. Many closed-end investment company shares sell at a discount to net asset value, while other investment company shares trade at a premium to net asset value. The gains and losses from holding shares in a closed-end investment company are determined by changes in the fund's net asset value and also by changes in the premium or discount to net asset value at which the shares sell. Investors in mutual funds do not have to worry about premiums and discounts, because mutual fund shares are sold and redeemed at net asset value.

What are unit investment trusts?

Unit investment trusts, also called *unit trusts* or *investment trusts,* have a different corporate structure compared to mutual funds and closed-end investment companies. Unit trusts offer diversification and the professional selection of assets, but their portfolios are unmanaged. The sponsor of an investment trust assembles a portfolio of assets and sells pieces of ownership of the trust, called *units,* to investors. Income earned by the trust is passed along to the trust's owners. The trusts are normally scheduled for liquidation on a particular date or, in the case of bonds, whenever the debts are redeemed. Unit trusts are particularly popular with investors who are interested in owning fixed-income securities, especially tax-exempt bonds. Trust units normally do not enjoy an active secondary market although the sponsor may agree to repurchase the units, which are then offered for resale. Unit trusts lack the liquidity of mutual funds and closed-end investment companies and are generally acquired by investors who anticipate a relatively long holding period.

9

CHAPTER

INVESTING IN FOREIGN STOCKS

Chapter summary

Reasons to own foreign investments ... Foreign exposure of domestic stocks ... The risks of holding foreign investments ... The importance of currency exchange rates to foreign investments ... Disadvantages of direct investments in foreign stocks ... American Depositary Receipts as indirect investments in foreign securities ... Tax implications of foreign investments ... Mutual funds as alternatives to individual stocks and American Depositary Receipts ... Closed-end investment companies with an international investment exposure

Is it difficult for individual investors to purchase stock in foreign companies?

It has become increasingly easy for individual investors to purchase foreign securities. In fact, it is no more difficult to become a shareholder of many foreign companies such Japan's Sony Corporation than it is to become a shareholder of a domestic company such as General Motors Corporation. The ordinary shares of some foreign corporations are traded in secondary markets in the United States. For example, the common stock of DaimlerChrysler, the large German-based automobile manufacturer, is traded on the New York Stock Exchange at the same time the shares are traded on Germany's Frankfurt Exchange. You need only call your broker and place an order to purchase shares of this foreign-based company. Other foreign firms, including Honda and BP Amoco, have chosen to have their shares traded indirectly in the United States as American Depositary Receipts. These receipts representing foreign shares of stock are actively traded and as easily purchased as shares of domestic corporations. In addition, many mutual funds and closed-end investment companies concentrate on foreign stock investments. Purchase shares of an international fund and you immediately become part owner of dozens of different foreign securities. It is also possible to invest in foreign stock market indices by purchasing iShares (formerly called *World Equity Benchmark Shares*, or *WEBS*) that are traded on the American Stock Exchange. Exhibit 9-1 summarizes investment vehicles that provide an international exposure.

Is it a good idea to invest in foreign companies?

Most academic research indicates investors can benefit from having at least a portion of their investments in foreign securities. The benefits of foreign investment exposure are gained either from direct ownership or indirect ownership of an investment company that specializes in foreign investments. Foreign economies and foreign stock prices often perform differently than the American economy and stock prices in the United States. European or Asian economies may remain strong at the same time that the United States economy is experiencing slow

EXHIBIT 9-1

Investments with an International Exposure

Foreign shares traded on a foreign exchange. Generally more complicated to buy and sell these stocks, in part because payment involves a foreign currency. Direct purchases generally occur through a U.S. brokerage firm that is affiliated with a brokerage firm in the country in which the shares are denominated and traded.

Foreign shares listed for trading in the United States. Offers limited selection, mostly stocks of Canadian companies. Most foreign firms are unwilling to incur the trouble and expense of listing their securities on an American exchange.

American Depositary Receipts traded in the United States. U.S. bank–issued receipts that represent indirect ownership of foreign shares. American Depositary Receipts offer a convenient vehicle for foreign investment exposure with all payments being in U.S. dollars rather than a foreign currency. Liquid markets for most ADRs make buying and selling these securities the same as trading regular shares.

Global or international mutual funds. Probably the best vehicles for achieving international investment exposure. Global and international funds allow you to acquire a diversified portfolio of foreign securities with a single investment. Alternatively, investments can be concentrated on a specific country or region of the world. International and foreign mutual fund shares are denominated in dollars, and dividends and distributions are made in U.S. dollars. Sales or redemption fees combined with operating expenses will reduce the return earned by a shareholder.

Closed-end investment companies. Especially attractive for investments in a single company that offers limited investment opportunities. Payments and distributions are in dollars. Shares of closed-end funds are generally actively traded on securities exchanges, causing you to pay brokerage fees but not sales commissions or redemption fees.

growth or a recession. Of course, the opposite can also occur and foreign economies may underperform the United States economy. Nonetheless, owing shares of stock in foreign companies provides additional diversification for your investment portfolio and can reduce the risk of your overall investment position. This reduction in risk assumes you don't overdo it and invest an unusually large portion of your funds in foreign securities, especially securities of companies in a single country or in one region of the world.

Do stocks of domestic companies provide at least some foreign exposure?

It is difficult to invest in the stocks of domestic companies and not be affected by many of the same factors that influence foreign stock prices. Currency exchange rates, foreign economic activity, domestic and foreign interest rates, and international politics each have an important influence on the revenues, expense, profits, and stock prices of many domestic companies. Most large U.S.-based corporations have at least part of their operations in foreign countries. Visit Europe for the first time and you will be amazed at the recurring presence of U.S. icons, including McDonald's, Coca-Cola, Pizza Hut, and Gillette. You are also likely to see much of the same clothing found at stores in the United States. Some domestic companies rely on foreign suppliers or maintain manufacturing operations in foreign countries. Other U.S. firms sell products or provide services to foreign customers. A few large domestic multinationals such as Coca-Cola actually earn more revenues and profits overseas than in the United States. Large corporations based in the United States and elsewhere have become ever more multinational in their business operations. Owning shares in a multinational corporation based in the United States will certainly provide you with an investment stake in the international economy.

If investments in domestic companies provide international exposure, why do I need to invest in foreign companies?

Not all U.S.-based corporations provide broad international exposure. Many companies have most or all of their operations and customers in the United States. Other firms have an international exposure but it is difficult for individual investors to determine the relative importance of foreign operations in the firms' overall valuations. Companies may decide to close or move foreign operations so their foreign exposure becomes a moving target. In addition, U.S. stocks, even shares of companies with international operations, tend to vary in value as a group and move differently in price compared to stock price movements on foreign exchanges. In short, investments in foreign companies provide better diversification than additional investments in domestic multinational corporations.

Aren't foreign stock prices affected by economic conditions in the United States?

Many foreign companies are heavily dependent on economic conditions in the United States. More than a few foreign companies sell a substantial portion of their products and services in the United States. In addition, an increasing number of foreign-based companies have established manufacturing facilities in the United States. With manufacturing operations and significant revenues derived from the United States, changes in the U.S. economy have a major impact on the revenues, profits, and stock prices of many foreign companies. Consider the importance of the U.S. market to European and Japanese automobile manufacturers. Likewise, a large portion of clothing purchased in the United States is manufactured or assembled overseas by foreign companies. Most electronic appliances purchased in the United States are manufactured in foreign countries. The world economy has become more integrated, so economic factors in a major market such as the United States affect domestic and foreign corporations alike.

What proportion of my investments should be in foreign stocks?

Financial experts recommend that the average investor should have from 8 percent to 15 percent of his or her total portfolio invested in foreign securities. This target range includes investments in ordinary shares or American Depositary Receipts and also in shares of mutual funds or closed-end investment companies that hold portfolios of foreign securities. For example, an individual investor's portfolio valued at $100,000 should include from $8000 to $15,000 of foreign securities. A portfolio should be periodically rebalanced so that the proportion of foreign securities remains within the desired range. Keep in mind that no specific percentage is appropriate for every investor at all times.

What types of risk exist for foreign investments?

Foreign stocks vary in price in the same manner as the stocks of domestic companies. Foreign stock values are affected by interest rates, inflation, economic activity, political considerations, investor expectations, and a host of other variables. Of course, these are variables in the host country, not the United States, which have the greatest impact on foreign stock values. In addition to risks in common with ownership of all stocks, foreign stocks also carry other potential dangers. Some countries suffer from unstable governments, a factor that can have a major impact on the values of stocks of companies domiciled in those countries. Consider the possibility of a newly elected government that nationalizes the assets of private businesses without compensating the owners. Political instability is an important risk in some countries. The same risk exists for U.S. companies that have foreign operations, although the impact on the stock values of these companies is likely to be less severe.

Are any other risks peculiar to foreign investments?

Stocks traded in foreign countries are denominated in foreign currencies, not U.S. dollars. For example, shares of Volkswagen, the German-based automobile company, are traded on the Frankfurt (Germany) Stock Exchange in euros, not dollars. Likewise, shares in Swiss Air, an airline based in Switzerland, are traded in Zurich in Swiss francs rather than U.S. dollars. Buying shares of these companies requires conversion of your dollar investment to the applicable foreign currency. Later, when the shares are sold, proceeds received in the foreign currency must be converted back to dollars. Changes in the rate at which dollars convert to the foreign currency and the rate at which the foreign currency later converts to dollars will affect the return you will earn from owning shares of a foreign stock. It would be unusual for the currency exchange rates to be exactly the same on the purchase date and the sale date. You will benefit if the dollar weakens relative to the foreign currency during the period you own a foreign security, and you will lose if the U.S. dollar grows stronger relative to the foreign currency. Investing in foreign securities is a bet on currency exchange rates as well as the market prices of the securities.

Can you provide an example of how the currency exchange rate can affect a foreign investment?

Suppose you are interested in buying 100 shares of Volkswagen stock at a time when the shares are trading on the Frankfurt Stock Exchange at 50 euros per share. At the time of your order the currency exchange rate of dollars to euros is .9 to 1. In other words, it takes nine-tenths of a do[llar]
euro. At this exchange rate the cost
.9 x 50 euros, or $45 per share, and
is $4500. Now move forward a ye[ar]
Frankfurt for 60 euros per share,

when the shares were acquired at 50 euros each. During the same year that VW shares increased in price by 20 percent, assume the dollar lost strength against the euro and now trades at parity on a one-for-one basis. The dollar is said to have weakened because it now takes more dollars (one dollar rather than 90 cents) to purchase one euro. Selling your 100 VW shares at a price of 60 euros per share nets 6000 euros, which convert to $6000 at the new exchange rate of one dollar per euro. Your profit is calculated as the difference between the initial $4500 cost and the proceeds of $6000, or $1500. The $1500 profit is equal to a percentage gain of 33 percent on the original investment of $4500 ($1500/$4500 = 33 percent), illustrating that the rate of return you earned on the Volkswagen shares was enhanced by a favorable change in the currency exchange rate. The currency in which your investment was denominated (euros) strengthened during the investment's holding period. Your investment increased in value both because of the increase in the stock price measured in euros and because the euro gained strength against the dollar.

How would the return have been affected if the dollar strengthened against the euro?

Your overall return on the transaction would have been penalized if the dollar strengthened during the period the Volkswagen shares were held. Remember, the Volkswagen shares you purchased are traded in euros, which would convert into fewer dollars in the event the dollar strengthened during the _____ you _____ y so _____ lar, or 90 cents, to buy _____ rate _____ of one Volkswagen sh _____ ened _____ the total cost for 100 _____ pur- _____ r, when VW share _____ shares _____ a 20 percent inc _____ change _____ $4800.

Your profit equals the difference between what you received from the sale and what you paid for the shares, or $300. The strengthening dollar has caused a reduction in your overall rate of return on this transaction to $300/$4500, or 6.7 percent. This compares with a return of 33 percent that was earned when the dollar weakened. The effect of a weakening and strengthening dollar on a foreign investment in London-traded British Telecom stock is illustrated in Exhibit 9-2. Notice that profits and losses are dependent on the value of the dollar relative to the British pound as well as the price of the shares of the telecom stock as measured in British pounds.

What causes changes in currency exchange rates?

Currency exchange rates are influenced by numerous factors. A country that buys more goods from foreign countries than it sells to foreign countries is likely to experience a decrease in the value of its currency relative to the currencies of the countries with which it trades. Likewise, a country with a strong economy may experience an increase in the value of its currency as foreign investors acquire the currency in order to invest in the country's growing economy. High rates of inflation tend to decrease the exchange value of a currency because it takes more of the currency to purchase goods and services. Speculation as to a currency's future strength or weakness will affect a currency's current exchange value as speculators attempt to beat the crowd by buying currencies they expect will appreciate in value and selling currencies they expect to depreciate in value. These are only a few of the things that cause changes in currency exchange rates.

Can I forecast future currency exchange rates in order to make better foreign investment decisions?

Individual investors are generally in no position to accurately forecast future movements in currency exchange rates when

EXHIBIT 9-2

How Currency Exchange Rates Can Impact a Foreign Stock Investment

You purchase 100 shares of British Telecom when the stock is trading in London at a price of 7.2 British pounds per share. At the
time of the trade the British pound has a value of 1.45 dollars. In
other words, 1 British pound will buy 1.45 U.S. dollars. Conversely, 1 U.S. dollar will buy 0.69 British pounds. The cost basis
for the purchase is calculated as follows:

Shares Purchased	Price per Share in British Pounds	Cost in British Pounds	Exchange Rate of Dollars for Pounds	Cost in Dollars
100	7.20	720	1.45	$1,044

During the next six months the stock price in London increases to
8.25 pounds, a 14.6 percent increase, while the exchange rate of
dollars to pounds increases to 1.60. The dollar is said to have
weakened against the pound because it now takes more dollars to
purchase 1 British pound. The new value of your investment is calculated as follows:

Shares Owned	Price per Share in British Pounds	Value in British Pounds	Exchange Rate of Dollars for Pounds	Value in Dollars
100	8.25	825	1.60	$1320

The value of the 100 shares of British Telecom has increased by
$276/$1044, or 26.4 percent. The dollar gain in the value of your
investment is due in part to the higher price of British Telecom
stock in British pounds and in part to the higher value of the British
pound in relation to the U.S. dollar. Remember, the stock is traded
in British pounds, so you benefit when the British pound strengthens relative to the U.S. dollar. In fact, you can earn a positive return
on your investment if the British pound strengthens even when the
stock price remains unchanged. Suppose in the last example the
stock remained unchanged at your initial cost of 7.2 British pounds
per share while the British pound strengthened to 1.60 dollars. The
value of your investment would now be calculated as:

EXHIBIT 9-2

How Currency Exchange Rates Can Impact a Foreign Stock Investment (*Continued*)

Shares Ownded	Price per Share in British Pounds	Cost in British Pounds	Exchange Rate of Dollars for Pounds	Value in Dollars
100	7.20	720	1.60	$1152

Suppose the stock price increased to 8.25 pounds per share but the British pound declined in value to 1.20 dollars per pound from the rate of 1.45 dollars per pound at the time of the purchase. The value of your investment would now be:

Shares Owned	Price per Share in British Pounds	Value in British Pounds	Exchange Rate of Dollars for Pounds	Value in Dollars
100	8.25	825	1.20	$990

In this last example your investment lost value in dollars even though the stock price increased in London trading. Unfortunately, the price gain in the stock was more than offset by the decline in the British pound relative to the U.S. dollar. Each of these examples illustrates how currency exchange rates are an important consideration of international investing.

even professionals who are paid for their expertise on these matters often make inaccurate predictions. Currency exchange rates are affected by so many variables that accurate forecasts of future changes are very difficult, especially for individual investors who have little or no training in economics. Who is to know if the dollar will buy more Swiss francs next year or even next month? It is best to simply remember that currency exchange rates fluctuate and the changes can affect the returns you earn from investing in foreign securities. On the positive side, changes in currency exchange rates are as likely to increase as to decrease your investment returns from the ownership of foreign stocks.

Do changes in currency rates affect the stocks of domestic companies?

The rate at which the dollar can be exchanged for foreign currencies can have a major impact on the financial performance of domestic companies and the values of their common stocks. A dollar that increases in value against foreign currencies causes U.S. products sold in foreign countries to become more expensive and less competitive in those markets. Suppose the exchange rate is such that one dollar is worth 1.1 euros. At this exchange rate, a U.S. vehicle manufacturer will need to charge 22,000 euros in order to receive $20,000 for each of its vehicles that is sold in Europe. Now suppose the dollar strengthens so that one dollar is worth 1.2 euros. The dollar is said to have strengthened because it can be exchanged for more euros than before. To earn the same $20,000, the U.S. manufacturer must increase the vehicle price in Europe by approximately 9 percent to 24,000 euros. Notice that the U.S. firm does not receive any additional dollar revenue or earn any additional dollar profit even though the vehicle is selling in the foreign country at a higher euro price. With a stronger dollar, the manufacturer must charge more euros in order to receive the same price in dollars. The problem for the manufacturer is that sales in Europe will suffer because consumers there are likely to buy fewer vehicles at the higher price. The bottom line for the domestic exporter is that a stronger dollar will cause a decline in foreign sales and a reduction in revenues and profits. Lower revenues and profits will most likely result in a reduced stock price.

Does a weaker dollar have the opposite effect?

A weaker dollar will result in U.S. companies being able to sell their products overseas at a lower price without sacrificing revenue and profits. Suppose in the above example the dollar weakens to parity and trades even with the euro. In other words, one dollar buys one euro. With a weaker dollar, the U.S. manufacturer is able to lower the price of its vehicles from 22,000 euros to 20,000 euros and still receive $20,000 when the euros are converted to dollars. Alternatively, the U.S. manufacturer could leave the price unchanged at 22,000 euros per vehicle so that revenues and profits measured in dollars increase. The increased profits resulting from a weaker dollar are likely to result in higher prices for the stocks of U.S. exporters.

What are emerging markets?

Emerging markets are countries that have recently instituted the public trading of securities. Trading is available either over-the-counter or on securities exchanges, but neither market is as highly developed as in Western Europe, Japan, and the United States. These emerging market countries have a semblance of political stability and a relatively low per capita income, and at the same time a potential for rapid growth. Securities traded in emerging markets are available for purchase by foreign investors who are able to exchange the local currency for Western currencies. The financial markets in these countries are often not considered particularly efficient, which means securities traded in these markets offer the potential for relatively large gains and losses. Investing in emerging markets can be quite risky compared to owning the securities of firms in more developed countries. Witness the meltdown of emerging Asian markets in the late 1990s.

Is it easy to obtain information about foreign stocks?

It is relatively easy to obtain information about foreign stocks but it isn't always easy to obtain financial information about the companies that issue the stocks. Foreign companies are not always subject to the same disclosure requirements as publicly traded companies in the United States. In addition, companies based in foreign countries are not always required to use the same accounting standards as companies in the United States, so assets, earnings, revenues, and other accounting information aren't necessarily comparable. In other words, you need to be careful because financial information provided by foreign companies is sometimes sparse and the information made available can't always be interpreted the same way as information reported by companies based in the United States.

Can I purchase foreign company shares traded on foreign exchanges?

Individual investors are finding it increasingly easy to purchase shares on foreign exchanges. Some brokerage firms have either acquired or affiliated with brokerage firms in foreign countries, through which they can funnel customer orders for securities that trade on foreign exchanges. Several discount brokerage firms offer direct investments in shares traded on certain foreign exchanges. Keep in mind that direct investments for securities traded on foreign exchanges tend to be risky. Information is often limited, regulations are spotty, and fees can be high. Individuals who prefer to invest in the stocks of individual companies are generally better off choosing American Depositary Receipts traded in U.S. markets rather than shares of stock traded on foreign exchanges.

How do American Depositary Receipts work?

The purchase of American Depositary Receipts (ADRs) represents the easiest method for U.S. investors to acquire an ownership stake in individual foreign companies. An ADR is a transferable receipt representing ordinary shares of stock in a foreign corporation. A trustee in the foreign corporation's home country issues the receipts against the actual shares of stock, which are held in safekeeping. The ordinary shares of stock of the foreign corporation serve to collateralize, or secure, the

ADRs that are issued to trade in the United States in the same manner as shares of stock. It is ADRs, not the actual shares of the foreign company, that trade in the United States. A single American Depositary Receipt may represent multiple and/or fractional shares of the foreign corporation. For example, BP Amoco ADRs each represent six shares of the British-based company's ordinary shares. BP Amoco's ordinary shares are traded in the United Kingdom, France, Germany, Switzerland, and Japan, while the ADRs are traded in North America on the New York, Chicago, Pacific, and Toronto stock exchanges. Exhibit 9-3 provides a select list of ADRs that trade in U.S. markets.

Can ADRs be converted into the underlying shares?

The convertibility of American Depositary Receipts is necessary to ensure that an ADR will trade at a price equivalent to the value of the underlying shares. So long as ADRs are convertible, any deviation between an ADR and its underlying shares will cause investors to enter into arbitrage transactions by purchasing the undervalued security and selling the overvalued security. For example, if an ADR sells for less than the value of its underlying shares, investors will buy the ADR and convert to the more valuable ordinary shares. Conversely, if an ADR is overvalued relative to its underlying shares, investors will sell the ADR short (sell borrowed shares that must eventually be replaced) at the same time they purchase the underlying shares. The ability to convert should make a conversion unnecessary.

Does the foreign company that issues ordinary shares also issue the ADRs?

American Depositary Receipts can be either sponsored or unsponsored. ADRs are classified as sponsored when the foreign company that issues ordinary shares is directly involved in the issuance of ADRs that represent the ordinary shares. Direct involvement includes selecting the depository bank to hold the ordinary shares, registering the ADRs with the U.S. Securities and Exchange Commission, and providing U.S. shareholders with regular financial reports in English. Owners of sponsored ADRs have voting privileges and the right to dividend payments. Unsponsored ADRs are issued by banks that serve as the depository for ordinary shares the bank purchases and holds in trust. Investors who own unsponsored ADRs have a right to dividends, but the depository bank is the owner of record of the underlying shares and retains the voting rights to these shares. ADRs are traded in dollars even though the value of the receipts is determined by the value of the ordinary shares that are traded in the currency of the firm's home country. Take the case of the previously mentioned BP Amoco ADRs that trade on the New York Stock Exchange. The dollar value of each BP Amoco ADR is determined by the market value of the six ordinary BP

EXHIBIT 9-3

Select List of ADRs Traded in U.S. Markets

Issuer	Home Country of Issuer	Where Traded
Alcatel	France	New York Stock Exchange
BPAmoco	United Kingdom	New York Stock Exchange
China Mobile	China	New York Stock Exchange
China Unicom	Hong Kong	New York Stock Exchange
Deutsche Telekom	Germany	New York Stock Exchange
Ericsson	Sweden	Nasdaq National Market
Nokia	Finland	New York Stock Exchange
Royal Dutch Petroleum	Netherlands	New York Stock Exchange
Serono	Switzerland	New York Stock Exchange
Taiwan Semiconductor	Taiwan	New York Stock Exchange
Tele Brasil	Brazil	New York Stock Exchange
Telefonos de Mexico	Mexico	New York Stock Exchange

Amoco shares that trade in London and are priced in English pounds. The dollar value of the ADRs is dependent on the pound value of the underlying shares and the rate at which pounds can be converted to dollars. Fortunately for U.S. investors, American Depositary Receipts embody the foreign stock price and currency conversion rate.

As an owner of ADRs, will I receive dividends in dollars or the home currency of the corporation?

ADRs overcome one of the great disadvantages of direct ownership of foreign stocks. That is, the trustee that issued the depositary receipts and holds the foreign shares will take care of converting any dividends from the foreign currency to dollars. Thus, dividends on your American Depositary Receipts will be paid in dollars, not the currency of the country in which your firm is based. A relatively modest fee is deducted from dividends in order to cover the expenses involved in converting currencies and safekeeping of the underlying securities.

Can owners of American Depositary Receipts participate in dividend reinvestment plans?

Many companies represented by American Depositary Receipts offer *dividend reinvestment plans* (DRIPs) that are operated by trustees, generally large money-center banks. The trustee uses quarterly dividend payments to acquire additional depositary receipts. As an owner of ADRs of a firm that offers a dividend reinvestment plan, you are free to choose whether to participate. Choosing not to participate means you will receive quarterly dividend checks. If you do participate, instead of dividend checks you will receive quarterly statements listing your total holdings in the plan along with the number of additional ADRs that were purchased with the latest dividend. Choosing to participate in one of these plans is not irrevocable, so partic-

ipants can opt out of the reinvestment plan and begin receiving
regular dividend checks if they wish.

Are the tax implications of investing in foreign stocks the same as investing in domestic stocks?

Any realized gains or losses in the value of foreign stocks or
American Depositary Receipts are treated as capital gains or
losses, respectively. The gains and losses are netted out against
gains and losses you may have realized on any other stocks or
ADRs sold during the same year. A $10,000 gain realized on
the sale of Sony ADRs is treated exactly the same as a $10,000
gain that is realized on the sale of General Electric stock. A
holding period of over a year qualifies a realized gain or loss as
long-term. Dividends may be somewhat more complicated.
Some countries require that foreign investors pay income taxes
on dividend income. In other words, you will be required to pay
British income taxes on dividend income you receive as an
owner of ADRs of BP Amoco, a British company. In practice,
the custodian will deduct and pay the tax before the dividend is
converted to dollars and paid to you. The dividend you receive
is net of foreign taxes. Fortunately, U.S. tax law allows you to
claim foreign taxes you are required to pay as a credit in calculating your U.S. tax liability. A credit results in a dollar-for-dol-
lar saving, so paying $500 in taxes to Britain reduces your U.S.
tax liability by an equal amount.

How do mutual funds compare with ADRs and direct investments in foreign stocks?

Mutual funds offer individual investors an opportunity to buy
into a professionally operated portfolio of foreign stocks. Some
mutual funds specialize in the stocks of a particular country or
a particular region of the world, while other mutual funds
assemble a global portfolio that represents most regions of the

world. Choosing a mutual fund relieves you of choosing which particular foreign stocks to buy and sell, because someone else makes the decisions for you. Mutual fund portfolio managers presumably stay abreast of the economics and politics of international investing because this is their livelihood. They have the time, expertise, and sources of information that are unavailable to most individuals. Of course, you must still select the appropriate mutual fund in which to invest.

What factors differentiate among the mutual funds that invest in foreign stocks?

Perhaps most importantly, mutual funds often tend to specialize in the categories of foreign stocks they hold. Some mutual funds concentrate their investments in the stocks of companies in a particular country or a particular region of the world. Mutual funds that concentrate their foreign holdings tend to produce more volatile investment returns for their shareholders, who have a chance to earn unusually high returns in good markets and absorb unusually large losses in bad markets. Imagine that all your foreign investment exposure is concentrated in the stocks of Japanese companies or Chinese companies. Political instability or economic recession in one of these countries will have a major negative impact on the returns you earn. Conversely, a extended period of economic growth is likely to produce unusually high returns. Specialized mutual fund portfolios result in magnified gains and losses compared to the returns you will earn from owning a mutual fund that holds stocks from many different countries.

Should I choose a large or small international fund?

Large international funds often hold substantial amounts of stock in large multinational companies based in foreign countries. Many of these large foreign companies conduct a substantial proportion of their business in the United States. To a surprising extent, investing in large multinational firms headquartered in foreign countries is not a great deal different from investing in large multinational companies headquartered in the United States. You will probably gain better international exposure by selecting a relatively small international or global fund that invests in small and medium-size companies that tend to conduct most of their business in their home country. Consider a company such as Nokia, the large high-tech firm headquartered in Finland. Nokia does a substantial portion of its business in Western Europe and the United States, the same as many U.S.-based companies. Many large international and global mutual funds hold a substantial position in Nokia, an active stock that is relatively easy to buy and sell in large volume. Smaller global and international funds are able to concentrate their investments in the stocks of smaller companies, many of which do not conduct much business in the United States. Thus, these smaller funds are likely to provide you with greater international exposure.

Are any other differences important in differentiating between these mutual funds?

You can expect to pay different fees depending on the mutual fund you choose. Global and foreign funds typically charge a sales fee, or load, and an annual fee to cover operating expenses. Some funds also charge an annual 12b-1 distribution fee and a redemption fee. These fees, which can vary considerably from fund to fund, may have a significant impact on the returns you will earn as a mutual fund shareholder. Thus, it is important to compare various fees you will be charged when you are in the process of comparing mutual funds to purchase. You will also find that mutual funds with a similar investment objective can have very different performance records. Some global and foreign funds have a history of providing their shareholders with above-average returns. Low expenses, superior investment selection, and, perhaps, some luck, can explain differences in investment performance, but it seems prudent to choose a mutual fund that has a history of beating its competition.

Are mutual funds that invest in foreign securities segmented into classifications?

The two major classifications for mutual funds that invest in foreign securities are *global funds* (also called *world funds*) and *international funds* (also called *foreign funds*). Global funds invest both in the stocks of U.S. companies and foreign companies. In other words, global funds hold stocks from many different countries including the United States. International, or foreign, funds invest only in stocks that trade outside the United States. International funds may concentrate their investments on companies in a single country or a limited region of the world. Regional mutual funds are a special type of international fund. A global fund may be the best bet if you desire some international exposure and don't currently have a significant investment in domestic stocks. A global fund provides both domestic and foreign investments in a single package. An international fund is probably a better choice in the more likely event that you already own domestic stocks or you hold shares in a mutual fund that limits it investments to domestic stocks.

Are all global and international funds actively managed?

Professional portfolio managers actively manage most but not all global and international funds. Increasingly popular international index funds hold an unmanaged basket of stocks designed to reflect the performance of stocks in a particular country or region of the world. Both international and domestic index funds generally enjoy low expenses because there is no need to pay portfolio mangers to buy and sell securities.

Do closed-end funds offer an international investment exposure?

Unlike mutual funds that continuously redeem and issue shares of their own stock, closed-end funds are established with a fixed number of shares that trade in the secondary market in the same manner as other common stocks. Exhibit 9-4 includes a select list of closed-end funds that provide an international exposure. Closed-end funds are especially popular for single-country investments, particularly countries in which investment opportunities and liquidity are limited. For example, some countries limit investments by foreign investors, a restriction that reduces shares available for purchase. Like all closed-end investment companies, shares of closed-end international funds may trade at a premium or a discount to net asset value. Thus, as a shareholder in a closed-end international fund, you are exposed to variations in the value of the securities in the fund's portfolio and also to changes in the discount or premium at which the fund shares trade to net asset value.

Do other international securities trade on U.S. stock exchanges?

Funds called *Ishares*, formerly called *World Equity Benchmark Shares,* or *WEBS,* are unmanaged mutual funds with stock portfolios designed to replicate the investment performance of a stock index for a particular country. Unlike most mutual funds, iShares are listed for trading on the American Stock Exchange and can be bought and sold just like other common stocks. You will pay a brokerage fee but no sales load to buy these securities. These iShares trade throughout the day, and prices and volume statistics are published in the financial pages of most newspapers. Dividends and capital gains distributions are paid periodically in dollars, the same currency in which their shares trade. These funds are very popular and offer a convenient way for individual investors to gain international exposure.

EXHIBIT 9-4

Select List of Closed-End Funds Offering an International Investment Exposure

Fund	Where Traded
Brazilian Equity Fund	New York Stock Exchange
China Fund	New York Stock Exchange
Europe Fund	New York Stock Exchange
First Australia Fund	American Stock Exchange
First Israel Fund	New York Stock Exchange
First Philippine Fund	New York Stock Exchange
France Growth Fund	New York Stock Exchange
India Fund	New York Stock Exchange
Japan Equity Fund	New York Stock Exchange
Korea Fund	New York Stock Exchange
Latin America Equity Fund	New York Stock Exchange
Mexico Fund	New York Stock Exchange
Singapore Fund	New York Stock Exchange
Southern Africa Fund	New York Stock Exchange
Spain Fund	New York Stock Exchange
Taiwan Fund	New York Stock Exchange

What is the best way to gain a foreign investment exposure?

The best choice for most individuals is a widely diversified international mutual fund. Foreign investing is tricky, and individuals generally lack the knowledge to make informed choices, especially regarding individual stocks traded on foreign exchanges. Even American Depositary Receipts traded in the United States can be a risky choice, especially if your total foreign exposure consists of only one or two different ADRs. Foreign funds that specialize in the stocks of a specific country or region, while not as risky as individual stocks, are not without their own disadvantages. Single country and regional funds tend to be volatile because the stocks of companies in a single country or a particular region of the world tend to move together. International funds holding stocks from many different countries do not suffer from this deficiency.

What should I look for when I choose an international mutual fund?

Investigate the fees you will be charged, both to buy shares and to own shares in the fund. Unless you have some reason to do otherwise, select a fund without a sales or redemption charge. Sales and redemption fees have nothing to do with a fund's performance. Also investigate the annual fees you will be required to pay as an owner. Operating expenses result in a direct reduction in the annual return you will earn. Try to avoid funds that charge an annual 12b-1 distribution fee that decreases the return you will earn. All of these fees and charges are presented in a fund's prospectus, which is available without charge to investors. You should also investigate the past investment performance of any funds you are considering. Compare a fund's investment performance over several years with the performance of other diversified foreign funds during the same period. Evaluate performance records over several years because short-term investment performance is not a reliable indicator of future performance. Information about fees and performance of international funds is available in several publications, including the *Value Line Mutual Fund Survey* and the *Morningstar Mutual Fund Survey*, two highly respected sources.

10
CHAPTER

TAX IMPLICATIONS OF STOCK INVESTMENTS

Chapter summary

Taxes are an important consideration for individuals who invest in stocks ... Dividend income is taxed the same as wages and interest ... Gains in value are taxed only when shares of stock are sold ... Realized gains receive favorable tax treatment when shares have been held over a year ... Federal income tax rates for dividends and short-term gains range from 15 percent to nearly 40 percent ... Gains and losses offset one another when calculating the tax on capital gains in any one year ... Net capital losses can be used to offset income ... Most states and many local governments tax income realized from stock investments, although generally at a lower rate than the federal government ... Gifts of stock can be used to reduce your income tax liability and the tax your estate may be required to pay ...

How are stock investments taxed?

Nearly all investments, including stocks, bonds, mutual funds, and real estate, are taxed in a similar manner. Income taxes must be paid on any gains in value that are realized when investments are sold. In addition, taxes must generally be paid on distributions that are received during the period the investments are owned. With regard to investments in shares of stock, this translates into taxes on dividend payments and on gains realized from shares of stock that are sold. In addition to federal taxes, it's likely you have to pay taxes to the state in which you reside, and perhaps taxes to the city as well.

Are taxes an important consideration in investments?

Taxes can consume a substantial portion of investment income. In fact, taxes are so important that you should always compare investment alternatives in terms of the after-tax return you can expect to earn. The comparison is obvious when you are deciding whether to purchase taxable or tax-exempt bonds, but it should also be put into practice when investing in stocks. The taxes you will be required to pay are an important consideration in deciding whether to concentrate on investments in stocks with substantial dividend payments or stocks that primarily offer the promise of gains in market value. Likewise, taxes become an important factor when deciding whether to sell stock, because the length of time shares have been held has a major impact on taxes you will be required to pay on realized gains in value.

Can I take any actions to save on these taxes?

A variety of actions are available to reduce the taxes you pay on stock investments. Some are relatively painless, while others are more burdensome. Regardless, it is important that you learn the tax laws applicable to stock ownership. Knowing the laws allows you to make informed investment decisions with regard to taxes. Not knowing them can lead you to make some faulty decisions that result in higher taxes.

How can I reduce the taxes I pay on my stock investments?

One action you can take to reduce taxes is to hold appreciated stock for over a year before it is sold. Realized gains from stock held over a year are taxed at a very favorable rate. Hold appreciated stock until your death and no income tax will be collected on the gains, either from you, your estate, or whoever inherits the stock. It is also possible to choose stocks in which you are more likely to profit from gains in value than from dividend payments. A more burdensome action is to move your residence to a state with a favorable tax environment. Several states, including Florida and Nevada, do not levy a tax on personal income, for example. Likewise, some states, including Georgia and North Carolina, do not tax the market values of intangible assets such as stocks and bonds. Tax laws vary significantly from state to state so moving to a state with a favorable tax environment can result in substantial tax savings. You might consider giving away shares of stock prior to death, either to a charity or to individuals. All these tax-saving possibilities are discussed in more detail later in this chapter.

Will I have to pay taxes if I buy mutual funds rather than individual stocks?

Mutual fund investments are taxed in the same manner as individual stocks. A mutual fund actually offers less flexibility with regard to the taxes you will be required to pay because the mutual fund manager, not you, decides when stocks in the mutual fund portfolio are sold and gains must be realized by the fund's shareholders. The tax liability for the gains that are realized and distributed to shareholders is passed along to these same shareholders.

Let's start at the beginning. How does the federal income tax system work?

The federal government taxes personal income, but not personal assets. In other words, the government taxes the income you earn from stock ownership, but it doesn't tax the market value of the stocks you own. The income tax is structured as a series of rates that increase with larger incomes. Applying higher rates against higher incomes qualifies the federal income tax as progressive. That is, progressively higher rates of taxation are applied against progressively higher levels of income. Exhibit 10-1 illustrates tax rates in effect when this book was written in early 2001. It is anticipated these rates will be reduced in the coming year, but the basics of the tax will remain unchanged. The rates for a single individual in the exhibit show that the federal government levies a 15 percent rate, the lowest current federal tax rate, against all taxable income up to a prescribed level of $27,050. A 28 percent rate is applied to taxable income in the next higher prescribed bracket of $27,050 to $65,550. Income above this second bracket is currently taxed at a rate of 31 percent. Higher rates of taxation apply to even higher levels of income, but you probably get the point. People who report large amounts of taxable income not only pay more taxes, they pay a higher percentage of their income in taxes compared to individuals who have lower levels of taxable income. At least, this is the way the tax is intended to work. In practice, people with high incomes are often able to utilize loopholes that allow them to substantially reduce the taxes they pay, but tax avoidance is the subject for another book.

If an increase in income causes me to pay taxes at a higher rate, will all my income be taxed at the higher rate?

The different rates apply to defined brackets of income, not total income. If an increase in income causes you to pay taxes at a higher rate, only the increased amounts of income included in the higher bracket will be taxed at the increased rate. The federal tax

E X H I B I T 10-1

Marginal Federal Tax Brackets for Tax Year 2001

Single Individual

Over	But Not Over	Tax	Plus	Of Amount Over
$ 0	$ 27,050	....	15%	$ 0
27,050	65,550	$4,057.50	28	27,050
65,550	136,750	14,837.50	31	65,550
136,750	297,300	36,909.50	36	136,750
297,300		94707.50	39.6	297,300

Married Filing Jointly

Over	But Not Over	Tax	Plus	Of Amount Over
$ 0	$ 45,200	....	15%	$ 0
45,200	109,250	$ 6,780.00	28	45,200
109,200	166,450	24,714.00	31	166,450
166,450	297,300	42,446.00	36	166,450
297,300		89,552.00	39.6	297,300

rates are known as *marginal rates* because the rates apply to brackets of income, not total income. Many people are under the erroneous impression that an increase in income will result in all of their income being taxed at the higher rate. Thus, they mistakenly believe a salary increase or additional dividends may result in less take-home income because the increased tax may exceed the increased income. This, in fact, is incorrect. The higher tax rate is applicable only to the extra income.

Can you provide an example?

Suppose you are single and expect to report $26,000 in taxable income this year. Calculating your tax liability from the brackets in Exhibit 10-1 indicates that you can expect to pay $26,000 x .15, or $3900 in federal income taxes. During the year you are offered another employment opportunity that will provide an additional $4000 of income, thus increasing the year's taxable income from $26,000 to $30,000. If you accept the new employment, your tax liability will be 15 percent of the first $27,050 plus 28 percent of the $3950 excess over $27,050. Thus, your tax liability will be $4057.50 plus $1106, or $5163.50. Notice that a portion of the increased income is taxed at 15 percent and part is taxed at 28 percent. Tax on the increase in taxable income is a mix of the two rates applicable to income that falls into two income brackets.

Does the federal government tax all my income?

A big difference often exists between total, or gross, income, and the amount of income that qualifies as taxable income. Certain deductions and exemptions are permitted in calculating the taxable income that must be reported to the Internal Revenue Service. Every taxpayer is permitted to claim whichever is larger—a variety of individual deductions or a standard deduction. For example, interest paid on a mortgage is an itemized deduction claimed by many homeowners. Likewise, most charitable contributions can be deducted in calculating taxable income. All these deductions can be used to reduce the amount of income subject to the federal income tax. Some types of income are not subject to taxation. For example, interest earned from most state and local debt securities is not taxable by the federal government. Likewise, scholarships, gifts, and inheritance you receive are not normally considered gross income and are not included in taxable income. These are exceptions, not the rule, and most income is subject to being taxed.

Do the same marginal tax rates apply to income from stock investments?

Dividends received from stock that you own are taxed in the same manner as wages received from your employer and interest earned on your bank account. Receiving a $500 dividend has the same effect on your tax liability as a $500 salary increase from your employer. All of this income is lumped together and taxed at the appropriate federal rates. If the dividend income added to other income causes your total taxable income to creep into a higher tax bracket, the dividends will be taxed at this higher rate. The highest federal tax rate is approximately 40 percent, although this high rate applies only to taxable income above $250,000. Most taxpayers are in either the 28 percent or the 31 percent tax bracket. Still, paying federal taxes at these rates means the government takes from a quarter to almost a third of the dividend income you receive.

Can I escape taxes on dividends that are reinvested in additional shares of stock?

Dividends are considered taxable income regardless of whether the dividends are spent, saved, or reinvested. The company that pays the dividend doesn't know or care what you do with its dividend check. It only knows that it is required to report the amount of the dividend payment to the Internal Revenue Service.

What if I enroll in an automatic dividend reinvestment plan?

All reinvested dividends, whether reinvested by you or by the company in which you own stock, must be reported as taxable income in the year the dividend is paid. Dividend reinvestment plans are a handy and inexpensive method of acquiring additional shares of stock, but enrollment in these plans doesn't result in a tax benefit. In fact, the fractional shares and varying prices of shares purchased over a long period of time in a dividend reinvestment plan are likely to cause headaches when and if you eventually sell the shares. The problem is one of computing capital gains and losses, however, not reporting the appropriate amount of dividend income.

What tax will be applied when I sell shares of stock?

The tax you will be required to pay when shares of stock are sold
depends on several factors including the price you paid for the
shares compared to the price you received when the shares were
sold. Brokerage commissions to buy and sell the shares are also
factored into the calculation and reduce the amount of the gain or
increase the amount of the loss. In addition, the length of time
between when shares were purchased and sold is a very important consideration in calculating the taxes you will owe.

How is the gain or loss calculated?

Gains or losses in the value of stocks you continue to own are
considered paper gains or paper losses that are not included when
calculating your taxable income and tax liability. Having paper
gains or losses doesn't mean you haven't earned or lost money, of
course, but only that you haven't earned or lost money for purposes of including the gains and losses in calculating your taxes.
A paper gain or loss must be converted into a realized gain and
loss through a sale of the shares before your tax liability is
affected. Once shares have been sold, the gain or loss is calculated as the net proceeds from the sale less the cost basis for the
shares. A gain is reported if the net proceeds exceed the cost
basis. A loss is recorded if the cost basis for the shares exceeds
the net proceeds. The federal government doesn't ask about the
price per share, but rather the total amount of money involved in
the purchase and the sale. You must also list the date the shares
were purchased and the date the shares were sold.

Can you provide an example?

Suppose you recently sold 100 shares of stock for $35 per share
that had been purchased several years ago at a price of $25 per
share. A brokerage commission of $40 was charged when the
stock was purchased and again when the shares were sold. Net

proceeds from the sale are $3500 less the $40 brokerage commission, or $3460, and the cost basis is $2500 plus the $40 brokerage commission, or $2,540. The capital gain to be reported is the net proceeds of $3460 less the cost basis of $2540, or $920. The net gain of $920 is the amount that will be subject to taxation. Smaller commissions would result in a larger gain and a slightly higher tax liability.

What if the transaction had resulted in a loss rather than a gain?

Let's use the same transaction but reverse the purchase price and sale price. In other words, assume you purchased 100 shares for $35 each and later sold the shares for $25 each. In this example, net proceeds from the sale are $2500 less a $40 brokerage commission, or $2460, and the cost basis is $3500 plus a $40 commission, or $3540. The resulting net loss of $1080 would be reported on your federal tax return. Notice that commissions have the effect of reducing the size of a gain and increasing the size of a loss.

Am I required to report a transaction when no gain or loss results?

You must report any transaction regardless of whether it produces a gain or loss. The Internal Revenue Service has a record of the proceeds from all your transactions, which will be matched against the transactions reported on your tax return. The two amounts must be equal or you will probably be asked for an explanation of the difference. Brokerage firms report to the Internal Revenue Service the proceeds of all the shares of stock you sell. Thus, the IRS knows the value of all the stock you sell but it does not know how much you paid for the stock. This is data you must supply to the IRS, which may ask for proof.

How are capital gains and losses treated for tax purposes?

Capital gains and losses receive special tax treatment and are reported on a separate tax form from ordinary income such as wages. A gain on stock held for more than one year qualifies as long-term and is currently taxed at a maximum rate of 20 percent. Stock acquired in 2001 or later and held for five years or more qualifies for a maximum rate of 18 percent. A gain on stock held for a year or less is classified as short-term and treated as regular income to be taxed at whatever marginal tax rate applies to your total taxable income. The 20 percent maximum tax on long-term gains is a major benefit for individuals who have substantial amounts of taxable income and pay relatively high marginal tax rates on their regular income. Essentially, these high earners are able to trim their tax bill by nearly half with capital gains as opposed to regular income. Suppose you and your spouse earn sufficient income so that dividends you receive are taxed at a rate of 36 percent. During the year, you sold shares of stock for $6000 that were purchased several years earlier for $2000. Because of the favorable treatment accorded to long-term capital gains, the $4000 gain will result in a tax of only $800, not the $1440 that would be required if the gain was treated as regular income.

Why do capital gains receive favorable tax treatment?

Proponents of the favorable treatment argue that a lower tax rate on capital gains encourages more investment, which in turn results in a more productive economy. A more productive economy results in more jobs and a higher standard of living. Opponents argue that the lower capital gains tax rate mostly benefits wealthy individuals who provide most of the financial backing for politicians who write the tax regulations. Regardless of the reasons, the lower tax rate on long-term capital gains exists, so you may as well take advantage of it.

What if my relatively modest income places me in the 15 percent tax bracket?

Even people with relatively low incomes are able to enjoy tax benefits from long-term capital gains. Individuals pay a rate of only 10 percent on long-term capital gains when their total taxable income qualifies for the 15 percent marginal tax rate. Stock held for over five years qualifies for a slightly lower tax rate. In other words, the tax rate for long-term capital gains is always lower than the rate an investor must pay on regular income. The problem is that many low income families don't have sufficient disposable income or financial resources to invest in stocks to begin with. The lower tax rate for capital gains offers little help to a family that doesn't own any stocks. Still, the low rate sounds good when capital gains legislation is discussed.

Is the lower tax rate the only benefit of capital gains as opposed to dividends?

One of the great benefits of capital gains stems from the tax being levied only when stock is sold and gains are realized. The benefit stems partly from the fact that you are allowed to determine the year of taxation by choosing the year when shares are sold. Not only that, you can choose which stocks to sell and even which shares of a particular stock to sell. The discretion you have over the timing of stock transactions is a great advantage in planning tax strategies. Compare this flexibility of timing for capital gains and losses with dividend payments over which you have no control: Directors of a company determine how much dividends to pay and when the payments are to occur.

What if I have both long-term and short-term gains during the same year?

Long-term and short-term capital gains are each calculated and grouped separately on the same tax form. All long-term gains will be taxed at the favorable 20 percent or 10 percent rate, depending on your tax bracket, while all short-term gains will be taxed at the rate applicable to your regular income. You must list the purchase date, cost basis, sale date, and net proceeds for each stock sold during the year. The process is somewhat more complicated if you have both gains and losses in the same year.

Are gains and losses realized in the same year combined?

If you sold a number of different stocks, and the sales resulted in multiple gains and losses, both short-term and long-term, you must first calculate the totals in each category. In other words, calculate total long-term gains, total long-term losses, total short-term gains, and total short-term losses. Total long-term gains are offset with total long-term losses to determine the net long-term gain or loss for the year. Total short-term gains are offset with total short-term losses to determine your net short-term gain or loss for the year. If one total is a net gain and the other total a net loss, the two totals must be netted to produce the net gain or loss that will be entered on your tax return.

What if I have a net loss for the year?

If netting all the gains and losses for a year produces a net loss, either short- or long-term, the loss can be used to offset regular income up to a maximum of $3000 per year. Net losses over $3000 must be carried over to future years when they can be used to offset net gains or again used to offset regular income up to the $3000 maximum. No time limit exists regarding how long losses can be carried forward.

Are dividends and capital gains reported on the same tax form?

The total for each category of income is reported on IRS Form 1040, the main federal income tax form. Total annual dividends of less than $400 do not require a separate form. If total dividends received during a year exceed $400, the amount of each stock's dividend payments and total dividends received for the year must be listed on Schedule B, which is also used to list taxable interest payments received during the year. Each of the companies paying dividends and interest must be listed along with the annual amount received. In the event stock is being held in your brokerage account, the payment will originate from the brokerage firm, and the brokerage firm—not the company paying the dividend—should be listed on Schedule B. Your brokerage firm should send an annual tax report along with instructions regarding where to enter amounts on your federal tax form.

Should I maintain a record of what I receive in dividends, interest, and proceeds from stock sales?

It is important to keep good records regarding the dates and prices paid for shares of stock you purchase and the dates and prices received when stock is sold. This information will be required to calculate gains and losses to be reported on your federal tax form. You should also maintain a record of the dividends you receive. You will receive annual tax information at the beginning of each year from each of your brokerage firms and from each company in which you own stock and hold the certificates. Form 1099-DIV, sent by each of these firms, will list the amount of dividends paid to you during the year. Your brokerage report will provide information on the proceeds received from any sale of stock as well as information on dividends received on shares of stock being held in your account.

Will money be withheld for taxes from dividend payments?

In general, no taxes are withheld from the dividends you are paid. No withholding means you will owe the full amount of the tax on dividends received during the year. Be certain to accumulate enough funds to take care of the taxes that will be due. You must also be careful not to forget to remit estimated quarterly payments if withholding by your employer is insufficient to satisfy government requirements. Postponing all of your tax payments until the April filing date is likely to result in a substantial penalty if you end up owing a substantial amount of taxes. The Internal Revenue Service publishes a worksheet to help determine if you should be paying quarterly estimated taxes.

What if I own shares of a foreign corporation?

Foreign corporations in which you own shares of stock are likely to deduct any taxes you owe to the country in which the firm is headquartered. For example, if you own American Depositary shares in BP Amoco, a British firm, the company will withhold income taxes due to Britain before sending your quarterly dividend check. Taxes paid to a foreign country can be claimed as a credit on your tax return to Uncle Sam. In other words, you are permitted to reduce the tax due the United States by the amount of the tax you pay the foreign government. Thus, a foreign tax shouldn't increase your overall tax burden, although it may complicate your financial life somewhat.

Will taxes be withheld from the net proceeds of a stock sale?

Taxes are not normally withheld from proceeds of a stock sale. Remember, a tax is calculated on a net gain resulting from a sale, not the proceeds from the sale. Withholding from proceeds doesn't make sense, because stock is sometimes sold at a loss. As with dividend income you receive, you need to make certain to have cash available to pay taxes that are due, either at the end of the year or as part of your quarterly estimate. With substantial income not subject to withholding, you may discover that you should be paying an estimated tax based on the gains you realize. A penalty for underpayment of taxes applies to your total tax bill, including taxes due from capital gains, not just income earned from dividends, interest, and as a result of employment.

How is stock ownership affected by state taxes?

Each state has its own tax system, so it is impossible to provide more than a general overview of how stock ownership is impacted by state taxation. Most but not all states levy both a personal income tax and a sales tax. Exceptions exist and some states have one or the other, but not both. Sales taxes impact spending, not income, and so this levy will not be addressed other than to say you get more for your money by living in a state without a sales tax. A state income tax simply results in an added burden for stock investors, who are required to pay additional taxes on dividend income and realized capital gains. Rather than retaining 72 percent of the dividends you receive (assuming you are in the 28 percent federal tax bracket), you may keep 65 percent or less if you reside in a state with a personal income tax. One positive aspect to a state income tax is that the tax payments are permitted as an itemized deduction on your federal tax return.

How do states treat capital gains for tax purposes?

Taxation of capital gains varies from state to state. Some states tax capital gains at a reduced rate, while other states tax even long-term capital gains at the same rate as regular income. If your state sets its state income tax as a percentage of your federal tax liability (for example, your state tax liability is calculated as a certain percent of your federal tax liability), you benefit from a reduced rate of taxation on long-term capital gains compared to other sources of income. However, some states tax all income at the same rate regardless of the source of the income. As a resident of one of these states, you would not gain any tax benefit from a realized capital gain as compared to a dividend.

Are other state and local taxes applicable to stock investors?

Some states levy an annual tax on the market value of all the securities that are owned as of a specific date each year, usually January 1. This levy, called an *intangible tax*, is a significant annual expense if you own a substantial stock portfolio. It is common for states that impose this tax to set the levy at one-tenth of 1 percent of the market value of securities that are owned. This rate results in a tax of $300 for an individual owning common stocks with a market value of $300,000. An intangible tax is separate from and in addition to taxes you are required to pay on income realized from stock ownership. Like state income taxes, this tax can be utilized as an itemized deduction when federal income taxes are calculated. The deductibility reduces the effective cost of these taxes by about a third.

Do any tax benefits derive from donating stock to a charity?

Substantial tax savings can result from donating appreciated stock to charitable organizations. The donor can claim as an itemized deduction the market value of such stock. The charitable deduction is effective only if you itemize rather than utilize the standard deduction in calculating your federal income tax liability. The key point here is that you are able to deduct the market value of the stock at the time of the donation, not the price you paid when the stock was acquired. It makes sense to donate only stock that has appreciated in price subsequent to the date it was purchased. Donating appreciated stock allows you to claim the full value of the shares as a deduction without being required to pay any taxes on a gain in the stock's value.

Should I consider donating stock that has declined in value?

The major benefit of donating appreciated stock is avoidance of the tax that would be levied on the capital gain if the shares were sold. Donated stock is given away, not sold, and so no realized gain results. This same benefit does not result when the donated stock has declined in value since the purchase date. Donate shares of a stock in which you have a paper loss and you will lose the tax savings that would result from the realized capital loss. You would be better off selling stock that has declined in value and using the realized loss to reduce your income tax liability. Claim the tax savings and donate cash to the charity. You can still gain a tax deduction from the donation of cash at the same time you gain a tax benefit from the realized loss. Never donate stock in which you have a paper loss. Turn the paper loss into a realized loss that can be claimed on your tax return. Remember that charitable organizations generally don't pay taxes and so are unable to gain a tax benefit from selling stock at a loss.

Can I benefit from giving shares of stock to my children?

Stock received as a gift assumes the cost basis of the donor or the market value at the time of the gift, whichever is lower. In other words, any paper gain that has resulted during your holding period will be passed along to your children. When your children eventually sell the shares, their gain will be calculated on the difference between the sale price and either your cost basis or the market value on the date of the gift. Thus, giving stock to your children does not generate the same tax benefit as giving the stock to a charity: You fail to gain the tax benefit of a charitable deduction, and any existing paper gain is passed along to your children.

Can you provide an example of how the tax is determined?

Suppose you purchased 100 shares of Mull Corporation several years ago for $28 per share. The stock has since climbed to $43, resulting in a paper gain to you of $15 per share, or $1500. You give the stock to your son who has been in and out of college and needs the money. Although your son may seem like a charity to you, your gift does not qualify for a charitable deduction and you are not permitted to deduct the market value of the gift when calculating next year's federal income tax liability. Likewise, your son is not required to report the gift as income so receipt of the gift is not taxable to him. Your son will assume a cost basis of $28 per share, which was the lower of your cost or the market value at the time of the gift. If the stock is subsequently sold, your son will calculate a capital gain or loss using the $28 per share cost basis.

Do any tax benefits result from the gift?

Actually, a couple of benefits may result from giving stock to a child. Part of any benefit depends on the tax rate applicable to your son's income. Following the gift, any dividend income from the stock will be taxed to your son at his tax rate, not yours. Likewise, if the stock is sold by your son, any capital gain that results will be taxed to your son. Even though your son will assume your cost basis for the stock, taxes on any gain are likely to be reduced if your son is in a lower tax bracket than you. Another advantage is that the gift removes the stock from your estate and, thus, reduces any federal estate tax or state inheritance tax that might apply.

Why does someone want to tax the stock that I own at my death?

It's not only your kids who want a piece of your financial pie, both while you are alive and at your death. The federal government currently levies a tax on large estates. Politicians often talk about doing away with the federal estate tax, and the discussions have become more serious in this era of federal government surpluses. Thus, the current estate tax may be reduced or eliminated by the time this book is published. However, the tax remains in place at the time this chapter is being written. Fortunately for most citizens, the tax is levied only on estates of substantial value. On the downside, the rate of taxation is quite high. The executor of your estate will be required to file a federal estate tax return that lists all of the things you own, including your home, bank accounts, life insurance, and stock. If the value of all these assets exceeds a specified threshold, a tax must be paid to the federal government on any excess above the threshold. Likewise, many states tax either the estates of the deceased or inheritances by heirs. Giving away stock decreases the value of your estate and reduces any tax that may be levied on the estate.

Does a limit exist on how much I can give away?

You are permitted to give $10,000 in any one year to as many individuals as you like. Your spouse can do the same with gifts that are in addition to your own. Thus, you and your spouse together are permitted to give away up to $20,000 per year to any number of people, with no tax consequence either to you or to the persons receiving the gifts. The gifts can be in cash, stocks, bonds, bank accounts, real estate, or virtually anything else. The $10,000 annual limit applies to the market value of the assets at the time of the gift. Unlimited gifts are permitted to your spouse without any tax being imposed.

What happens to stock owned at my death?

Shares of stock along with all the other assets in your estate will be distributed according to your will or, if you die without a valid will (e.g., die *intestate*), according to the laws of

the state of your residence. Assets held in joint name automatically pass to the other person or persons who have ownership rights. Having a valid will is important because the law
in your state may disburse your assets in a manner you would
not choose. Perhaps your children receive more and your
spouse less that you would have liked. Heirs of your estate
inherit shares of stock at the market values of the shares at the
time of your death. In other words, if stock is part of your
estate, your heirs will assume a cost basis equal to the current
market value. If you made wise stock investments that appreciated in value, your heirs will avoid the substantial capital
gains tax that would have been paid upon selling the stock
prior to your death.

Are any tax changes on the horizon?

Proposals for a reduction in capital gains taxation are always
on the table, especially prior to a national election. Some
politicians propose lowering the rate on long-term gains from
the current 20 percent to a reduced level of 15 percent or even
10 percent. The lower rate would benefit all stockholders.
There seems to be increasing political support for eliminating
the federal tax on estates, although it is difficult to know if
such a plan will be enacted. Current law calls for a gradual
increase in the size of an estate not subject to taxation. In addition, proposals for reductions in marginal tax rates are always
in the hopper. In each case, it is impossible to know if these
changes will be put into place. Opponents argue that any federal budget surplus should be used to reduce the national debt
rather than reduce taxes. They also argue that most of the tax
reductions outlined above would benefit the wealthy and offer
little relief for others.

Would the value of my stock investments be affected if Congress substituted a national sales tax for the current income tax?

Replacement of the income tax by a national sales tax would most likely stimulate investments in stocks and bonds. Think of the advantage of not being required to pay a tax on dividend income or capital gains. It might also influence stockholders to demand that companies increase their dividend payments if they were no longer subject to taxation. On the other hand, a sales tax would result in an increased cost for purchasing goods and services and have a negative impact on consumer spending. In fact, one of the major points voiced by proponents of a national sales tax is the incentive it would provide for individuals to save rather than spend. Increased savings, in turn, would stimulate investment spending by businesses and result in a more productive economy. Although a national sales tax occasionally receives media attention, political considerations indicate you shouldn't count on this change in the near future. Change is unlikely because many individuals and institutions have a vested interest in maintaining our current complicated tax system.

11

CHAPTER

THE RISKS OF STOCK OWNERSHIP

Chapter summary

Stocks are generally considered risky assets to own because of the uncertainty of the returns they will provide to their owners ... Most of the risk of owning stock involves fluctuations in market price ... Inflation, interest rates, and other economic factors can have a major impact on stock values ... Stocks of small companies tend to be especially risky to own but offer the potential for high returns ... Stocks of companies in different industries and different countries can be combined in a portfolio to reduce certain types of risk ... Beta is a mathematical measure of market risk

Are stocks risky investments to own?

Stock ownership certainly involves risk, although different stocks are subject to various degrees of risk. Remember, shares of stock represent ownership of a business, and businesses tend to be risky enterprises. Businesses can suffer from reduced profits, shoddy accounting, employee theft, inept management, rising interest rates, government regulation, union unrest, customer and employee lawsuits, and uncertain government tax policies. The list goes on but you probably get the idea; a lot of things can go wrong to reduce the value of a business enterprise, sometimes to zero. From your standpoint as part owner of a business, lots of things can go wrong to reduce the market value of the shares you own. The possibility of a decline in a stock's market price is only one of several risks you face as a stockholder.

Exactly what constitutes risk?

Risk is the uncertainty of a particular outcome. The less certain the outcome, the greater the risk. For example, not knowing for certain if you will return unhurt from a mountain climbing expedition makes the outing a risky endeavor. The less certain you are of your safe return, the more risky the expedition. Likewise, betting your paycheck on the spin of a roulette wheel is a risky proposition because there is substantial uncertainty that you will win the bet. Uncertainty regarding the return you will earn from a particular investment is generally considered the major risk of investing in an asset. The less certain the return it will provide, the riskier the investment. The more certain the return it will provide, the less risky the investment.

What investments involve little risk?

Investments that provide an assured return have little risk. Invest in a one-year insured certificate of deposit and you know exactly how much interest income you will earn, when the interest will be paid, and the date your principal will be returned. An insured certificate of deposit provides a guaranteed rate of return and a guaranteed repayment of the principal. Invest in a U.S. Treasury bill and you know exactly how much you will be paid and when the payment will occur. The U.S. Treasury guarantees the payment, so there is no risk that you will not receive the promised return.

Are you saying there is no risk to owning these investments?

Unfortunately, every investment subjects its owner to some degree of risk. With respect to the investments noted above, no risk exists regarding the return you will earn for a defined period. You will realize the promised income, and your principal will be repaid on the date specified. You don't have to worry about these promised payments unless the government collapses or refuses to make payment, two unlikely prospects. However, a risk does exist regarding the return you will be able to earn in the event the principal is to be reinvested in subsequent periods. Invest in a one-year certificate of deposit and you know how much you will earn for the year but not what the investment will earn in subsequent periods. The risk of an uncertain return on reinvestments is particularly important for investments in short-term fixed-income investments such as certificates of deposit, short- and intermediate-term bonds, and money market mutual funds. On the other hand, if you intend to spend the principal and interest when the CD or bond matures, reinvestment risk is unimportant because there will be no reinvestment.

Are stocks riskier to own than bonds?

In some respects stocks are a riskier investment than bonds, and in other respects stock is the less risky investment. Several types of risk are applicable to most investments, and determining the riskiness of a particular investment depends on the types of risk you consider most important. Most experts believe stocks tend to entail more overall risk than bonds because stock values are much more difficult to forecast. This means you are uncertain what your shares of stock will be worth at any future point in time. Still, an increasing number of experts are coming to believe that stocks may actually be less risky to own than bonds over long periods of time. One thing is certain, however: Stocks vary proportionately more in market value than bonds, so shares of stock can be a very risky investment, especially if you may unexpectedly need to sell.

What types of risk apply to stock ownership?

The risk most investors associate with an investment is the potential for a loss of asset value. What is the possibility of a decline in value and how large a decline can occur? With respect to stocks, this risk translates into the possibility of a reduction in market price of the shares. Stocks certainly do decline in price, sometimes to the point that they lose nearly all their value. Many Internet stocks experienced price declines of 70 to 90 percent during 2000. Even respected blue chip stocks can decline quite suddenly in price. In March 2000 the common stock of Procter & Gamble, one of America's great old corporations, declined nearly 33 percent in a single day after the firm reported it would be unable to meet quarterly earnings forecasts. Big price movements in stocks seemed to become the norm in the stock market boom of the 1990s. Many things can go wrong and result in a declining stock price. Stocks sometimes decline in price for no apparent reason.

Don't stock prices usually recover from declines?

Not all stocks recover from major price declines. Remember, companies can actually go out of business, in which case a firm's common stock may become worthless. One of America's leading transportation companies, Eastern Airlines, suffered years of financial distress and finally went out of business, with the common stockholders losing their entire investment. This is the worst case, of course, but it occurs more often than you might think, especially to small firms. Even companies that remain in business can produce major losses for their stockholders, and the losses can linger for years. The great glamour stocks of one decade may become the also-rans of the following decade as competitors grab their customers or consumers move on to different products.

What can cause a company to go out of business?

Companies go out of business for various reasons. Bankruptcy often results from too much borrowing and an inability to meet the required payments of interest and principal. In other words, companies are sometimes unable to pay their lenders. Many companies face cyclical sales that result in periodic revenue declines that make it difficult for the firms to cover their expenses. Companies sometimes operate in a fading industry with poor long-term prospects. Other firms end up in failure after attempting to diversify into new fields in which they know little. Even an unexpected event such as a huge lawsuit and jury award can cause a firm to seek bankruptcy. In short, all kinds of bad and unpredictable events can cause a company to fail. The potential for these events represent risks that can cause a stockholder to lose substantial amounts of money.

Does a firm's size influence the risk of owning its stock?

In general, stocks of small companies (often called *small-cap stocks*) are more risky to own compared to the stocks of larger companies, especially large companies that have been in business for many years. Small companies often have short operating histories and suffer from limited financial resources, a major disadvantage if they must compete with much larger firms. Large companies, especially firms that simultaneously operate in several business sectors, are better able to withstand lean years in part of their operations, while small companies often depend on a single product or service. Having said this, the Procter & Gamble example noted previously indicates that even large companies can encounter difficulties that result in major losses to their shareholders. Also, keep in mind that some of America's largest firms have ended up in bankruptcy.

To what degree is a company's debt important in evaluating my risk as a stockholder?

Nearly all companies rely to some degree on borrowed funds to pay for many of the expenses that are required to conduct business. Companies borrow to buy real estate, purchase equipment, and acquire inventories. They also borrow to pay their employees, their utility bills, and the rent. Companies sometimes borrow money to repay existing debt that comes due. A firm's managers may choose to borrow more money than is prudent, thereby placing the company and its stockholders at risk. Excessive borrowing tends to magnify positive returns to the company during the good times, but it can result in financial catastrophe in bad times, especially if the bad times linger. The value of the owners' investment is likely to parallel the ups and downs of the economic fortunes of the company in which they own stock. Borrowing results in fixed expenses that must be met in both good and bad times. Companies are required by law to meet interest and principal payments for the money they have borrowed. These fixed financial obligations can place the entire organization at risk during periods of unfavorable business conditions.

Are you saying that a large amount of debt can cause a firm to go out of business?

Heavy indebtedness can cause a company to fail. Creditors who have not been paid interest or principal can force a company into bankruptcy. However, even if the worst case is avoided, a company's financial condition can deteriorate to the point that the investment community worries about the firm's future. Investor concern about a firm's viability will most likely cause a fall in the stock price and a loss for the firm's stockholders. Stock values reflect expectations, and large debts can result in bleak expectations.

Are all companies susceptible to having too much debt?

Companies operating in different industries are able to handle different amounts of debt. In general, the more stable and predictable a firm's revenues, the more debt the firm can comfortably handle. For example, regulated utilities are generally better able to handle large amounts of debt compared to companies with very cyclical revenues. Still, any firm without significant amounts of debt is generally considered to be less risky. Keep in mind the other side of the equation: Companies with debt attempt to use financial leverage to earn a high return on the shareholders' investment. Debt allows a company to acquire more assets without having to issue additional shares of ownership. Fewer shares of ownership mean that profits are split fewer ways. Debt is a double-edged sword that produces both increased risk and the possibility of increased returns to shareholders.

What other risks exist for an investor who buys stock?

A company's directors might decide to decrease or eliminate the firm's dividend, a decision that reduces the shareholders' current income. The announcement of a dividend cut, especially if the news is unexpected, is likely to negatively affect the firm's stock price, an added risk to owners of the firm's stock. The possibility of a reduction in dividend income is an important consideration for many individuals who invest in stocks, particularly investors who choose to own stock in order to earn quarterly dividend income. The possibility of a cut in current income is a greater risk for stock investors than it is for investors who buy bonds of the same company because firms guarantee interest payments to lenders but they do not guarantee dividend payments to stockholders.

Is inflation also a risk for stockholders?

Inflation is an increase in the prices you must pay to purchase goods and services. In other words, inflation causes you to have to pay more money for the same amount of food, gasoline, clothes, housing, and so forth. While not every good or service increases in price during a period of general inflation, enough prices go up so that the purchasing power of a given amount of money declines. Just as inflation means a dollar is worth less, it also causes the dollar value of investments to be worth less in terms of the amount of goods and services that can be purchased. A $20,000 portfolio of stocks buys less goods and services following a year of inflation than after a year of stable prices. Inflation causes a fixed amount of financial assets to command less purchasing power. You hope that your stocks will increase in value by more than the rate of inflation, but this is a separate issue. Inflation means a given amount of money has reduced purchasing power.

Is it true that stock is a good hedge against inflation?

Stocks sometimes serve as a hedge against inflation, especially over a long period of time. However, stock prices do not always rise on inflationary news, and in fact may be negatively affected by bad inflation news. Stock prices can go up or down during inflationary periods but the fact remains that inflation causes a dollar to be worth less, and so a given dollar value of stock is worth less in terms of the goods and services it can buy. Shares of stock can rise in price and still have reduced purchasing power if consumer prices go up proportionately more than stock prices. The manner in which inflation affects the company in which you own stock is a separate issue.

What does this mean?

Some businesses tend to benefit from periods of general inflation, while other companies do not. For example, companies that own and extract or harvest natural resources such as petroleum, timber, and coal are likely to enjoy increased revenues and profits during periods of inflation. These firms benefit from higher prices for the products they sell and from the higher market value of the assets they own. A large petroleum company that owns substantial reserves of crude oil has more value when oil is selling at $30 per barrel than when oil is selling for $15 per barrel. Companies that hold large amounts of real estate often benefit from periods of inflation when land prices increase. On the other hand, the owners of some businesses may see profits erode during periods of inflation when they are unable to pass along increases in the cost of doing business. Companies with large labor costs can suffer lower profits during periods of inflation, especially when unemployment rates are low and wages are rising. Public utilities often suffer during inflationary periods when they are unable to gain approval for price increases to cover their increased costs. General inflation affects different businesses differently and, as a result, affects different stockholders differently.

Does inflation have any other effects on stock prices?

Inflation is likely to cause concern for government officials and may trigger the Federal Reserve, the government board in charge of domestic monetary policy, to hike short-term interest rates. The thinking is that higher interest rates produce slower growth in economic activity, which in turn slows increases in consumer prices. Interest rate changes often have a strong impact on stock values, especially if a change in rates is unexpected. Increases in interest rates mean higher yields from certificates of deposit and bonds, investments that compete with stocks for investors' money. In other words, higher interest rates are likely to cause investors to shift some of their savings from stocks to bonds or CDs, thereby resulting in reduced demand and lower prices for stocks. Wouldn't you be more likely to place your savings in stocks when CDs were paying 5 percent interest rather than 9 percent interest?

Don't stock prices reflect investors' anticipation of some inflation?

Stock prices do indeed take into account the inflationary expectations of investors, and share prices will suffer little if expectations become reality. When investors expect an annual inflation rate of 3 percent, little reaction can be expected from stock prices if the government announces the economy is experiencing a 3 percent annual inflation rate. However, if an inflation rate of 5 percent is announced when investors are expecting 3 percent inflation, the reaction in stock prices is likely to be much different. Afraid that the Federal Reserve will act to increase interest rates, investors are likely to sell stocks and drive down stock prices. The bottom line is that inflation at a higher-than-expected rate is likely to cause the stock market to suffer. On the other hand, if inflation occurs at a lower-than-expected rate, stocks can be expected to rise in value. Not all stocks, mind you, but most stocks. Remember, some companies actually benefit from inflation, and so a report of lower inflation is likely to depress the stock prices of these firms.

Do interest rates affect stocks in any other manner?

Companies often borrow large amounts of money in order to finance their assets. Rising interest rates increase borrowing costs, which in turn reduce profits. Reduced profits tend to result in a falling stock price. Some companies are more dependent on short-term borrowing and are immediately impacted by rising interest rates. Other companies, which primarily rely on long-term borrowing, may not feel the impact of increased interest rates unless the firms require large amounts of capital or the higher rates persist for a relatively long period. Regardless, any firm that borrows large amounts of money is likely to be negatively affected by increasing interest rates.

Are you saying that fluctuating interest rates represent yet another risk of owning stock?

Exactly. Because rising interest rates tend to have a negative effect on stock values, one of the risks of owning stocks is the possibility of rising interest rates. A strong rise in interest rates is likely to depress the value of your stock portfolio. Of course, an increase in interest rates will also have a negative impact on the value of any bonds you own. On the other hand, falling interest rates often produce increased stock prices.

Does inflation affect both short-term and long-term interest rates?

Inflation and inflationary expectations have a greater impact on long-term interest rates than short-term interest rates. The Federal Reserve has several methods for impacting short-term interest rates, but investor expectation regarding inflation is the primary factor affecting long-term interest rates.

Does stock ownership present any other risks?

Some stocks suffer from a lack of liquidity, or the inability of an investor to buy and sell shares at a fair price. It is nice to know the price you will receive if you decide to sell shares of stock. This doesn't mean that liquidity demands you know the price a year ahead of time. Rather, liquidity means you should know the approximate price you will receive based on a recent price quotation for the stock. Suppose you enter an order to sell your shares after determining that the last trade took place at $40 a share. You expect to receive approximately the same price only to discover that your shares bring only $38.50 per share. Some stocks are very actively traded and enjoy excellent liquidity, while other stocks trade infrequently and are relatively illiquid. Owning a stock without liquidity means you may be required to accept a price you consider inadequate in the event you need to sell shares fairly quickly.

How can I judge a stock's liquidity?

Daily trading volume is a good measure of a stock's liquidity. Heavy volume indicates good liquidity, in which case you should be able to buy or sell shares with no impact on the market price of the stock. Light volume is a warning sign that liquidity is likely to be limited, which means you may discover that even a moderate-size trade impacts the stock's price. Daily trading volume is published for stocks listed on the major exchanges and on Nasdaq's National Market System. However, some stocks that trade only on a regional exchange or in the over-the-counter market offer limited liquidity. Check the trading history of a stock prior to committing money to the security, especially if you expect a relatively short holding period for the stock.

Are stocks listed on the New York Stock Exchange more liquid than stocks traded over-the-counter?

At one time stocks listed on the New York Stock Exchange offered superior liquidity compared to stocks traded over-the-counter. As a generalization, this comparison is still accurate because of the many OTC stocks that are relatively inactive. However, liquidity for many OTC stocks is excellent, especially stocks that are included in the National Market System. The bottom line is that liquidity varies more by stock than by market, so you should check on the daily trading volume of a stock before investing your money.

Can I reduce my risk by sticking to the stocks of big, well-known corporations?

Even large corporations with years of profitable operations occasionally face difficulties that sometimes turn out to be permanent. The sinking stocks of Procter & Gamble and Eastern Airlines were mentioned earlier. Numerous railroads once considered the country's transportation backbone went bankrupt during the business depression of the 1930s. IBM, once the sole colossus of the computer industry, was overtaken and subsequently surpassed by more nimble competitors. Restricting your investments to big, well-known corporations is certainly not a foolproof method for avoiding risk. In addition, limiting your investments to the stocks of mature corporations can result in a drag on the profitability of your portfolio.

Do stock investments involve other risks?

It is the nature of stock prices to fluctuate. Fluctuations in price occur in a random manner during the trading day and from day to day. These random price changes are apart from and in addition to the advances and declines in value that can result from earnings reports, management changes, or shifting economic forecasts. The random fluctuations aren't necessarily large but they are continuous. Random fluctuations are not important unless you may be required to sell stock on short notice. The risk of a quick sale means that you may need to sell at an inopportune time when the stock price has taken a downward bounce. These short-term fluctuations aren't particularly important, but they should be a consideration if you are not planning a reasonably long holding period.

All these risks are confusing. Can I develop a simple strategy to reduce the risk from owning stocks?

Actually, it isn't particularly difficult to develop a strategy of risk reduction. First you need to understand that two broad categories incorporate all of the risks you will confront. These two categories take into account all of the risks already discussed in this chapter, including interest rate changes, unexpected inflation, management changes, excessive debt, falling profits, and so forth. The two categories also take into account some risks we haven't discussed, such as fluctuations in foreign currency exchange rates. One of these categories is called *systematic*, or *market risk*. The other category that includes all the other risk factors is called *unsystematic*, or *non-market risk*.

What is non-market risk?

Non-market risk refers to risks that are specific to a particular business. For example, timber companies face potential losses from fires, pine beetles, government regulation of forests, liability lawsuits, and so forth. Each of these possible events is likely to impact a timber company's stock price. Airlines face potential damage from soaring fuel prices, plane crashes, labor disruptions, bad weather, government restrictions on international flights, gate limitations at major airports, and more. All of these factors are likely to affect an airline's stock price. Each business and each industry faces special risks that are unique to that business or industry. These industry-specific risks are called non-market risks because they are independent of the overall market.

How does market risk differ from non-market risk?

Market risk incorporates uncertainties that are faced by all firms. For example, an increase or decrease in interest rates generally impacts all companies, if not to the same degree, at least in the same direction. Rising interest rates cause a downward pressure on the overall market and on nearly all individual stocks. Likewise, changing expectations regarding inflation affect most firms and the prices of the shares of stock of these firms. Movements in the market tend to carry stocks along in the same direction. A rising stock market carries most stocks upward, and a falling market places downward pressure on the prices of individual stocks. Although market movements affect nearly all stocks, individual stocks are affected to a different degree. Some stocks are strongly affected by market movements, while other stocks do not have a strong relationship to market movements. For example, stocks of companies in certain industries such as food retailing and pharmaceuticals tend to hold up better during bear markets.

What do these classifications have to do with my investment strategy?

Understanding how risks can be grouped into these two major categories allows you to devise an investment strategy to reduce the risk of your stock portfolio without sacrificing the return you can expect to earn. Reducing risk without reducing the expected return may sound too good to be true, but many academicians who have studied the stock market believe it can be accomplished. Assembling a diversified portfolio of securities substantially reduces the importance of non-market risk, or unique risk. Acquiring a number of stocks with different investment characteristics means your portfolio is not overly affected by the peculiarities of any one stock. A pine beetle infestation may be a major risk of a southern timber company, but the risk to you is manageable if the timber company's stock represents a limited part of

your overall portfolio. The same reduction applies to other risks
that are unique to a particular industry or to a particular company.
For example, owning a portfolio that includes both petroleum
companies and airlines tends to negate fluctuations in the price of
crude oil. An increase in the price of crude oil will affect an airline
stock negatively (higher fuel costs) at the same time your investment in a petroleum company should benefit from higher oil company profits. Banks are subject to unique risks that can, at least in
part, be offset by owning investments in manufacturing sectors of
the economy. Invest all your money in companies concentrated in
a single industry, or even worse, a single stock, and the value of
your portfolio will be subject to substantial non-market risk as
well as market risk.

Can you clarify the relationship between risk and diversification?

Exhibit 11-1 illustrates the relationship between investment
risk and the number of securities comprising a portfolio. Risk is
measured on the vertical axis (higher on the axis represents
more risk), and the number of securities, or diversification, is
measured along the horizontal axis. Risk declines swiftly at
first as new securities are added to a limited portfolio with little
diversification. As a portfolio grows, risk decreases little as new
securities are added. In other words, the addition of another
security to an existing portfolio of a hundred different securities
will not result in much risk reduction. Notice that all the decline
in total risk is caused by a reduction in unique, or non-market
risk, as the portfolio diversification improves

How many different stocks are required to eliminate non-market risk?

First, you can reduce but not completely eliminate non-market
risk. Adequate diversification requires that you own at least 8 to

EXHIBIT 11-1

Investment Risk and Diversification

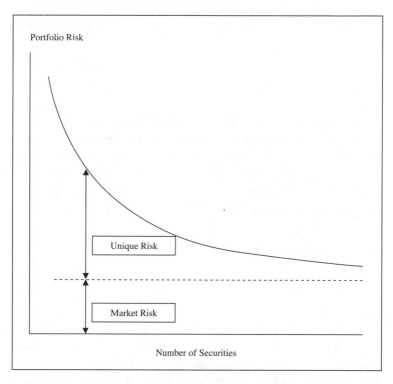

Portfolio Risk

Unique Risk

Market Risk

Number of Securities

12 different stocks. Some analysts recommend more than 12 stocks, partly because many companies have become more specialized in the products or services they provide. A properly diversified stock portfolio should not include five Internet stocks and five retailing stocks, although this is certainly better than owning only one or the other. Diversification works best when you acquire the stocks of companies that operate in different industries. Your portfolio might include stock investments in an airline, a computer manufacturer, a petroleum company, a computer chip manufacturer, a software company, an electric utility, and so forth. The more different stocks you

own and the more diversified your portfolio, the more non-market risk is reduced.

Are you saying that more stocks are better than fewer stocks?

Increasing the number of stock issues will improve diversification, but the law of diminishing returns sets in after a portfolio includes 10 to 12 different stock issues. Adding a thirteenth, fourteenth, or fifteenth stock issue to your existing portfolio will produce additional diversification but the reduction in risk is relatively small. Adding a second stock to a one-stock portfolio results in greater risk reduction than adding a thirteenth stock issue to a 12-stock portfolio. As a practical matter, owning dozens of different stocks makes it difficult to monitor your investment portfolio and complicates your financial life.

How do I minimize market risk?

Market risk is a different matter entirely. The diversification that reduces non-market risk has no effect on market risk. Owning a dozen stocks can substantially reduce non-market risk, but it isn't helpful in lessening the impact of overall market movements. Market risk is a measure of the degree to which market returns affect the returns on a particular stock or a portfolio of stocks. In other words, market risk determines how a particularly strong or weak market affects the price of a stock. Substantial market risk is identified by a strong link between the performance of the overall stock market and the performance of a particular stock or portfolio of stocks. Conversely, the weaker the link between a stock's returns and market returns, the smaller the market risk of owning the stock.

How is market risk measured?

Market risk is measured by a variable called *beta*. The mathematical calculation for determining a stock's beta is fairly complicated and better left to academic texts. Suffice it to say that beta is determined by establishing the mathematical relationship between the returns on a stock and returns on the market. The market beta is defined as 1 because a comparison of the returns from the market with itself is perfect. A stock with a beta of greater than 1 has more risk than the market as a whole, while a stock with a beta of less than 1 has less risk than the overall market. Most calculations use the S&P 500 as a measure of market performance.

What does this mean?

Beta is a measure of a stock's market risk. A stock with a higher beta entails greater risk of ownership because the stock's returns are more volatile than the returns of the overall market. Stocks with high betas tend to do very well when the stock market is booming and very badly when the stock market is plummeting. A stock with a beta of 2 can be expected to outperform a rising market (produce a higher return than the overall market) and underperform a falling market. At the other end of the scale, a stock with a beta of .6 can be expected to underperform a rising market and outperform a falling market. The higher a stock's beta, the greater the variations in that stock's return, both on the upside and on the downside.

Is beta always an accurate measure of a stock's risk?

Beta is considered an accurate measure of a stock's risk only when the stock comprises part of a diversified portfolio. By itself, a stock has both market and non-market risk. As part of a diversified portfolio, an individual stock produces mostly market risk. Critics of beta claim that historical financial data do not necessarily provide an accurate indication of the present or the future. In other words, betas of individual stocks can change over time, and so betas calculated from historical returns are not necessarily the same as the betas for the same stocks today or during future years. Still, the theory is sound and beta appears a practical method for evaluating the risk of owning a particular stock.

Where can I locate the betas for individual stocks?

Stock betas are calculated and published by several investment advisory services, including the *Value Line Investment Survey*. Value Line is available in most public libraries and so is probably the most accessible source of stock betas. Many online investment services and brokerage firms also provide individual stock betas.

How do I calculate the beta for a portfolio of stocks?

The beta of a stock portfolio is the weighted average of the betas of the individual stocks that comprise the portfolio. Suppose you own the six stocks shown in Exhibit 11-2. Your total portfolio has a current market value of $103,750 distributed unevenly among the six stocks. Your most valuable current investment is in 500 shares of Union Pacific, which represent 25.53 percent of the overall portfolio. Your smallest investment is in 500 shares of Compaq Computer, which represent 11.49 percent of your total portfolio. The six stocks have individual betas that range from a low of .47 for Union Pacific to a high of 2.58 for AOL Time Warner stock. The relative weight of each stock's importance to your portfolio is multiplied by the stock's beta to calculate that stock's weighted beta. The final step is to add the six weighted betas to calculate the beta of the overall portfolio. This calculation shows that your overall portfolio has a beta of 1.1488. This is slightly higher than the overall market beta of 1, which means your portfolio is subject to greater than average market risk.

Will portfolio risk increase if I sold shares of Union Pacific and use the proceeds to buy shares of Microsoft?

Substituting a high-beta stock for a low-beta stock will increase the market risk of the overall portfolio. Conversely, selling shares of Microsoft and using the proceeds to purchase shares of a stock with a relatively low beta will reduce the overall portfolio beta. Keep in mind that beta measures market risk, not non-market risk. Thus, putting most of your money in a single stock with a low beta is not a low-risk investment strategy.

What size portfolio beta should I shoot for?

There is no best beta that all investors should seek. The beta of your portfolio should be inversely related to the amount of sleep you lose over your investments. If your heart begins a rapid beating each time you turn to the financial section of the morning newspaper, you should probably assemble a portfolio of low-beta stocks. If you invest with a goal of earning relatively large returns and can stomach the price volatility, construct a portfolio with a beta greater than 1. The higher the beta of your portfolio, the greater the volatility of returns.

Is an easier method available for reducing the risk I face from investing in stocks?

Mutual funds are convenient vehicles for acquiring a diversified stock portfolio. A mutual fund may hold 50 or more different issues of stock, which makes buying shares in the fund equivalent to assembling a portfolio with a large number of different stocks. Most individual investors are unable to achieve diversification anywhere near that achieved by many mutual funds. Diversification with individual stocks is especially difficult for investors who have relatively small amounts of money to invest. Splitting a total investment of $10,000 among 10 or

EXHIBIT 11-2

Calculating the Beta of a Stock Portfolio

Stock	Beta	Shares	Stock Price	Market Value	Proportion of Portfolio	Weighted Beta
AOL Time Warner	2.58	250	$47.80	$11,950	11.52%	0.2972
Coca-Cola	0.69	400	57.75	23,100	22.27	0.1537
Compaq Computer	1.27	500	23.85	11,925	11.49	0.1459
Microsoft	1.81	300	60.80	18,240	17.58	0.3182
Tyco International	0.98	200	60.25	12,050	11.61	0.1138
Union Pacific	0.47	500	52.97	26,485	25.53	0.1200
Total Portfolio				$103,750	100.00%	1.1488

With a beta of 1.1488 the portfolio is slightly riskier than the overall market that has a beta of 1.

more stocks is not really practical because of the substantial transactions costs that are likely to result. Transaction costs are less of a problem for investors who trade online. Mutual funds are about the only way many small investors are able to achieve proper diversification.

Do all mutual funds offer appropriate diversification to reduce risk?

Some mutual funds offer excellent diversification by holding stock portfolios representing many industries. Other mutual funds hold portfolios comprised of both stocks and bonds. However, many mutual funds offer little diversification. Specialized mutual funds became all the rage in the stock market boom of the 1990s when investors became interested in placing their bets on particular industries rather than the overall economy. Specialized funds hold stocks representing a particular industry or a particular region of the world. Shares in one of these funds offer at least some diversification compared to investing all your money in one or two stocks, but specialized funds certainly don't offer real diversification. If you want a diversified portfolio, stick to mutual funds with portfolios that mirror one of the broad stock indexes.

Will risk increase if I hold stocks of foreign corporations as part of my portfolio?

Research has demonstrated that incorporating foreign stocks in your portfolio will reduce the overall investment risk. Estimates of the best proportion of foreign stocks range from 7 percent to 15 percent of the overall market value of a portfolio. Foreign stocks can be purchased directly, but are most conveniently acquired as part of a mutual fund that specializes in foreign investments.

Any last hints relative to reducing the risks of stock ownership?

Don't put all your eggs in one basket. This means you shouldn't invest in just one or two stocks, or even three or four. However, this also has a broader meaning: You should never bet the farm on stocks to the exclusion of other investment vehicles. Bonds, tangible assets, and a money market account all have a place in any individual's investment portfolio. The historical record of returns from stock investments has been excellent over long periods of time, but there is no guarantee that the past will accurately forecast the future, especially during the period of time you will hold your investments. Always plan for the unexpected. Emergencies can shorten planned holding periods, and you may be required to sell some of your investments sooner than expected. Long-term holding periods can terminate early when you are in desperate need of money.

12

CHAPTER

SOURCES OF STOCK INFORMATION

Chapter summary

Interpreting stock quotations ... Stock information available via the Internet by computer ... Brokerage firm and financial services company Web sites ... Recommended publications to learn about investing ... Financial resources that are available in most public libraries ... Books that provide investment information ... Sources of mutual fund information ... Recommended sources for industry and economic information ... Radio and television programs offering investment information

Where can I locate information about common stocks?

There is certainly no shortage of readily available information about stock investments and the cost ranges from free to exorbitant. Daily newspapers now often devote substantial space to business stories and financial data of interest to investors. Sunday editions of metropolitan newspapers are particularly good sources for information about specific companies and stock investments. A large number of books about investing are shelved in the business section of any public library or bookstore. Although the titles may not specifically identify common stocks as the main subject, all but the most specialized books about investments devote substantial attention to stocks. In fact, most books on investing concentrate on stocks. Investigate the table of contents if you are in doubt about whether information about stocks is included. Weekly and monthly business and personal finance periodicals often devote a majority of their pages to a discussion of stock investments. Some articles concentrate on specific stocks or groups of stocks while other articles deal with investment techniques. Television and radio have developed an array of programs designed to attract individual investors, to the point that some networks now air business information most of the day. All types of stock information from financial data to programmed instruction on investing are available to individuals with access to the Internet. Internet sources are especially valuable because they are often continuously updated to provide the most current information. In addition, Internet Web sites are able to offer specialized topics that would be uneconomical for a book or magazine publisher that needs to appeal to a large audience.

How do I interpret the stock price information published in a newspaper?

Major metropolitan newspapers typically include daily data for stocks listed on the New York Stock Exchange, Nasdaq, and, less frequently, the American Stock Exchange. Because of space considerations, newspapers typically omit data for inactive stocks. Most papers also include the closing share values of popular mutual funds. Stock listings generally include the closing price, or the last price at which the stock traded on the previous day, and the net price change. Net change represents the change in price between the most recent closing price and the closing price on the prior trading day. Suppose the listing in the Tuesday morning paper indicates Coca-Cola closed Monday at $55.55 per share with a net change of +$1.00. The net change shows that Coca-Cola stock increased in price by $1.00 per share compared to the closing price on the previous trading day, when its last trade was at a price of $54.55. Most newspaper listings also include information on the volume of trading, usually expressed in hundreds of shares, although sometimes in thousands of shares. The volume, closing price, and net change are the three basic pieces of data available in most newspapers. Some papers also publish a listing of each stock's current annual dividend and the price-earnings ratio based on the most recent reported earnings and closing stock price. Less frequently, newspapers will include the highest price and the lowest price at which each stock traded during the day. Exhibit 12-1 provides an interpretation of a complete newspaper stock listing.

Are other important stock data available in the newspaper?

Newspapers nearly always report the prior day's closing value and change in value for popular stock indexes and averages, including the Dow Jones Industrial Average, the Nasdaq Composite, and the S&P 500. These broad-based indexes indicate the performance of the overall stock market during the previous day's trading. Most newspapers include a market diary or market summary segment that lists the 10 or 15 stocks with the greatest daily trading volume on the New York Stock Exchange, the Nasdaq, and the American Stock Exchange. This section sometimes lists stocks that experienced the biggest daily gains and losses in percentage or dollar value. Also of

EXHIBIT 12-1

Interpreting Stock Price Quotations

Major newspapers often carry several pages of stock price and volume data. The completeness of these listings varies with some papers publishing only the closing prices of selected stocks while other papers include substantial details about the daily trading activity of each listed NYSE stock, some Amex stocks, and most OTC National Market System stocks. A complete listing generally appears as:

| 52-Week | | | | | | | | Net | |
Hi	Lo	Stock	Div	PE	Yld	Hi	Lo	Close	Chg
27.3	48.25	Young Industries	0.30	8	1.5	21.12	19.75	20.25	+0.40

52-Week Hi and Lo: The highest price and lowest price at which the stock traded during the previous 52-week period. In this example, Young Industries stock traded as high as $27.34 and as low as $8.25 per share during the past year. A comparison of the closing price with the 52-week high and low indicates whether the stock is trending higher or lower. The difference between the high price and the low price is called the *range*.

Div: The annual dividend per share. Young Industries currently pays an annual dividend of 30 cents per share. You would receive $30 in dividends if you held this stock for a year. Most companies pay dividends quarterly.

PE: The price-earnings ratio is calculated by dividing the stock price by earnings per share. Young's earnings per share of $2.53 can be calculated by dividing the stock price of $20.25 by the PE ratio of 8.

Yld: The dividend yield that is calculated by dividing the annual dividend by the closing stock price. Young's current dividend of 30 cents per share provides owners of the stock with a yield of 1.5 percent based on the current stock price. Dividend yield does not include any actual or potential returns from changes in the price of the stock.

Hi: The hightest price at which the stock traded during the day.

Lo: The lowest price at which the stock traded during the day.

Close: The price at which the stock last traded during the day.

Net Chg: Net change, or the difference between the closing price and the closing price on the previous day the stock traded. Young's stock closed up 40 cents at $20.25 per share which means it closed the previous trading day at a price of $19.85.

interest is a listing of the number of stocks that advanced in price compared to the number of stocks that declined in price during the day's trading. A quick look at the number of advances and declines will indicate whether a change in the market averages was broad-based or influenced primarily by price changes in a limited number of major stocks.

What other important financial information is available in the business section of a newspaper?

Many business sections include a listing of the exchange rates for major foreign currencies. Keeping track of changes in currency exchange rates will keep you current on whether the dollar is gaining or losing strength against foreign currencies. Currency exchange rates have an important influence on the country's balance of trade, corporate profits, and stock prices. A strengthening dollar tends to hurt U.S. companies that sell a lot of their goods in foreign countries. Newspapers often publish data about interest rates and the bond market. Interest rates, especially long-term interest rates, have a major influence on stock values. Rising long-term interest rates generally have a negative impact on stock prices, while falling long-term interest rates are favorable for stock prices. Many newspapers list recently declared dividends along with relevant dates for owning stock to receive the dividends. Dividend data is of special interest to investors who invest for current income. Reports of increased or decreased dividends can have a major impact on stock values.

What type of stock information is available on the Internet?

The Internet provides every possible kind of stock information you want or will ever need, if only it can be located. All of the statistical data you can digest is available for individual companies, industries, stocks, and the overall stock market. A large number of Web sites provide current information about stock prices, market averages, the most active issues of the day, and the biggest daily gainers and losers. This is similar to the information provided by daily newspapers, but utilizing the Internet means you don't have to wait until the morning paper arrives. Plus, you can access up-to-date information about these statistics at any time of the day. Most sites provide stock price information with a 20-minute delay. In other words, the stock price on the screen represents the price at which a trade took place 20 minutes earlier. Most sites that cater to individual investors are operated either by online brokerage firms or by firms in the business of disseminating financial information. Brokerage company sites are primarily designed to provide information that can be used by their customers. Most of these sites require a password for all but the most basic information. For example, real-time stock quotations are generally available only to individuals with accounts. Brokerage firm Web sites also generally provide some type of sales presentation intended to convince potential customers that their firm offers more and better services than its competitors. Brokerage firm sites are good places to obtain current information on the overall market and stock prices, but you are likely to be excluded from most of the premium information such as real-time stock quotes and research unless you become a customer of the firm.

Do brokerage firm Web sites provide information about their commission rates?

Commission rates are included in all the brokerage firm sites. Each firm will post separate commission schedules for stocks, bonds, and options. Some firms levy an additional charge for limit orders in which you specify a minimum price for stock you wish to sell or a maximum price for stock you wish to purchase. This may be an important consideration if you prefer to specify a price with your orders. Brokerage firm sites also generally provide information about the interest rates charged for loans to purchase securities on margin, and the cost of various services including delivery of certificates, transfer of securities, bond redemptions, share exchanges in mergers, and so forth. Most brokerage firms make their account forms available online so you are able to open an account without calling or sending for a package of information. Brokerage firm sites include an email address and phone number in the event you have questions that are not answered by information provided on the Web site.

How good are investment-related Web sites not associated with brokerage firms?

Some nonbrokerage financial Web sites provide comprehensive financial information about a wide variety of issues related to stock investments. Companies involved in some manner with an investment product or service sponsor some of these sites, while other sites are sponsored by news information organizations such as CNN and CBS. Many of these sites are very comprehensive and offer a one-stop center for investment information. They often include information about companies, investment techniques, and links to other investment-related sites. Some sites provide "investment learning centers" in which individuals can pace themselves through informational segments directed at specific investment topics. These sites typically provide current business news and columns about investing, in addition to stock prices and market averages. Some sites also include chat rooms that allow users to correspond with other investors who have similar interest. Exhibit 12-2 includes a select listing of Internet Web sites that are devoted to providing comprehensive investment information.

Do most companies have their own Web site?

Any firm with publicly traded stock will almost certainly have its own Web site. Type the company name in a search engine, and you will be able to determine the Web address for the site. Realize that company sites are often designed to promote the company and its products or services, not provide comprehensive information to investors. Still, you can often obtain current financial statistics on sales, profits, and assets of the company. Many company sites also provide a link to the firm's stock price and provide current news relative to the company and its operations. Still, these sites don't approach the usefulness of the more comprehensive Web sites that are available to investors.

Can I find useful investment information in Internet chat rooms?

Chat rooms have become an important source of investment information for many individuals, especially investors who are interested in rapid trading of stocks that exhibit big price movements. The problem is the difficulty in knowing if information posted in these chat rooms is accurate or, even worse, intentionally misleading. A well-publicized 2000 episode involved a

E X H I B I T   12-2

Select Web Sites Providing Comprehensive Investment Information

CBS MarketWatch	http://cbs.marketwatch.com
CNNfn	http://cnnfn.cnn.com
Microsoft MoneyCentral	http://moneycentral.com
Morningstar.com	http://www.morningstar.com
The Motley Fool	http://www.fool.com
Quicken.com	http://quicken.com
TheStreet.com	http://www.thestreet.com
Wall Street City	http://www.wallstreetcity.com
Wall Street Research Net	http://wsrn.com

teenager who earned hundreds of thousands of dollars by purchasing shares in thinly traded OTC stocks and then posting favorable stories about the stocks in investment chat rooms. Prior to leaving for school, the student entered limit sell orders that were triggered when buyers reading the postings drove the stock prices upward. Most of the postings were apparently made not on any factual basis, but rather to drive up the prices of the stocks. The morale is: It is not a good idea to make investment decisions based on information obtained from Internet chat rooms.

How about investment chat rooms? Are they useful for obtaining investment information?

Investment chat rooms can be a good place to obtain answers to technical questions about investing or about interpreting investment data. Perhaps you have a question concerning an article you recently read about how companies calculate earnings per share or how cash flow differs from reported earnings. You are likely to encounter someone in a chat room who can answer these types of questions. You will also probably be able to find someone who knows how to locate dividend information specific to a particular company, or someone who can tell you about short selling or how to transfer a security. You may be interested in other opinions about which online brokers offer the best service or the lowest commissions on stock transactions. Maybe you have wondered how difficult it is to transfer your account to another brokerage firm, or you want to know how interest is charged on margin accounts. Chat room participants are likely to provide answers to these kinds of questions. It is important to understand that the answers you receive may or may not be correct. It's not like you are asking a tax question of a Certified Public Accountant who is paid to provide accurate advice. Still, chat rooms can be a good place to obtain answers to specific questions and to learn about investing, so long as you understand the limitations of not knowing the expertise of the persons supplying the answers.

What publications should I read to learn more about investing?

You should start with a subscription to the *Wall Street Journal*, the daily business newspaper published by Dow Jones & Company. Read the paper every day and you will learn a lot about investing as well as keep abreast of important business developments. The paper is available in any public library, but you are more likely to miss important and useful information if you don't have time to leisurely browse each issue. Occasional articles about personal finance and investing in the Money and Investing section are some of the most useful you will find in any publication. Because the paper is published daily, the information is more up-to-date than similar information available in weekly or monthly periodicals. You don't have to read completely through every issue, of course, and few people do so. Many of the articles report news about companies in which you are likely to have no interest. Still, you will gain useful information about accounting and economics, and you will almost certainly pick up investment ideas from these stories. Most libraries will have back copies of the *Journal* available on microfilm in case you have a need for historical information. Perhaps you are involved in an estate tax matter and need the closing price of Texaco stock on January 12, 1942. Dow Jones also publishes *Barron's*, a weekly financial newspaper, but this is written more for advanced or professional investors than for occasional individual investors. *Barron's* contains a great deal of useful statistical information, including each firm's most recent quarterly earnings, which are compared with the prior year's earnings for the same period. *Barron's* is also a readily available source of dividend dates for individual stocks. *Investor's Business Daily*, the other daily newspaper aimed at individual investors, has more statistical data than the *Wall Street Journal*, but it lacks the overall business news and commentary that make the *Journal* so useful.

What are some other good sources for general stock market information?

The Outlook, published weekly by Standard & Poor's Corporation, provides current information on the overall stock market and on specific industries and companies. This is an excellent publication that is written in a no-nonsense and easy-to-read manner. *The Outlook* is available in most large public libraries and in university libraries that offer a program in business. The New York Stock Exchange, American Stock Exchange, and Nasdaq each publish an annual fact book that provides a wealth of statistical information about the two securities exchanges and the over-the-counter market for the respective year. None of the three publications provides general investment information, but you may have an interest in annual trading volume, new listings, and a historical look at market averages. Large libraries are likely to carry at least one of these publications, and all three are available at nominal cost from the exchanges.

Do you have any suggestions on magazines to read?

Several magazines provide useful information for individual investors. *Smart Money* and *Individual Investor* are two informative monthly magazines targeted primarily at individual investors. Both have numerous articles of interest to both novice and experienced investors. Each can generally be found at large bookstores and public libraries. One of the best general interest personal finance publications is *Kiplinger's Personal Finance*, a monthly magazine that is widely available in bookstores and public libraries. *Kiplinger's* covers a variety of financial topics, including insurance, retirement, and home buying. Each issue usually contains several useful and easy-to-understand articles about stock investments. *Forbes*, a general business magazine published twice a month, contains articles about specific companies that can provide you with some new investment ideas. Each issue includes columns written by industry professionals who discuss the stock market. The columnists often recommend specific stocks to buy or sell. *Worth* is a monthly magazine directed at a more upscale audience, although inexperienced investors can learn something from most of the articles.

Can you recommend any other resources?

Value Line Publishing, one of the oldest and most respected investment advisory services, publishes the *Value Line Investment Survey*, which is available at most public and college libraries. Ask at the reference desk about the location. The publisher regularly offers three-month trial subscriptions at nominal cost, so you may want to become a subscriber. The *Value Line Investment Survey* is an excellent publication that provides historical data, current financial statistics, and recommendations for all major publicly traded stocks. Information for each company includes dividend payment dates, earnings estimates, cash flow estimates, debt obligations, and a chart illustrating historical stock prices and trading volume. The *Survey* is published in 13 weekly editions that together provide coverage for over 1300 companies. The publication classifies each stock into one of five groups, depending on the analyst's estimate of the stock's potential for gaining market value. Academic studies have indicated that investors acting on Value Line recommendations by investing in Group I stocks (the highest rating) can earn above-average returns compared to the overall stock market. An accompanying Selection and Opinion section includes an overview of the overall stock market along with an individual stock selection that the firm's analysts feel is a particularly attractive purchase. A sample page from the *Value Line Investment Survey* is shown in Exhibit 12-3.

EXHIBIT 12-3

Sample Page from the *Value Line Investment Survey*

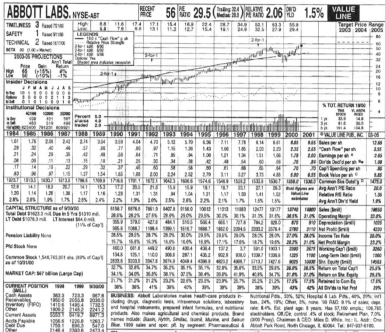

Can you recommend similar publications that are available in the library?

Two of the country's premier financial information services, Standard & Poor's and Moody's, each produce an excellent publication for individual investors. *Standard & Poor's Stock Reports* is a quarterly publication that consists of 12 paperback volumes: four volumes each for all companies with stocks listed on the New York Stock Exchange, all companies with stocks listed on the American Stock Exchange, and nearly 2000 companies with stocks traded over-the-counter. Companies are listed in alphabetical order, and each listing includes two pages filled with historical information, including quarterly earnings, dividend dates, a graph of the stock price, and 10 years of important financial data. Each listing includes a summary of recent developments and a short-term earnings estimate. This is an excellent but expensive publication that is carried by most large public libraries and college libraries. Exhibit 12-4 illustrates a typical report from this publication. As with many financial publications, *Standard & Poor's Stock Reports* is available online, an option that many space-starved libraries find desirable. The electronic version includes additional information, including recent news and an industry analysis.

Moody's produces the *Handbook of Common Stocks,* a quarterly publication that provides financial data and a brief analysis for more than 900 widely held common stocks that are listed on the New York Stock Exchange and the American Stock Exchange. Moody's also publishes a companion *Handbook of OTC Stocks* for companies with stocks traded over-the-counter. Both publications provide information about dividend dates and quarterly earnings, and an overview of each firm's financial structure (debt and equity). Historical statistical information includes earnings per share, shares outstanding, sales, debt, and a bar graph illustrating the stock's annual price range. Both Moody's publications are relatively inexpensive and can be found in nearly any public or college library. The information provided for each company is not as complete as the information available in *Standard & Poor's Stock Reports,* mentioned above. The S&P and Moody's publications are generally located in the library's reference section. Another publication, the *Wall Street Transcript,* is an excellent but expensive weekly newspaper that provides more investment information than you will have time to digest. Each issue contains brokerage firm recommendations with graphs, earnings estimates, and stock price targets. Both fundamental and technical information about stocks are included in each issue. The *Transcript* also has periodic roundtables in which industry experts are brought together for a discussion about a particular industry, but it is generally available only in larger libraries.

Can you recommend some good books on investing?

The number of books about investing boggles the mind: Visit a major bookstore or large library and you will be confronted with hundreds. Books will provide you with advice about investing in real estate, bonds, collectibles, mutual funds, and stocks. Some books tell you about investing in all these things and more. Many investment books offer a get-rich-quick pitch with little useful information for the average investor interested in learning about the basics. It's nice to think you can get rich with no money down and without the possibility of a loss, but as many people can attest from actual experience, this isn't the way the world works. Beginning investors should start with a general investments book that provides information about risks, returns, and details about all of the major investment vehicles. General information is useful even though you may only be interested in stocks. Find a book that presents both the positives and negatives of investing. It is impossible to make informed investment decisions unless you understand the risks. *Fundamentals of Investing* by Hirt and Block (McGraw-Hill) is an excellent text that is used in beginning investments classes at

EXHIBIT 12-4

Sample Entry from *Standard & Poor's Stock reports*

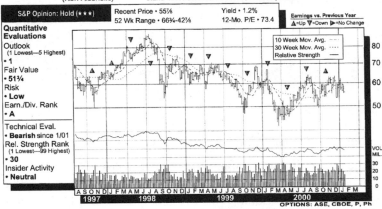

STANDARD &POOR'S
STOCK REPORTS

Coca-Cola

NYSE Symbol **KO**

In S&P 500

20-JAN-01

Industry:
Beverages
(Non-Alcoholic)

Summary: Coca-Cola is the world's leading soft-drink company and has a sizable fruit juice business. Its bottling interests include a 40% stake in NYSE-listed Coca-Cola Enterprises.

S&P Opinion: Hold (★★★)

| Recent Price · 55⅝ | Yield · 1.2% |
| 52 Wk Range · 66¾-42⅞ | 12-Mo. P/E · 73.4 |

Earnings vs. Previous Year
▲=Up ▼=Down ▶=No Change

Quantitative Evaluations

Outlook
(1 Lowest—5 Highest)
· **1**

Fair Value
· **51¾**

Risk
· **Low**

Earn./Div. Rank
· **A**

Technical Eval.
· **Bearish** since 1/01

Rel. Strength Rank
(1 Lowest—99 Highest)
· **30**

Insider Activity
· **Neutral**

10 Week Mov. Avg. --
30 Week Mov. Avg. ····
Relative Strength —

OPTIONS: ASE, CBOE, P, Ph

Overview - 27-NOV-00

Revenues should rise 9% to 10% in 2001, as 5% to 6% higher volumes and 3% to 4% higher concentrate prices outweigh unfavorable currency exchange translations. Continued weakening of foreign currencies (particularly the euro) may pressure earnings since the company has chosen not to hedge euro exposure for 2001. Operating margins should widen, aided by operating efficiencies and benefits of restructuring activities. A modest rise in equity income is seen, reflecting an improved earnings outlook for bottlers. Rising free cash flow should allow for debt reduction and a resumption of share repurchases. We anticipate that EPS will rise 17% in 2001, to $1.70, from an anticipated $1.45 in 2000. Our estimate includes the net effect of reductions in bottler concentrate inventories and realignment savings for 2000. Longer term, annual EPS growth of 15% is expected.

Valuation - 27-NOV-00

We continue our hold opinion on the shares, reflecting concerns about KO's ability to achieve long-term volume growth objectives as the company implements a massive organizational realignment. The company's new decentralized operating structure and aggressive new product development activity should improve its ability to operate more effectively at the local market level. Volume growth of 4% for the third quarter of 2000 matched expectations, and provided further evidence that business trends are improving as international markets continue to improve and stabilize. Shares may be volatile in the near-term, as the company considers a potentially dilutive acquisition of Quaker Oats. Despite trading recently at 34X our 2001 EPS estimate, a significant premium to the S&P 500, we believe KO's superior margin structure and dominant market position make the shares a worthwhile holding.

Key Stock Statistics

S&P EPS Est. 2000	1.44	Tang. Bk. Value/Share	3.18
P/E on S&P Est. 2000	38.8	Beta	0.69
S&P EPS Est. 2001	1.70	Shareholders	394,603
Dividend Rate/Share	0.68	Market cap. (B)	$138.4
Shs. outstg. (M)	2479.8	Inst. holdings	52%
Avg. daily vol. (M)	4.356		

Value of $10,000 invested 5 years ago: $ 15,784

Fiscal Year Ending Dec. 31

	2000	1999	1998	1997	1996	1995
Revenues (Million $)						
1Q	4,391	4,428	4,457	4,138	4,194	3,854
2Q	5,621	5,379	5,151	5,075	5,253	4,936
3Q	5,543	5,195	4,747	4,954	4,656	4,895
4Q	—	4,931	4,458	4,701	4,443	4,333
Yr.	—	19,805	18,813	18,868	18,546	18,018
Earnings Per Share ($)						
1Q	-0.02	0.30	0.34	0.39	0.28	0.25
2Q	0.37	0.38	0.48	0.52	0.42	0.35
3Q	0.43	0.32	0.36	0.40	0.38	0.32
4Q	—	-0.02	0.24	0.33	0.30	0.26
Yr.	—	0.98	1.42	1.64	1.38	1.18

Next earnings report expected: late January

Dividend Data (Dividends have been paid since 1893.)

Amount ($)	Date Decl.	Ex-Div. Date	Stock of Record	Payment Date
0.170	Feb. 17	Mar. 13	Mar. 15	Apr. 01 '00
0.170	Apr. 19	Jun. 13	Jun. 15	Jul. 01 '00
0.170	Jul. 20	Sep. 13	Sep. 15	Oct. 01 '00
0.170	Oct. 18	Nov. 29	Dec. 01	Dec. 15 '00

EXHIBIT 12-4

(Continued)

STANDARD
&POOR'S
STOCK REPORTS

The Coca-Cola Company

20-JAN-01

Business Summary - 27-NOV-00

The Coca-Cola Company is the world's largest producer of soft drink concentrates and syrups, as well as the world's largest producer of juice and juice-related products. Finished soft drink products bearing the company's trademarks have been sold in the U.S. since 1886, and are now sold in nearly 200 countries. Sales and operating profit in 1999 by geographic region were distributed as follows: North America (38% of revenues, 32% of profits), Greater Europe (23%, 23%), Middle & Far East (26%, 23%), Latin America (10%, 18%), and Africa (3%, 4%).

The company's business may be the most focused and efficient of any in the world, and is, quite simply, the production and sale of soft drink and non-carbonated beverage concentrates and syrups. These products are sold to the company's authorized independent and company-owned bottling/canning operations, and fountain wholesalers. These customers then either combine the syrup with carbonated water, or combine the concentrate with sweetener, water and carbonated water to produce finished soft drinks. The finished soft drinks are packaged in authorized containers bearing the company's well-known trademarks, which include Coca-Cola (best-selling soft drink in the world, including Coca-Cola classic), caffeine free Coca-Cola (classic), diet Coke (sold as Coke light in many markets outside the U.S.), Cherry Coke, diet Cherry Coke, Fanta, Sprite, diet Sprite, Barq's, Surge, Mr. PiBB, Mello Yello, TAB, Fresca, PowerAde, Minute Maid, Hi-C, Fruitopia, and other products developed for specific markets, including Georgia ready to drink coffees. KO has equity positions in approximately 42 unconsolidated bottling, canning and distribution operations for its products worldwide, including bottlers that accounted for about 58% of the company's U.S. unit case volume in 1999.

In the third quarter of 1999, the company completed the $970 million acquisition of Cadbury Schweppes plc beverage brands in 161 countries worldwide (excluding the U.S.), representing 85% of the world's population. Brands acquired include Schweppes and Canada Dry mixers (such as tonic water, club soda and ginger ale), Crush, Dr. Pepper, and certain regional brands. The proposed acquisition of these brands in several remaining countries is still undergoing regulatory review.

KO typically enters into forward exchange contracts, and purchases currency options (principally European currencies and Japanese yen) to reduce the risk that its eventual dollar net cash inflows resulting from sales outside the U.S. will be adversely affected by changes in exchange rates. The company has elected to not to hedge its exposure to the euro for 2001, reflecting a belief that the euro will rebound from its low levels.

Per Share Data ($) (Year Ended Dec. 31)	1999	1998	1997	1996	1995	1994	1993	1992	1991	1990
Tangible Bk. Val.	3.06	3.19	2.67	2.18	1.77	1.79	1.55	1.34	1.55	1.31
Cash Flow	1.30	1.67	1.89	1.59	1.36	1.14	0.97	0.83	0.70	0.60
Earnings	0.98	1.42	1.64	1.40	1.19	0.99	0.84	0.71	0.60	0.51
Dividends	0.64	0.60	0.56	0.50	0.44	0.39	0.34	0.28	0.24	0.20
Payout Ratio	65%	42%	34%	36%	37%	39%	40%	39%	39%	39%
Prices - High	70 7/8	88 7/8	72 3/8	54 1/4	40 1/4	26 3/4	22 5/8	22 3/4	20 1/2	12 1/4
- Low	47 1/4	53 5/8	51 1/8	36 1/8	24 3/8	19 1/2	18 3/4	17 3/4	10 3/4	8 1/8
P/E Ratio - High	72	63	44	39	34	27	27	32	34	24
- Low	48	38	31	26	21	20	22	25	18	16
Income Statement Analysis (Million $)										
Revs.	19,805	18,813	18,868	18,546	18,018	16,172	13,957	13,074	11,572	10,236
Oper. Inc.	4,774	5,612	5,627	4,394	4,546	4,090	3,485	3,080	2,586	2,237
Depr.	792	645	626	479	454	382	333	310	254	236
Int. Exp.	337	277	258	286	272	199	178	171	185	231
Pretax Inc.	3,819	5,198	6,055	4,596	4,328	3,728	3,185	2,746	2,383	2,014
Eff. Tax Rate	36%	32%	32%	24%	31%	32%	31%	31%	32%	31%
Net Inc.	2,431	3,533	4,129	3,492	2,986	2,554	2,188	1,884	1,618	1,382
Balance Sheet & Other Fin. Data (Million $)										
Cash	1,812	1,807	1,737	1,658	1,315	1,531	1,078	1,063	1,117	1,492
Curr. Assets	6,480	6,380	5,969	5,910	5,450	5,205	4,434	4,248	4,144	4,143
Total Assets	21,623	19,145	16,940	16,161	15,041	13,873	12,021	11,052	10,222	9,278
Curr. Liab.	9,856	8,640	7,379	7,416	7,348	6,177	5,171	5,303	4,118	4,296
LT Debt	854	687	801	1,116	1,141	1,426	1,428	1,120	985	536
Common Eqty.	9,513	8,403	7,311	6,156	5,392	5,235	4,584	3,888	4,426	3,774
Total Cap.	10,865	9,514	8,560	7,573	6,727	6,841	6,125	5,090	5,611	4,650
Cap. Exp.	1,069	863	1,093	990	937	878	808	1,083	792	642
Cash Flow	3,223	4,178	4,755	3,971	3,440	2,936	2,521	2,194	1,872	1,600
Curr. Ratio	0.7	0.7	0.8	0.8	0.7	0.8	0.9	0.8	1.0	1.0
% LT Debt of Cap.	7.9	7.2	9.4	14.7	17.0	20.8	23.3	22.0	17.6	11.5
% Net Inc.of Revs.	12.3	18.8	21.9	18.8	16.6	15.8	15.7	14.4	14.0	13.5
% Ret. on Assets	11.9	19.6	24.9	22.4	20.7	19.9	19.0	17.9	16.6	15.8
% Ret. on Equity	27.1	45.0	61.3	60.5	56.2	52.4	51.8	45.7	39.6	39.3

Data as orig. reptd.; bef. results of disc. opers. and/or spec. items. Per share data adj. for stk. divs. as of ex-div. date. Bold denotes diluted EPS (FASB 128). E-Estimated. NA-Not Available. NM-Not Meaningful. NR-Not Ranked.

Office—1 Coca-Cola Plaza, N.W., Atlanta, GA 30313. **Tel**—(404) 676-2121. **Website**—http://www.thecoca-colacompany.com **Chrmn & CEO**—D. N. Daft. **Pres & COO**—J. L. Stahl. **EVP's**—J. E. Chestnut, C. S. Frenette, J. R. Gladden, C. Ware. **SVP & CFO**—G. P. Fayard. **Secy**—S. E. Shaw. **Investor Contact**—Larry M. Mark. **Dirs**—H. A. Allen, R. W. Allen, C. P. Black, W. E. Buffet, D. N. Daft, S. B. King, D. F. McHenry, S. Nunn, P. F. Oreffice, J. D. Robinson III, P. V. Ueberroth, J. B. Williams. **Transfer Agent & Registrar**—First Chicago Trust Co. of New York, Jersey City, NJ. **Incorporated**—in Delaware in 1919. **Empl**— 37,400. **S&P Analyst:** Richard Joy many colleges. Although pricey, this book covers the entire realm of investing in an easy-to-understand manner. One of the best books for an understandable overview of the theory of stock investing is *A Random Walk Down Wall Street* by Berton Malkael. This well-written book has been through several editions because it provides good, solid information about investing that is useful to experienced and inexperienced investors alike. *The Stock Market* by Teweles, Bradley, and Teweles (Wiley) provides excellent coverage of the workings of the stock market. Although the book probably goes into more detail than you might like, it is well written and includes information you are unlikely to find in most other books about stock investing. *Wall Street Words* by Scott (Houghton Mifflin) is an excellent glossary (if I do say so myself) for individual investors, regardless of experience.

Are corporate annual reports a good source of investment information?

Annual reports tend to be produced by public affairs people who are more interested in promoting their company than providing useful information to investors. These reports include basic financial information, including a current balance sheet, income statement, and statement of cash flows, all of which are available from the sources mentioned above. You will be able to obtain all of the financial information contained in a firm's annual report on the Internet long before the report can be published and mailed. One item of interest in annual reports is corporate management's discussion of the year's results along with its opinion of the firm's future operations. Most companies are happy to send their annual report to interested individuals who submit a request. Appropriate corporate addresses are available in the *Value Line Investment Survey*, *Standard & Poor's Stock Reports*, and Moody's *Handbook of Common Stocks* and *Handbook of OTC Stocks*, which were discussed

above. Names and addresses are also available on corporate
Web sites. Some publications such as the *Wall Street Journal*,
Fortune, and *Forbes* offer select annual reports to their readers.

Where can I obtain information about mutual funds?

Mutual fund information is available in newspapers, magazines, books, and on the Internet. Information about specific
funds can be obtained at brokerage firms where the funds are
sold or directly from the mutual fund. Most newspapers publish
price quotations for many of the more popular mutual funds.
The Wall Street Journal and *Investor's Business Daily* both
devote substantial space to mutual fund price quotations. You
will also find good articles about mutual funds in each of these
newspapers. Mutual fund price quotations are also available on
many Internet sites, including most brokerage company Web
sites. A variety of books are available to help you learn about
mutual funds and how they are operated. Some of the better
ones are *Getting Started in Mutual Funds* (Wiley), *The Guide
to Investing in Mutual Funds* (Globe Pequot), and *Common
Sense on Mutual Funds* (Wiley).

What can I read to help in the selection of a mutual fund?

Several publications are available to assist in the selection of a
mutual fund. The most popular and best known mutual fund
investment service is *Morningstar Mutual Funds*, a periodical
that includes a full page of information on each of 1600 mutual
funds. Each fund is rated on a system of one to five stars (five is
best) according Morningstar's evaluation of the fund's risk-
adjusted return. In the Morningstar rating system, mutual funds
with higher risk are expected to produce higher returns in order
to obtain a favorable rating. The write-up for each fund
includes information about historical performance, fees, the
fund's largest portfolio holdings, a short descriptive analysis,

and various services offered by the fund. This biweekly publication is a very complete mutual fund service and is available in many public libraries. Morningstar usually offers a three-month trial subscription at nominal cost. Exhibit 12-5 illustrates a sample page from *Morningstar Mutual Funds*. Value Line Publishing publishes the *Value Line Mutual Fund Survey*, a biweekly service that is very similar to the Morningstar service. Both firms make their information available online, on CDs, or biweekly via mail. Several business periodicals, including *Forbes* and *Business Week*, publish special issues devoted to mutual funds in which they rate individual funds.

Where can I obtain information about particular industries?

A variety of publications provide industry information. Many brokerage firms publish research about industries along with recommendations about the stocks of particular companies within an industry. These reports can be obtained, generally without cost, by calling or visiting an office. Brokerage firms occasionally advertise the reports in financial publications and welcome readers to request a copy. The purpose, of course, is to reach potential customers who will like the research and open an account. Both *Forbes* and *Fortune* publish special issues that provide an analysis of major industries and companies. *Standard & Poor's Industry Survey* may be the best source of industry information. The *Survey* includes historical industry information along with an S&P analysis of the industry's outlook. This publication can be located in most large public and university libraries and is available in many brokerage company offices. As mentioned earlier, weekly editions of the *Wall Street Transcript* often include an industry roundtable in which experts discuss a specific industry and companies that operate within the industry.

EXHIBIT 12-5

Sample Page from *Morningstar Mutual Funds*

Published January 8, 2001. Reprinted by permission of Morningstar.

Fidelity Magellan

Ticker FMAGX	**Load** Closed	**NAV** $119.30	**Yield** 0.2%	**Total Assets** $92,568.1 mil	**Mstar Category** Large Blend

Prospectus Objective: Growth

Fidelity Magellan Fund seeks capital appreciation.
The fund invests primarily in common stocks and convertible securities. It features domestic corporations operating primarily in the United States. domestic corporations that have significant activities and interests outside the U.S. and foreign companies. No limitations are placed on total foreign investment, but no more than 40% of assets may be invested in companies operating exclusively in one foreign country.
The fund closed to new investment in 1995 and reopened in 1981. It closed again in 1997.

Historical Profile

Return	Above Avg
Risk	Average
Rating	★★★★ Above Avg

| 79% | 90% | 95% | 93% | 98% |

Investment Style
Equity
Average Stock %

▼ Manager Change
▽ Partial Manager Change

Fund Performance vs. Category Average
▪ Quarterly Fund Return
+/- Category Average
▬ Category Baseline

Performance Quartile
(within Category)

1989	1990	1991	1992	1993	1994	1995	1996	1997	1998	1999	12-00	**History**
59.85	53.93	68.61	63.01	70.85	66.80	85.98	80.65	95.27	120.82	136.63	119.30	NAV
34.58	-4.51	41.03	7.02	24.66	-1.81	36.82	11.69	26.58	33.63	24.05	-9.29	Total Return %
2.90	-1.39	10.54	-0.60	14.60	-3.13	-0.71	-11.28	-6.78	5.05	3.01	-0.19	+/- S&P 500
-3.46	-0.49	8.59	-0.64	14.92	-2.28	-0.78	-10.48	-6.45	4.95	2.72	1.91	+/- Wilshire Top 750
2.60	1.42	2.46	1.93	1.22	0.18	0.88	1.41	1.57	0.72	0.63	0.20	Income Return %
31.98	-5.93	38.57	5.09	23.43	-1.98	35.94	10.28	25.03	32.91	23.42	-9.49	Capital Return %
9	64	11	53	5	66	20	98	65	2	56		Total Rtn % Rank Cat
1.24	0.83	1.30	1.25	0.75	0.13	0.59	1.10	1.25	0.67	0.73	0.27	Income $
3.82	2.42	5.43	8.82	5.50	2.64	4.69	12.65	5.21	5.15	11.36	4.68	Capital Gains $
1.08	1.03	1.06	1.05	1.00	0.99	0.99	0.92	0.64	0.61	0.56	0.74	Expense Ratio %
2.13	2.54	2.47	1.57	2.11	1.07	0.35	0.95	1.75	0.77	0.86	0.46	Income Ratio %
87	82	135	172	155	132	120	155	87	31	28		Turnover Rate %
12,699	12,325	17,119,257	17,22,268	31,705	31,36,441	53,702	53,988	63,798	83,552	105,308	92,588.1	Net Assets $mil

Portfolio Manager(s)

Robert E. Stansky, CFA. Since 6-96. BA'78 Nichols C.; MBA'83 New York U.

Performance 12-31-00

	1st Qtr	2nd Qtr	3rd Qtr	4th Qtr	Total
1996	1.79	1.00	1.67	6.85	11.69
1997	-0.58	16.55	9.67	-0.40	26.59
1998	14.22	3.37	-11.05	27.22	33.63
1999	7.39	5.93	-5.97	15.97	24.05
2000	4.85	-1.94	-0.58	-8.40	-9.29

Trailing	Total Return%	+/- S&P 500	+/- Wil Top 750	%Rank All Cat	Growth of $10,000
3 Mo	-8.40	-1.58	0.80	75 66	9,060
6 Mo	-8.93	-1.21	0.08	73 69	9,007
1 Yr	-9.29	-0.19	1.61	73 55	9,071
3 Yr Avg	14.56	2.30	2.79	16 17	15,035
5 Yr Avg	16.28	-2.04	-1.53	17 54	21,258
10 Yr Avg	18.31	0.86	1.06	10 13	53,729
15 Yr Avg	17.04	1.03	1.41	7 8	105,948

Tax Analysis	Tax-Adj Ret%	%Rank Cat	%Pretax Ret	%Rank Cat
3 Yr Avg	12.93	16	88.8	38
5 Yr Avg	13.65	55	83.9	59
10 Yr Avg	15.33	29	83.7	52

Potential Capital Gain Exposure: 37% of assets

Analysis by Scott Cooley 10-18-00

Bob Stansky is as big an Internet bull as ever.

Plenty of Internet-related stocks have gotten pummeled in 2000, but Fidelity Magellan's manager has sidestepped much of the carnage. While some of his peers loaded up on Internet-content stocks, which have gotten hammered, Stansky has focused on companies that participate in the Internet-infrastructure buildout, which he believes is still in the early stages. As of September 30, 2000, the fund's top-10 holdings reflected this conviction: Cisco Systems, EMC, and Sun Microsystems were among the fund's largest holdings. For the year to date through October 17, 2000, each of those stocks was in the black, while many "pure" Internet issues had shed half of their value or more.

That focus on Internet-infrastructure stocks is one of the biggest reasons this fund has edged past the S&P 500 so far in 2000. Another is Stansky's preference for

financials with plenty of fee income; those names have handily outperformed regional banks, which he has largely avoided. Gains in those areas have offset the fund's substantial losses in retail, which Stansky has overweighted throughout 2000. Long-time top-10 holding Home Depot has lost about half its value this year.

Right now, it appears that Stansky is continuing to run the portfolio with a mildly contrarian bent. He cut about 50 stocks from the portfolio during the third quarter, suggesting that he had sold strong-performing mid-caps and deployed the proceeds in larger stocks, which have been hard-hit in 2000. Fidelity also reports that Stansky has been doing some buying among beaten-down tech stocks. In some ways, the current environment might be similar to 1998's third-quarter tech sell-off. At that time, Stansky loaded up on tech and reaped huge gains when it rebounded.

Address:	82 Devonshire Street Boston, MA 02109 800-544-8888
Web Address:	www.fidelity.com
Inception:	05-02-63
Advisor:	Fidelity Mgmt. & Research
Subadvisor:	FMR (U.K.)/FMR (Far East)
NTF Plans:	Fidelity Inst.

Minimum Purchase:	Closed	Add: $250	IRA —
Min Auto Inv Plan:	Closed	Add: $100	
Sales Fees:	3.00%L		
Management Fee:	57%+.52% mx/.27% mn.(G)+(-).20%P		
Actual Fees:	Mgt: 0.57%	Dist: —	
Expense Projections:	3Yr: $532	5Yr: $704	10Yr: $1202
		Income Distrib: Semi-Ann.	
Total Cost (relative to category):		Below Avg	

Risk Analysis

Time Period	Load-Adj Return %	Risk %Rank All Cat	Morningstar Return Risk	Morningstar Risk-Adj Rating
1 Yr	-12.02			
3 Yr	13.40	65 59	1.32 0.88	★★★
5 Yr	15.57	70 65	1.08 0.90	★★★
10 Yr	17.95	72 70	1.29 0.93	★★★★

Average Historical Rating (181 months): 4.6★s

1=low, 100=high

Category Rating (3 Yr)		Other Measures	Standard Index S&P 500	Best Fit Index S&P 500
(2)(3) ...		Alpha	1.9	1.9
(1) (4)(5)		Beta	1.06	1.06
Worst Best		R-Squared	96	96
		Standard Deviation	21.87	
Return	Above Avg	Mean	14.56	
Risk	Average	Sharpe Ratio	0.48	

Portfolio Analysis 03-31-00

Share change since 09-99 Total Stocks: 372

	Sector	PE	YTD Ret%	% Assets
⊕ General Elec	Industrials	39.2	-8.00	4.69
⊖ Microsoft	Technology	25.5	-62.80	4.10
⊕ Cisco Sys	Technology	93.3	-28.50	3.74
⊕ Home Depot	Retail	39.7	-33.30	2.53
⊕ Intel	Technology	30.1	-26.80	2.78
⊕ Texas Instruments	Technology	29.2	-1.79	2.51
⊖ Citigroup	Financials	19.2	23.57	2.40
⊕ ExxonMobil	Energy	20.7	10.24	2.05
⊕ Time Warner	Services	NMF	-27.50	2.05
⊕ Tyco Intl	Industrials	20.9	42.45	1.94
⊕ Wal-Mart Stores	Retail	38.2	-22.70	1.44
⊕ AT&T	Services	9.9	-85.20	1.44
⊕ American Intl Grp	Financials	42.3	36.98	1.44
⊕ Lucent Tech	Technology	36.5	-80.70	1.29
⊕ EMC/Mass	Technology	NMF	21.74	1.27
⊕ IBM	Technology	20.7	-20.80	1.27
⊕ Chase Manhattan	Financials	11.7	-10.00	1.21
⊕ Oracle	Technology	25.8	3.74	1.28
⊕ Motorola	Technology	29.1	-56.50	1.07
⊕ Nokia Cl A ADR	Technology	74.9	-6.70	1.06
⊕ Warner-Lambert	Health		46.73	1.06
⊕ Sun Microsystems	Technology	45.0	-28.00	1.02
⊕ Eli Lilly	Health	33.2	41.33	1.01
⊕ America Online	Technology	64.4	-54.10	0.99
⊖ Merck	Health	33.3	41.77	0.98

Current Investment Style		Stock Port Avg	Relative S&P 500 Current Hist	Rel Cat
Style Value Blnd Growth				
	Price/Earnings Ratio	32.2	1.02 1.19	0.98
	Price/Book Ratio	7.3	0.95 1.27	0.95
	Price/Cash Flow	24.9	1.04 1.07	1.00
	3 Yr Earnings Growth	22.6	1.36 1.45	1.20
	1 Yr Earnings Est%	23.4	1.06	0.94
	Med Mkt Cap $mil	80,094	1.2 1.7	1.34

Special Securities	% assets 03-31-00
Restricted/Illiquid Secs	0
Emerging-Markets Secs	Trace
Options/Futures/Warrants	No

Composition	% assets 03-31-00	Market Cap	
Cash	2.0	Giant	63.1
Stocks	98.0	Large	28.5
Bonds	0.0	Medium	7.8
Other	0.0	Small	0.5
		Micro	0.1
*Foreign	4.6		
(% stocks)			

Sector Weightings	% of Stocks	Rel S&P	5-Year High Low
Utilities	0.0	0.0	9 0
Energy	6.5	0.9	25 1
Financials	17.1	0.7	17 7
Industrials	9.9	0.9	31 10
Durables	2.0	1.3	16 2
Staples	2.3	0.3	10 0
Services	15.6	1.4	17 10
Retail	9.8	1.6	11 2
Health	8.1	0.6	15 2
Technology	33.5	1.6	42 4

MORNINGSTAR Mutual Funds

Where can I locate information about the economy?

Economic information includes data such as economic activity, consumer prices, producer prices, government spending, interest rates, currency exchange rates, and so forth. Economic statistics are very important to investors because the economy plays such an important role in stock valuations. *Barron's*, the weekly sister publication of the *Wall Street Journal*, is a readily available source for many economic statistics, including interest rates, monetary data, and economic activity. *Barron's* is published each Monday and can be found at many newsstands and in nearly all public libraries. Being a weekly publication results in more current data than can be found in monthly publications. Public and college libraries will generally carry several government publications that provide useful economic data. These include the *Economic Report of the President*, *Business Conditions Digest*, *Economic Indicators*, the *Federal Reserve Bulletin*, and the *Monthly Labor Review*. Ask at the library reference desk for any of these publications, which include just about any bit of economic data you need. The annual *Statistical Abstract of the United States* is an excellent source of historical economic data and is available in virtually all public and college libraries.

Do you have any suggestions for radio or television programs?

The amount of airtime devoted to financial news seems to be increasing every month. Increased public participation in the stock market has caused interest in the financial markets to soar, and both radio and television have scrambled to feed the public appetite for more financial news. On the radio, "Sound Money" is an excellent weekly program about investing as well as other personal financial topics. Produced by Minnesota Public Radio, this hour-long program includes commentary, answers listeners' questions, and generally includes a guest expert who provides information and advice on a specific financial topic. The program also attempts to educate its listeners with information and conservative investment advice. Many National Public Radio stations carry this show, usually on Saturday mornings. Call your local NPR affiliate and inquire about the time the program is aired in your locale. *Wall Street Week* is an excellent weekly half-hour television program about investing that is carried by most affiliates of the Public Broadcasting System. The program is aired on most public television stations on Friday evenings at 8:30 P.M. and provides a review of weekly market activity, answers several viewer questions, and includes a guest who addresses a specific topic about investing. Weekly guests include investment professionals who discuss specific industries or investment strategies and recommend stocks they consider candidates for purchase.

INDEX

About the Author

David L. Scott, Ph.D., is professor of accounting and finance at Georgia's Valdosta State University. The author of nearly 30 books on finance and investing, including *How Wall Street Works* and the bestselling reference *Wall Street Words*, Dr. Scott has been a guest on numerous radio and television venues, including CNBC and NBC's *Today*.